Tales Of The
Big Potato

Jack R. Christmas

Copyright © 2011 by Jack R. Christmas

All rights reserved. No part of this book may be used, reproduced, stored in a retrieval system, or transmitted in any form whatsoever — including electronic, photocopy, recording — without prior written permission from the author, except in the case of brief quotations embodied in critical articles or reviews.

FIRST EDITION

ISBN: 9781936989294

Library of Congress Control Number: 2011940726

Published by
NewBookPublishing.com, a division of Reliance Media, Inc.
2395 Apopka Blvd., #200, Apopka, FL 32703
NewBookPublishing.com

Printed in the United States of America

Dedication

*I dedicate this book to my beloved wife and
best friend Joan, for her support and inspiration
during the writing of these articles and
her many hours of hard work bringing this book
to a conclusion during my lifetime.*

Table Of Contents

Introduction 7
Acknowledgements 8
Foreword: In The Beginning 9

Chapter 1 – The Early Days
    Coacoochee 11
    History Of The Town Of Apopka 13
    Peter Buchan 15
    D. B. Stewart 17
    William A. Lovell 19
    Mrs. M. E. Buchan 21
    Henry Witherington 23
    Zelotes Mason 25
    The Prince Family 27
    Dudley Adams 29
    Masonic Lodge 31
    Joseph G. Roberts 33

Chapter II – Pioneers & Communities
    John Anderson 37
    Colorful History Of Lake Apopka 38
    Industrious Pioneers 41
    Pioneer Women 43
    Mysterious Underground Waters 45
    The English Colony Of Narcoossee 47
    McDonald 49
    Consumers Veneer & Lumber Co. 51
    Plymouth 53
    Bayridge 55
    Merrimack 57
    Frank H. Davis 59

Chapter III – Early Days Of Apopka
    Four Early Disasters 61
    Steamboats On Wekiva 63
    Clay Springs/Apopka Railroad 65
    Early Apopkans After Civil War 57
    Florida Cracker Horses 69
    Lula Bowers 71
    Zellwood 73
    The Heritage House 76
    Early Days In Apopka 78
    Apopka Baseball 80
    Apopka's Early History 84

Chapter IV – The William Edwards Era
    Piedmont Wineries 87
    Orange – Lake Boundaries 89
    The Road That Was Straight 91
    Lake Standish Hotel 93
    Tangerine 95
    Fred Marden 97
    William Edwards 99
    Turpentining In The Apopka Area 101
    The Great Freezes Of 1894-95 103
    Grace Richmond 105
    Waite Davis House 107
    Eldredge House 109
    The Apopka Chief 111

Chapter V – The Train Wreck/ Tornado Hits Apopka
    The Great Train Wreck of '05 113
    Apopka Water, Light & Ice Co. 115

Plymouth Citrus Growers 117
Sawgrass Jones 119
T. J. Smith 121
Apopka Roads Improved 123
Dr. Charles McCall 125
John Grossenbacher, Sr. 127
Old Spring Place 129
Oaks Hotel 131
1918 Tornado In Apopka 133

Chapter VI – Apopka's Illustrious Residents
Mallory Welch 135
Ryan Brothers 137
Moonshine In Apopka 139
Mabel Raulerson 141
The Mahaffey Boys 143
Edgar King 145
Annie Belle Driggers Gilliam 147
Grover Robinson 149
George McClure 151
Dr. Tommy McBride 153
W. R. McGuffin 155
Warren "Ed" Lockeby 157
T. A. Shepherd 159
Walter Stokes 161
John Talton 163
Bill Arrowsmith 165
Catherine "Kit" Land Nelson 168
Earl Nelson 170
Fred Brummer 173

Chapter VII – Sportsmen's Club And Old Hotels
Mt. Plymouth Hotel 177
The Palms Hotel 179
Life Before Air Conditioning 181
Henry Land's Essay 183
Ryan Field 185
Sportsmen's Club 187
Dr. Cole Carroll 189

State Bank of Apopka Bank Robbery 191
Richard Whitney 193
Edward's Field 195
Hall's Feed Store 197

Chapter VIII – World War II and Heros
World War II 199
Albert Martin 201
Dick Wells 202
Harold Caldwell 203
Jack Grossenbacher 204
Observation Tower 206
Harvey Caldwell 208
Ted Waite 210
Sneed 212
Zellwood Drainage District 214

Chapter IX – The Johnnys Come Marching Home
Johnie McLeod 217
John Land 219
Dr. Charles Henry Damsel 222
Coach Howard Beckert 224
Charles H. Damsel, Jr. 226
Tommy Staley 228
Roger A. Williams 230

Chapter X – Apopka's Finest
Jack Hall 233
"Fireball" Roberts 235
Bob Pitman 238
Rodney Brewer 241
Country Singer – John Anderson 243
Glenn Hubbard 245
Zack Greinke 247
Marion McDonald 249
Phil Orr 251

Table Of Contents, Continued

Chapter XI – The Lazy 50's
- Hickerson's Gorget 253
- Lake Apopka Fishing 255
- Martin Marietta 257
- The Ambs Family 259
- Gunnery Sergeant Carlos Hathcock 262

Chapter XII – Seventies
- Agriculture Lost Prominence In Apopka ...265
- Ed "Possum Slim" Meyers 267
- Corn On The Cob...................................269

Chapter XIII – From A Small Boy's Eyes: Memories Of Growing Up
- Soap Box Derby......................271
- Our Dog Jack 272
- Moss Yards 274
- Youthful Memories Of Growing Up..........276

- Foxfire......................................278
- Hobos.......................................280
- Medicine Show 282
- City Gangs................................284
- Dream Lake 286
- History Of Apopka Foliage Industry 288
- Slat Shed Heating 290
- Parris Island I 292
- Parris Island II 294
- The Old First Baptist Church...................296
- Gator Hunt 298
- Stonebird..................................300
- The Sycamore Tree..................302
- Sycamore Bears Mayor's Name 304
- References................................306
- Sponsors...................................307
- About The Author ....Inside Back Cover

Introduction

Jack Christmas wrote a weekly article in *The Apopka Chief* entitled "Historical Tidbits," from 2007 until 2011. These articles were generally about Northwest Orange County, Florida. They came from the archives of the Museum of Apopkans, personal memories or interviews with the subjects involved. When writing articles from the Museum archives, he did everything possible to give proper credits to the various authors. Sometimes, however, the author was unknown.

During the 16th century, the Acuera tribe of the Timucua confederation lived on the eastern shores of Lake Apopka, fishing, farming, and trading with other tribes. They called the area "Ahapopka," which means "potato eating place." By the 19th century, the Seminole Indians occupied the area and called the lake "Big Potato." From those days forward, Apopka was known as "The Big Potato."

Acknowledgments

I would like to give my thanks to the many people who encouraged me to write the weekly articles in *The Apopka Chief* about the history of Northwest Orange County and urged me to have them published.

This applies especially to my wife, Joan, who has shared every bump along the way. I would also like to give a special thanks to my beloved granddaughter, Kristen Reilly, and my daughters, Joan Bailey, Ginger Goff and Cindy Christmas for their help in proofing.

Thanks also to Angela Nichols, Belle Gilliam, Larry and Hilda Ludenburg of the Apopka Historical Society for their support and love of history.

Without John Ricketson, publisher of *The Apopka Chief,* and the support of his wonderful staff, I could never have ever written "Historical Tidbits", which supplies the content of this book.

Pat McGuffin and his staff at Reliance Media did a superb job in guidance and assistance in publishing the book.

My special appreciation goes to Mayor John Land for his encouragement to get the stories into book form and the City of Apopka for funding it.

Forward: In The Beginning

Apopka has been the community and trading center for Northwest Orange County since the area was settled a little more than a hundred years ago. In his 1885 directory of information about the area, Wanton S. Webb, an adamant Florida promoter, described the little town as, "situated about midway of the rolling belt of pine lands" between Lake Apopka on the west and the headwaters of the Wekiva River on the northeast. According to Webb, this strip of land was about seven miles wide, "interspersed with hundreds of lakes," and its soil was, "of the very best quality."

Probably the youngest part of the land area of the United States, Florida rose from the sea about forty-five million years ago. Most of it is underlain with several hundred feet of limestone formed by marine deposits during the long period when it was submerged. Extending from beyond the northern Florida boundary to the southern edge of the central ridge district is the Florida aquifer, which contains huge volumes of underground water. Since the limestone is soluble, the water occasionally causes it to give way.

A sinkhole forms wherever this occurs, accounting for the numerous surface lakes which dot the central Florida region. While both the Gulf and Atlantic coastal areas and the region south of Lake Okeechobee are low and sometimes almost flat, the central ridge with its rolling terrain extends from northern Florida down the peninsula, becoming narrower just south of Orange County, and finally disappearing northwest of Lake Okeechobee. Apopka and Northwest Orange County lie on the eastern edge of the central ridge, accounting for the desirable qualities which Webb found there. High enough to be well drained in most places and dotted with many lakes, the low, rolling hills were well suited to the purposes of the settlers who were coming into the area in the late 19th century.

Fossil remains show that during the Cenozoic geology era, perhaps because of ice covering much of the continent, Florida was inhabited by wolves, bears, sloths, camels, saber-toothed tigers, and mastodons. Fossils of some of these animals, dating from the Miocene epoch approximately seventeen million years ago, have been found at Rock Springs.

Although man came much later, archaeological excavations are continually pushing back the date of his earliest habitation of Florida. Until a few years ago, it was believed that man came to the state comparatively recently. Excavations of the past few decades have proven otherwise, and it is now generally known that the peninsula was the dwelling place of human beings at least 10,000 years ago. In early 1980, a young woman found remains in Marion County which strongly suggest humans were here at least 40,000 years ago. Whether that is correct or not, it is likely that the earliest human inhabitants of the Lake Apopka area lived on the northeastern edge of the lake around 7,500 years B.C.

The Zellwood archaeological site, which is located two miles west of Apopka and about a mile from the present lake shore, was excavated in the early 1970s. When the Indians lived at the site, their village was on the edge of the lake, but drainage in recent times has moved the shoreline back toward the southwest. The earliest inhabitants sustained themselves by hunting, but an agriculturally oriented society developed later. Since food and shelter were comparatively easily obtained either from the lake itself or from cultivation of the fertile soil adjacent to it, life along the shore of Lake Apopka for those early inhabitants seems to have been rather simple. Still, remnants of several dugout canoes have been recovered from the mucklands which once formed the lake bed, suggesting that trade was carried on with other villages. It is believed that they may have used water transportation to trade as far away as the west coast of Florida. Although there is no direct evidence of this, it is probable that these early lake dwellers had contact with other tribes only seven miles away on the Wekiva River. Unexcavated mounds near the river in present-day Wekiwa Springs State Park suggest prehistoric settlements were located there as well.

The layering of artifacts at the Zellwood site – trianguloid knives, crude scrapers, knife points, Citrus and Hernando arrow points, St. Johns Incised pottery, Pasco tempered pottery, and Deptford sand-tempered pottery – support the probability that it was inhabited from about 7,500 B.C. to the first century A.D., then abandoned for about four hundred years. It was probably a different cultural group which came to the lake shore about 500 A.D. or so, bringing ceramics and simple forms of agriculture. These later inhabitants also abandoned the site hundreds of years before Columbus discovered America.

When the Spaniards arrived in the 16th century, the Timucuan group inhabited northeast and central Florida, having migrated into the peninsula and down the St. Johns River from the north. A Timucuan tribe called the Acuera inhabited the Oklawaha River valley and probably camped on Lake Apopka. The Acuera, like other Timucuan tribes, grew corn, fished, and carried on extensive trade. When Hernando de Soto camped in the Ocala province in 1539, he bought corn from the Acuera. According to the de Soto narratives, the Acuera were located a two-day journey southeast of Ocala. This should place them along the Oklawaha River in the vicinity of the lake. There was an encounter between the Acuera and a Spanish military expedition in 1604, but the group was not mentioned by the Spaniards after 1656. Like most of the aboriginal tribes, the Acuera were probably decimated by European diseases, European wars in which Indian tribes were pitted against each other, and several revolts against Spanish authorities.

Only a few Timucuans remained after British Colonel James Moore's raid in 1702. Florida was virtually depopulated of its aboriginal inhabitants by 1730.

Chapter I - The Early Days

Coacoochee

Long before any of the Buchans, Lovells or Stewarts arrived in the Apopka area, the shores of Lake Apopka were inhabited by the Acuera tribe of the Timucua Indian Confederation. They hunted, fished, grew crops, and traded with neighboring tribes. By 1730, diseases brought in by the Spaniards had decimated the tribe.

In the early 19th century, the Seminoles had villages on Lake Apopka and remained there until the outbreak of the Seminole War.

Coacoochee was a Seminole chief famed for his intelligence, eloquence, and fearlessness as a warrior. He was also known as "Wild Cat." Coacoochee was born about 1809, near Ahapopka (Apopka), Florida. His father was Philip (Emathla), his mother was the sister of Micanopy, and Coacoochee was heir apparent to the throne of the Seminoles. Five feet, eight inches in height, he was physically well proportioned, with dark, full, and expressive eyes, and presented an extremely youthful and pleasing appearance. He governed his tribe with skill and firmness and obtained a reputation as a brave and daring warrior. He also had a reputation for his fluency of speech, vivid imagination, and spirituality.

When the Florida war began, Coacoochee was living near Lake Ahapopka (Lake Apopka), but soon he and his band of 250 warriors sought refuge in the swamps and hammocks ranging from Ft. Melon (Sanford) to the Atlantic coast, south to Ft. Pierce, and west to Lake Okeechobee. Coacoochee soon became known as the most dangerous chieftain in the field. He roamed swiftly throughout the countryside, laughing at and taunting the soldiers when they became mired in the mud and water while chasing him through the swamps.

On September 9, 1837, General Joseph M. Hernandez attacked the camp of Philip (Coacoochee's father) and captured him and eleven members of his tribe. Subsequently, Philip sent a tribal member to Coacoochee with a message in which he urged his son to surrender. Under a flag of truce, Coacoochee and Osceola came in to see the general. Fearing they would not surrender, the general had them seized on October 21, 1837. They were imprisoned in Ft. Marion at St. Augustine. A little over thirty days later, Coacoochee escaped and joined his band at the headwaters of the Tomoka River. They met with other Seminole chiefs on their way to surrender at St. Augustine and persuaded them to continue to fight, prolonging the war. Osceola was taken to Ft. Moultrie, near Charleston, South Carolina, where he eventually died.

Coacoochee had become the war chief most respected by the U.S. Army, and was believed to have led raids on the St. Johns River settlements and taken part in the murders along the Georgia state line from 1840 to 1841. On March 5, 1841, Coacoochee, who was then living at the Big Cypress Swamp, south of Lake Ahapopka, came in again under a white flag to Fort Cummings (Lake Alfred), at the invitation of General Walker K. Armistead to discuss bringing in his band. To the amazement of the soldiers, Coacoochee was arrayed as Hamlet, while another member of his party was dressed as Horatio, and a third member as Richard III. The costumes had been stolen from a traveling acting troupe they had attacked in May of 1840. Their meeting with the general was interrupted when Coacoochee's twelve-year-old daughter, also a captive in the camp, heard her father's voice and joined him. Overcome that his daughter was reunited with him, Coacoochee wept.

He then eloquently spoke:

"The whites dealt unjustly by me. I came to them, they deceived me. The land I was upon I loved, my body is made of its sands; The Great Spirit gave me legs to walk over it; hands to aid myself; eyes to see its ponds, river, forests, and game; then a head with which I think. The sun, which is warm and bright as my feelings are now, shines to warm forth our crops, and the moon brings back the spirits of our warriors, our fathers, wives, and children.

The white man comes; he grows pale and sick, why cannot he live here in peace? I have said I am the enemy to the white man. I could live in peace with him, but they first steal our cattle and horses, cheat us, and take our lands. The white men are as thick as the leaves in the hammock; they come upon us thicker every year. They may shoot us; drive our women and children night and day. They may chain our hands and feet, but the red man's heart will always be free. I have come here in peace, and have taken you by the hand; I will sleep in your camp though your soldiers stand around me like the pine. I am done; when we know each other's face better I will say more."

For the next few years, the U.S. Army constantly used Coacoochee to influence his people to give up and immigrate to Oklahoma Territory. He was very successful, and a majority of the Seminoles did leave; however, a few retreated into the Everglades and never gave up or surrendered to the Army.

Coacoochee said, "I am alone, I am going to my new home in Arkansas. I have thrown away my rifle and buried my hatchet. With the bright eyes of my sister looking at me from the pebbled bottom of my own Ahapopka, I have washed the dark stains of blood from my clothes and person, and I now say unto my white fathers, take care of me." In January of 1857, Coacoochee contracted small pox and died. He was only forty-eight years old.

History Of The Town Of Apopka

While researching some of these old authors from many years ago, I ran across someone who expressed himself in such an eloquent manner that I just have to pass it on to you. One of these authors is Ralph Grassfield, special staff writer for the Orange County Chamber of Commerce, who wrote this article on the history of the town of Apopka back in the early 1900s:

"Wealthy in terms of primitive life were the Indians that had their home on the northeast shore of Lake Apopka, for tradition assures us that this tribe of Seminoles, known as Apopkans, was industrious. The territory held by them was particularly fertile. They planted, harvested, and danced to the moon and the stars. Their Gods of wind and rain and sunshine were kindly, giving abundant life. The forest was full of deer and bear and winged life, while the lakes provided food throughout the semi-tropical year.

The waters of the great lake, with more than fifty miles of shoreline, and the scores of other and smaller lakes wound about through the territory held by the Apopkans, each with their particular charm, were full of fish to be caught with primitive hooks or speared with their harpoons made from bamboo or the straight and strong hardwood sapling. Rolling hills and broad stretches of prairie lands, with here and there a marsh bordering a lake, gave to these peace-loving and home-loving natives a range that was more than ample for their few needs.

Hills and flat lands were densely covered with semi-tropical growth of pine and evergreen oak, gum and magnolia, while in the lower lands and around the lakes, the palm trees lifted their tufted crests to the sun and moon. The rustling of the gentle breeze throughout the year in the forest of the Apopka territory, the kindly climate, the advantages of game in the forest and the fish in the lakes, inspired the Indian to a home life and a primitive agriculture, which in turn brought fame to this tribe throughout the Floridian peninsula. The success of their agriculture effort in raising potatoes gave them the name "Apopka" for this, according to tradition means, "big potato."

Chronological history of an aboriginal race is unfortunately impossible. Speculation on the mode of living of these Apopka Indians is indeed interesting. Fragmentary facts handed down from the chiefs and medicine men who first had contact with the white man indicate the prosperity suggested here.

The early explorers, who trekked across the Floridian peninsula during the years immediately following the coming of Ponce de Leon, noted the character and fertility and recognized the future of this country. The Apopka Indians were not hostile toward the first white men. They gave to them their substance and provided shelter for those first hardy and intrepid Spaniards who braved the perils of the forest to discover and report on the character of this great inland country.

The years rolled on and the Indians continued to live in peace and quiet. Then the early nineteenth century arrived, when wars and aggression swept over the Florida country. The Indian, strong in his defense of his native territory, could not withstand the insistence of the paleface and he finally succumbed. Weaker races give way to the strong, and those who will not make full use of their opportunities must submit to those who will build a greater civilization. Nowhere in the world is this emphasized more strongly than the territory of Apopka.

Forest and lake, hill and prairie yielded their natural endowment to the new civilization. The years preceding the Civil War, settlers from the North, principally from Georgia, came into the country. They cleared the land, established roads, built homes, and schools and produced crops of cotton, sugar cane, and vegetables."

Peter Buchan

Upon arriving in America, Peter Buchan, a Scottish silversmith of noble birth, settled in LaGrange, Georgia. Becoming discontent with the production of cotton in Georgia, he began to look further south to the virgin soils and beautiful rolling hills of Central Florida for production of his crops. Moving would give him a chance to practice his art as a silversmith in a new territory.

In the late 1830s, he decided to hitch his four mules to a wagon and migrate to Central Florida. He started the journey with his family, slaves, and all his worldly goods seeking a new life in a new land. He was well aware of the difficult 500-mile journey ahead. Family accounts of the journey had him going through Columbus, Thomasville, and on down the Wild Grass Trail, an Indian trail that took him through Live Oak, Lake City, and Starke on his way to Palatka. It was at this point that he put his family and possessions on board a barge heading south. This was a good-sized barge that had catwalks from stem to stern on each side, giving the slaves a place to stand and pole the vessel upstream. You can just imagine the labor it took to pole this barge with so many tons aboard. They continued their very difficult journey up the St. Johns until they reached the Wekiva, where they poled on up to Clay Springs.

It was here that Buchan homesteaded land in between Clay Springs and Apopka and proceeded to clear the land and planted cotton as his major crop. During this clearing process, Peter spotted many panthers and bears in the wild. As new settlers arrived, the panthers migrated farther south and became very scarce in this area. Peter also began practicing his trade as a silversmith and soon became known as an expert in this field. People came on horseback from all over Florida for his services.

When the Civil War broke out, Peter took his family to Indian River City on the east coast, somewhere around Titusville. They only stayed there for one year. When the Buchans moved back from the east coast, they came on a barge built for the purpose of paddling, not poling. They brought all their belongings, including several barrels of salt made by evaporating seawater from the ocean. Salt was precious at that time and it was sold at a high price. Their only fear was that the Federal soldiers then in Florida might find and confiscate it.

Soon, other settlers joined them in the Rock Springs area. The Stewarts, Major Delk, Lovells, McFaddens, and the Shoros were some of them. Jack and Mary Winters, who were freed slaves, homesteaded there also. About this time, most of the land in the area was cleared and producing good yields of cotton. There was a cotton gin on the Wekiva that was operated by water power and was ginning most of the cotton grown in the area.

Henry S. Sanford, who had a branch store in Clay Springs, was giving credit to the farmers who consigned their crops to him, Robert Barnhart put in a sawmill on the Little Wekiva at Shepard's Spring, using the flowing water to power his mill. It was here that the first Masonic Lodge was located before later being moved to Apopka.

One of the beautiful items that Peter made was a sword of gold for his grandson. It bore the slogan "I make sure," which was thought to be the family coat of arms. For sure, Peter Buchan made a contribution to the early days in Apopka.

D. B. Stewart

When D.B. Stewart passed away in March of 1916, he was the last of the original settlers in the Apopka area. His was the second family to settle in the area behind Peter Buchan, who had homesteaded a few years earlier a little closer to Rock Springs.

It was not long after Stewart's birth that his parents moved from Jasper to what is today known as Ocala. In 1853, the family moved farther south into Orange County. On Christmas Day, the party camped at Clay Springs where they had their Christmas dinner. A few days later, they settled on the land that for more than half a century was to become their home. This was the J.O. Welch property, located only a few miles south of the Peter Buchan homestead. One morning, Peter woke up to the sound of a rooster crowing, and that is when he knew he had a neighbor.

At that time, there were very few settlements in the county and the Indians roamed the land without restraint. In 1855, the Indian Chief Taliahasse and his tribe camped all winter at what is now Oakland, on the southern shore of Lake Apopka. There were signs everywhere that the Indians had recently occupied the land.

In 1861, Stewart married Miss Missouri Goolsby, whose family had moved from La Grange, Georgia, in 1854 to settle in Zellwood. They had three children, Mrs. S.W. Eldredge, S.W. Stewart, and Mrs. J.O. Welch.

The Stewarts' life, like that of all pioneers, was filled with constant adventure. They owned slaves who tilled the soil and raised cotton, which was ginned by machinery run by water power at what is now called Mill Creek. The ginned cotton was hauled to Fort Melon (Sanford) and from there it was shipped to Savannah or Charleston.

Stewart was among the first to become interested in growing oranges, and at one time, he became very wealthy, having an annual income that was almost princely for the area at that time. A typical example was the 1882 sale of 130,000 oranges for $15 per thousand. Using that money, he invested in more land and groves, but the big freezes of 1884 and 1885 deprived him of the greater portion of his wealth. Fortunately, however, they did not damage his indomitable spirit.

As is the case in sparsely populated areas, the citizens took a huge interest in all public affairs. In the early 1860s, Stewart was judge of probate, and in the late '60s, he was the high sheriff of Orange County, the area of which was about triple the size of the county today. Later, he resigned his position, because he didn't want to carry out the stern decrees of the law that conflicted with his conscience.

For six years during the 1880s, Stewart served as a county commissioner and was on the board when the courthouse and jail were built. He served on the board with Dr. King Wiley, F. Whitner of Sanford, and Clinton Johnson.

Stewart always took a deep interest in educational matters. His daughter, Mrs. S. W. Eldridge, graduated from Wesleyan College in Atlanta, Georgia, the oldest female college in the country. She is probably the first woman born in Orange County to hold a college diploma.

With the leadership of pioneers such as D.B. Stewart, the northwest section of the county grew at the same pace as the rest of the state, and boasted every modern convenience available at the time.

Although he was in favor of progress, D.B. Stewart was not inclined to be governed by the whims or fads of the public. He was a typical frontiersman, kind-hearted and a loyal friend, as well as a good neighbor and an indulgent father. Measured by the standard of the day and times, he stands out clearly against the background of the period as one of the leaders of men. And his name must ever stand high in the history of Orange County, which he helped wrest from its primitive state and carry into the foremost ranks of progress.

William A. Lovell

William A. Lovell has always been considered one of Apopka's earliest pioneers, along with Peter Buchan, the Shoros, the McFaddens, and Major Delk. Prior to the Civil War, the Lovells moved from Cartersville, Georgia, to Mellonville (Sanford, Florida), where William established himself in the business community. While living in Mellonville, he took a summer home in Apopka to get his family away from the mosquitoes on the river. At that time, he buried five bales of cotton on his land north of Apopka.

It was during this period that the War Between the States started and William enlisted in the Confederate Army for three years. He was captured by Federal Forces and was released at the end of the war. One day, the old rooster was crowing and seemed to his wife to be saying, "Pa's coming home," and Pa did come home. He immediately went to where he had buried the cotton and only three bales were left. Someone had stolen the other two bales. At any rate, he sold the three bales of cotton for $1.25 a pound, bringing Lovell more than $4,000, enough money to buy one square mile of land. The land that he bought is now downtown Orlando.

William built his home on the site of what is now the old Orange County Courthouse. He built a store on the southeast corner of Main and Central and built a hotel on Summerlin. It is said that he brought the first kerosene and the first glass windows into Orlando. His cow pen was where the library is now and he had a potato patch and a large garden on the shores of Lake Eola. He also planted cotton and operated a sawmill and three cotton gins. In 1869, he was superintendent of the Orange County school system.

In the 1860s, the average home was a log building with two large rooms, an open breezeway between the kitchen and bedroom on the back and a broad porch on the front. In the rear of William's house were chinaberry trees for shade, a scuppernong grapevine, and a trellis under which the laundry was done – the water being heated by an open fire under an iron kettle. The water was drawn from an open well by a long sweep. A fence surrounded the house to keep the cattle and hogs out. In the yard were bushes of Cape Jessamine and the red Cracker rose. The yard was sand and was continually swept clean. Many people had a cane patch from which "long-sweetening" was made, as well as a melon field and guava and citrus trees.

In 1878, the Lovells purchased the property on the corner of 7th and Alabama in Apopka and moved there with their eleven children. William Lovell operated a general store located on McGee Street where the Burger King is now. At that time, the Apopka House Hotel was nearby, where a service station stands today. The Apopka House would eventually become The Wayside Inn. Their rates ran $5 per week or $16 per month. Across the street from the hotel was the Masonic Lodge. To the west where the Silver Palms Motel now stands, Narcissus (William's wife) ran a drug store in a two-story building. A dress shop occupied the second floor. Lovell also operated a livery stable at the present site of World-O-Suds, at Highway 441 and Alabama.

In addition, he founded Lovell's Landing, a landing dock on Lake Apopka a little north of Magnolia Park, consisting of 250 acres. From there, he operated a freight service on the lake and points north. At Clay Springs (Wekiwa), he operated a wharf for shipping and receiving supplies via the Wekiva River. He was also president of a company which bought a steamboat to operate on the Wekiva and St. Johns River. This started out to be a thriving business, because many kinds of merchandise were brought down the river. Before long, however, the railroads proved to be too much competition. One of these was a narrow-gauge railroad that operated from Sanford to Orlando. Wagons were used to haul freight from Longwood to Apopka.

W.A. Lovell kept a dry goods store around this time. The Honorable James L. Giles, who would later become mayor of Orlando twice, was a clerk in this store when he was ten years old. Mr. Lovell left the business with this youthful assistant for some months, during an absence from Apopka. While he was gone, the boy purchased five thousand cigars from a traveling man, on the condition that they should be labeled Giles' Best. Upon his return, Lovell was very disturbed by this transaction, but the supply of Giles' Best cigars was exhausted within a year's time.

Later, the Florida Midland Railroad was built. Its station was located across the street from where the Catfish Place is today. The coming of the railroad caused the town to spread westward. The Tavares, Orlando and Atlantic (Seaboard) laid tracks even farther west, with a station at Central and Sixth Street, and the town began to move in that direction. A.J. Lovell was in charge of building a clay road from the "Old Town" to the newer town. The citizens contributed labor one or two days a week, some bringing teams of mules and wagons, and the ladies brought dinner. Everyone enjoyed the occasion and it did not cost the city one red cent.

The first effort to provide telegraph service to Apopka occurred in 1880, when William G. Lovell and others incorporated the Orange County Central Telegraph Company to build a line from Apopka through Zellwood and on to Lake Eustis. It was eventually acquired by the International Ocean Telegraph Company, a firm that ran wire services between the United States and Cuba on a route through Florida.

William Lovell raised his eleven children in Apopka. His oldest son Jack was on the committee to secure the charter for the "Town of Apopka City." His youngest son Fred, also known as "Bull," had three children – Charles, Justin, and Mildred (married name Savage) – who continued to live in the old Lovell home site on the Rock Springs Road north of Florida Hospital Apopka. In fact, the land where the hospital stands was owned at one time by Fred.

Mrs. M. E. Buchan

This is a story of one of Apopka's earliest pioneers as printed in The Apopka Chief on February 23, 1934:

"Tomorrow, February 24, Apopka's oldest pioneer, Mrs. M.E. Buchan, will observe her 95th birthday. She was born in Glen County, Georgia, in 1839 and came to Apopka with her father's family in 1855. She has been a resident here ever since, with the exception of about a year during the War Between the States when she lived in Indian River City, on the east coast, then known as Sand Point. Mrs. Buchan has two sons and two daughters. One of the sons is Chip Buchan of Apopka. Her husband passed away 35 years ago.

Mrs. Buchan is a remarkable personage with a mind that is still active. She clearly recalls events of 85 years ago and has watched, with the keenest interest, the development of Central Florida from an unbroken forest to its present modern state. She makes her home with her son, Chip in a modest cottage on the Rock Springs Road, a short distance north of Apopka. The home is still in the midst of pines and evergreen oaks. In the rear to the east, there are about 30 acres of cleared land that produces crops year round.

This venerable woman tells of the time when practically all that wild section was under cultivation, producing a good yield of cotton. That was about the time of the war. Around Rock Springs, cotton was grown abundantly and there was a cotton gin

Mrs. M. E. Buchan

Apopka, Resident
Who celebrates her 95th Birthday Anniversary tomorrow

and sawmill there, operated by water power. In later years, all that section returned to the wild state. Mrs. Buchan recalls many of the old neighbors, including pioneers whose descendants still live here – the Stewarts, Major Delk, the Lovells, McFaddens, and Shoros. She also remembers some of the former slaves that lived in that neighborhood of Rock Springs, including Jack and Mary Winters, who were freed and homesteaded here.

Mrs. Buchan told of experiences with bears and panthers, then very plentiful, and now only occasionally seen in the swamps.

When the Buchans moved back to Apopka from the coast, they came on a barge built for the purpose, poling up the St. Johns to Sanford and then the Wekiwa River to Wekiwa Springs, then known as Clay Springs. They brought all their belongings on the barge, including several barrels of salt, which they secured by evaporating waters of the ocean. Salt was precious at that time and it was later sold at a good price. Their only fear was that the Federal soldiers, then in Florida, might find and confiscate it.

Though bowed by the weight of years, Mrs. Buchan is sprightly and happy in the autumn of her life. She will no doubt receive many callers on her birthday anniversary tomorrow."

Henry Witherington

Henry H. Witherington was born in Tuscaloosa County, Alabama in 1862, the son of S.S. and Louise Witherington; his father was a farmer in Alabama and a plantation overseer during slavery days. Henry attended the schools of his native state, and was employed in a country store in Alabama for two or three years.

Witherington came to Apopka in 1884, when he was only twenty-two years of age. He was attracted to Florida by the orange industry and to Apopka in particular for its high ground and rolling hills. For a short time after his arrival, he was a clerk for the J.J. Combs store in Apopka. By 1886, he had built his own store on Central Avenue and operated a grocery and then hardware store for the next twenty years.

Henry Witherington never aspired to political honors, although in 1896 he was appointed to the Board of Public Instruction of Orange County to fill the unexpired term of the Honorable T.G. Hyers. He was later elected to the position and served for fourteen additional years.

In 1901, Henry, along with John B. Steinmetz of Clay Springs, started the first telephone service in the area by erecting a line from Clay Springs to Apopka. Operating as the Apopka Telephone Company, they ran lines to Orlando in 1902, to Lake County in 1905, and to Winter Garden in 1907. The Orange County Commission permitted the firm to use county right-of-ways for their lines. In about 1912, Witherington leased the company's lines and equipment to Arthur J. Walker, who incorporated them into his Winter Garden system.

Apopka struggled with the depression of 1890 and the devastating freezes of 1894-95. The population of 1,500 had declined to 350 by 1905. The city government had become almost non-existent. Determined to end the stagnation, Apopka started over by electing new city officials. Henry Witherington was elected to the Apopka City Council and appointed to a committee to revise the town ordinances.

The new ordinances continued the requirement that all able-bodied males, aged eighteen to forty-five, must work three days a year on the streets unless they paid one dollar a day or hired a substitute. The new ordinances also stated that, "no person may run animals upon the new streets....or break horses to harness or saddle in the streets." They also prohibited hitching horses to "shade trees, awning posts, lamp posts or any fence."

Witherington actively pursued early conservation measures, such as licenses for commercial fishermen in Lake Apopka and game laws for the protection of deer, turkey, etc. Henry said, "Young turkeys were being killed when frying size, the young deer were dying from no protection, the fish were being dynamited, seined, trapped, and caught by the thousands." Those who were interested in the conservation of game and fish were the same people who eventually formed the Apopka Sportsman Club.

John J. Anderson of Piedmont and Witherington were appointed by the Apopka Board of Trade to a committee that was to stimulate an interest in growing new crops in the area. They were to give "liberal assistance" to the planting of 300-500 acres. Both tomatoes and watermelons were planted in the next few years and, although they were damaged by an unusually long drought in 1913, sizeable shipments of both tomatoes and watermelon left Apopka that year. Witherington was among the tomato growers, and S.W. Eldridge was one of those who shipped watermelons by rail.

Henry served as postmaster for two years, starting in 1919. Beginning in 1923, he served two years in the Florida Legislature.

When the Brokers Mortgage Company of Orlando opened a branch in Apopka in 1926, Henry was appointed to the board of directors and served on their loan committee. The hurricane of 1926 helped bring an end to the land boom, and the mortgage company left Apopka.

Around 1920, Lake Apopka's fishing was attracting national attention. The City of Apopka built a dock, clubhouse and picnic grounds at Lovell's Landing and urged the county road engineer to build a road leading from the landing to the Apopka-Ocoee Road. Witherington served on the committee to secure the necessary right-of-way. They were successful, and Dock Road was opened in 1922.

I know Henry would have been proud of his son Harry, who also served terms as an Orange County Commissioner representing Northwest Orange County and was very active in community affairs. You can rest assured that we are proud of them both.

Zelotes Mason

In 1870, Dr. Zelotes Mason was a very sick man with a bronchial disease and he was looking throughout the state of Florida for some high, rolling land where he could build a home. He wanted to be as far away as possible from the swamps or any other areas that were not beneficial to his affliction.

That same year, he found the land of his dreams in Apopka, so he settled about a mile northeast of Orange Lodge and soon became one of the region's most enthusiastic boosters. In an 1875 article entitled "The Invalid's Refuge," he declared "the Apopka climate well-adapted for those suffering from bronchial diseases," assuring readers that "ample accommodations will be provided" as soon as "assurance is given that invalids will resort to the interior to spend their winters." Posing the question, "Who should come to Florida?" Mason also wrote that, "Florida offers inducements not only to the invalid, but also, to those who wish to make profitable investments in building hotels…purchasing orange groves or growing sugar cane."

A little later, the *Apopka Citizen* boasted that there had not been a single funeral in the community for an entire year. The editor thought this remarkable, since "we see about us every day numbers of people who came here mere skeletons, hardly able to crawl, who are now hale and healthy, recuperated both in health and in wealth." While such assertions were probably read with the caution they deserved, Florida in general and Central Florida in particular were becoming known as a healthy and prosperous place to live.

When F.A. Taylor, editor of the *Apopka Citizen,* went back to his native Missouri for a visit, the newspaper turned the trip into a promotional event. It stated, "The great change that had taken place in Taylor's physical condition since his residence in Florida will do more to convince his friends that the Florida climate possesses a recuperative power to restore health than many written assertions. He may be termed a traveling advertisement for Florida, and will no doubt, be instrumental in bringing many persons to Orange County."

So, as you can see, Dr. Mason was not the only one who thought the Apopka area did possess this recuperative power. The doctor quietly settled into being a good citizen in Apopka and was active in the Masonic Lodge and Orange County School Board, while also serving as a Baptist Deacon and farming his citrus grove.

Apopkans and their neighbors supported their local schools and were active in the county system as well. The original county board, which convened in late 1869, was composed of W.C. Roper, A.C. Caldwell, and Zelotes Mason. W.A. Lovell was the superintendent.

At various times between 1871 and 1889, Zelotes Mason, Nicholas Prince, and George F. Foots conducted examinations and certified teachers for the Apopka area schools.

For many years Apopka was known as "the Lodge," and the name "Apopka" was not adopted until 1887. The reason for this rather curious name is that Dr. Zelotes Mason and Peter Buchan, influential members of the Masonic Fraternity, lived in Apopka.

Dr. Mason sold the First Baptist Church some land near Edgewood Cemetery for $25 to build a new church. Even with aid from the Baptist Convention's building fund, the church committee, consisting of W.A. Lovell, J.D. Dorsett, M.A. Stewart, L.H. McConnell, and S.A. Dunaway, was unable to complete it until 1883.

The Presbyterian Church was organized in 1873 by Zelotes H. Mason and J. M. Auld as ruling elders, and a Rev. Wallace who served as supply minister for several years. After having met at the Lodge for a while, the Presbyterians began to hold their services in the Methodist Church until the completion of their own church at Highland Avenue and Fifth Street in early 1886. The Rev. S.V. McCorkle, having moved to Maitland for his health in 1881, served as minister for Apopka, Maitland, and Oakland for fourteen years. He preached at Apopka on the third Sunday, always staying overnight at Dr. Mason's home, where a room was permanently reserved for him.

The Prince Family

Many Southern families lost all of their possessions after the War Between the States, and a good portion of them packed their remaining goods and headed to the Sunshine State for a new beginning. This is an article about one such family who relocated from Tuscaloosa, Alabama, to Apopka, Florida.

This article is from the Prince Family History, written by Annie Bradshaw Mansfield, the granddaughter of Nicholas W. Prince.

"It was a sad day for our family in 1867 when my grandfather and his three sons Rufus, James, and Oliver started on their journey to the new land where Nicholas had high hopes of retrieving his fortune lost during the War Between the States. He took with him a few colored house servants, several white laborers, twenty mules, and a covered wagon. They traveled overland in the direction of Apopka, Florida where they hoped to locate in the vicinity of the "Masonic Lodge" where all of the Princes were active Masons.

After the boys were fairly well located on the west side of Apopka, they sent for the girls. Now, "Mammy," who had nursed all of the children, was heartbroken that she was not allowed to make the trip, however, she was quite old, and it was thought the trip would be too hard on her, so she was left with the son who stayed in Alabama.

Traveling in those days entailed many discomforts. The first part of the journey was a delight, especially to the younger members of the family. From Tuscaloosa, they traveled down to Mobile on one of the large steamers that plied the Black Warrior River. In Mobile, they visited in the home of our grandfather's sister, Charity, who had married Richard Knott.

Leaving Mobile, they crossed the Gulf in a small steamer. A terrible storm arose, and it took three days to make the crossing, nearly all on board were suffering from seasickness as well as fright.

The next stage of the journey was from Cedar Key to Jacksonville on a very primitive train. There were no coaches, only a string of flat cars where everyone sat for hours in the scorching Florida sun while the slowly moving engine belched forth smoke and cinders on the hapless passengers.

Arriving in Jacksonville, there was a wait of a few days for the steamer that was to take the party down the St. Johns River. The time was spent in purchasing supplies for their new home. The trip down the St. Johns River was a novel experience, the tropical vegetation and unusual sights serving to keep alive their enthusiasm.

At last, they reached Mellonville, about two miles from where Sanford is now located, their worldly possessions and all the family were put in wagons drawn by mules, and the last stage of the hard journey had begun. It was thirty five miles over sandy Florida roads to their destination. With the soft sand a foot deep much of the way, it took sixteen hours to make the trip, and at the end there was nothing but a rough wooden house that the boys had built in the woods---the beautiful orange grove of their dreams was not yet a reality.

This pioneer spirit was what brought Nicholas Prince's ancestors from England to Virginia in 1639, just as it brought his father, Edmond Prince, from Virginia to Alabama, and now in 1868, it had led him to Florida. But for him it was too late. It is true that his dream of a beautiful orange grove and fields of cotton became a reality but he was too old to begin anew and not strong enough for this kind of farming, and the hardships endured. He was stricken with a paralysis and died on April 7, 1880. He was buried in the old cemetery at Apopka, as is his wife, Mary Hill Foster Prince. Just a short time before his death, his home burned, destroying his beloved books, as well as practically everything of value.

Nicholas and Mary left seven children, one being Edmond Rufus Prince who was a senior at the University of Alabama when the war started, studying to be a doctor. He joined a company in the Confederate Army started at the University and served all four years. He was wounded at Corinth, Mississippi when in battle a cannon rolled over him. He was picked-up, placed on the cannon, and carried out in that manner. He recuperated in a hospital in Richmond, Va.

After the close of the war, he went to Baltimore and studied dentistry and graduated from Baltimore Dental College. He started practicing in Greensboro, Alabama. Immediately after his marriage, he came to Florida and practiced dentistry in Orange County. As was the custom at that time, in the sparsely settled country, he made many calls on horseback. Due to a knee injury received in the war, he was forced to retire, so he became a merchant and later a banker in Apopka.

Dr. Prince built his fourteen-room home in 1879 at the corner of Main Street and Edgewood Drive where Bank First now stands. That was sort of a coincidence as a bank now stands on the corner where Apopka's first banker built his home. Dr. Prince opened Apopka's first bank in 1885; however, it was short lived due to the freeze of the same year. Dr. Prince sold his house (that was later to become the Oaks Hotel) and property in order to settle his debts. He moved to Tampa and later passed away."

Dudley Adams

In the late 1870s, the Honorable Dudley W. Adams of Massachusetts spent two winters in Florida looking for the right location to build a home and spend the rest of his life. When he came upon the Tangerine area, he wrote some of the following impressions that I think you will enjoy:

"One January evening, I came upon the hills overlooking Lake Beauclaire just as the sun was going down in a blaze of glory. The air was as soft as the breath of peace. The pines, the palms, the gorgeous coloring of the clouds and sky and setting sun were repeated in mirrored waters. To the north, Lake Dora half encircled Beauclaire in her crimson embrace, while to the south Ola and Carlton glistened through the pines like gems of the purest water, in emerald settings. Back from the lake for miles sweep the grand swelling hills and lovely secluded valleys, all adorned with those long leaved pines, tall, slender and graceful, the sure indication of a soil peculiarly adapted to the growth of the famous Florida orange. Here and there, less in size, but no less beautiful, Lakes Angeline, Fanny, Lilly, Gem, Victoria, Bonnet, Lena, etc., add beauty to the landscape and adorn a spring of sparkling water delights and entices the thirst.

Here and there are commanding hills in these beautiful valleys by these sparkling waters, among these health-giving pines, surrounded by lovely lakes to furnish sport to the angler, food to the hungry, and to bear freights and pleasure yachts; here is Tangerine, our home, the gem of Florida. From this point, the waters flow north by the Ocklawaha River, east to the St. Johns and west to the gulf. Located as we are on this high rolling plateau, the summit of the peninsula, midway between the ocean and the gulf, we are constantly refreshed and our climate equalized by the ever-recurring sea and gulf breezes, and are comparatively exempt from the gales that sweep the coasts. The summer days are cooled, and with the same agency, the frost is taken from the winter winds. Just northwest of this, a cluster of five large lakes, Harris, Griffin, Eustis, Dora and Beauclaire, furnishes an additional equalizer, giving us a location eminently adapted to the culture of very tender plants and trees. Even the great freezing cold wave of December 30, 1880, spent its fury on the northern shores, and here the lime and lemon, the most tender of all the citrus family, were uninjured in leaf, twig and blossom.

There is no diminutive 'town site' owned by speculators and held at high prices, but a broad expanse of the finest orange land in Florida, miles in extent, sufficient for a large and powerful settlement, owned and occupied by actual settlers. We have made roads, planted 15,000 orange and lemon trees, and established mail routes, sawmills, a post office with daily mail, stores, schools, Sunday school and religious services. We have a Justice of the Peace who never had a trial, and a doctor who rarely has a patient. Steamers now land goods at our doors, and the frequency of their visits will increase with our increasing numbers and wants.

Our inhabitants are moral, intelligent, progressive, and almost of cosmopolitan origin; consequently they are broad and tolerant in their opinions and associations. We want more people, as that means better roads, more steamboats, more schools, bigger stores, more society, and a higher civilization. There is room for many. The soil is a fine light sandy loam with a clay subsoil. It produces sweet potatoes, cassava, conch and cow peas, Sea Island cotton, watermelons etc. It responds with alacrity to the application of manure, and will produce an immense variety of crops in perfection.

The cost of provisions is about the same as in New England, but somewhat higher than the Northwest. It costs much less here for rent, fuel and clothing than in either. Numerous men of liberal means are planting groves here, and this furnishes employment to such settlers who wish to labor for wages until their groves come into bearing. Wages for labor in the groves are $1.25 a day, mechanics proportionately higher. Choice five-acre lots, suitable for groves and homes, can be bought for $175 to $200 each. It costs about $16 per acre to clear, $2.50 to plow and 45 cents per rod to fence. Orange and lemon trees are from 25-75 cents each. I can show you a tree eleven years old from seed, thirty-nine inches around the trunk in the smallest place, which has borne $20 worth of oranges each year for two years. I can show others of the same age that never bore an orange. One grove near here of one-half an acre has produced from $900 to $1,500 for three years in a row. Does it pay? Come and see.

The route to Tangerine is by steamers on the St. Johns River to the railroad in Astor. You take that railroad to Tavares on the north shore of Lake Dora, and then take a steamer to Tangerine. A large hotel will be opened by October 1. The Tangerine Development Society has issued a map of the locality with a circular."

Masonic Lodge

The isolation of the first settlers in Northwest Orange County in the 1800s drew men together in a bond of fellowship that resulted in the organization of a Masonic Lodge, the first in Orange County. Master Masons from Orlando, Sanford, Kissimmee, Tavares, Sorrento, Fort Mason, and other settlements began meeting at Robert Barnhart's mill on the Little Wekiva River at Shepherd's Spring.

Due to the efforts of Dr. Zelotes Mason, Peter Buchan, and others, Orange Lodge No. 36 F. & A.M. was warranted on January 14, 1856, with 14 members. Orange Lodge received a warrant, not a charter, and is one of the few lodges in the state to have such. Immediately after the new Masonic lodge had been granted a warrant, the members sought larger and more efficient quarters. A building committee was formed and it was decided to give Robert Barnhart, who had a sawmill, the contract to build the original Masonic lodge near his mill. A few months later Barnhart asked to be excused from the contract because his mill had broken down.

It was not long until the location for the lodge was moved from near Barnhart's mill to the home of John L. Stewart. It was at this time that the members began serious discussions to construct the lodge on a two-acre site purchased from John L. Stewart. This site was located in the area that grew to be the center of the Town of Apopka City. This was part of a 40-acre tract he had obtained in a deed signed by President Franklin Pierce in 1855. On November 26, 1858, another building committee was appointed, consisting of J. R. Worthington, Amos Newton, Matthew A. Stewart, L. A. Newton, and J. L. Stewart. The new building was presented to the lodge with appropriate ceremonies on October 21, 1859.

Beginning on March 28, 1860, the lodge rented the lower floor one Sunday a month to the Baptists, and J. M. Jackson rented it one Sunday a month for the Methodists. On the other two Sundays, it was used by other Christian denominations.

This lodge was designated as a "moon lodge," with meetings scheduled on the Friday before each full moon, from "two o'clock to candle light." As it was the only lodge in the county (much larger than it is today) and members came from settlements quite a distance away. They had to travel for miles at night and would be able to find their way with the light of the moon.

In the 1860s and 1870s, the lodge became the center of a small, but growing, community, which ultimately became the Town of Apopka City. In 1868, the lower floor of the building was sold to William Mills who, in partnership with Matthew Stewart, opened a general merchandise store. With lodge members from all over the county coming to meetings, with church services being conducted here, and with the only general store for miles around, the lodge attracted increasing attention. So it was appropriate that when the Town of Apopka City was incorporated in 1882, its organizational meetings were held in the lodge building, which was then known as Fudge Hall.

It was known as Fudge Hall because in the 1870s, James D. Fudge, Apopka's first mayor, bought the ground floor from Mills and Stewart. He formed a partnership with William A. Lovell, an experienced merchant and former Orange County School superintendent (1869). They immediately started Apopka's first school on the ground floor of the lodge.

In 1884, J.J. Combs bought it, installed a ceiling, and sold it to parties in England. The lodge bought back the ground floor in 1907, and started operating a printing office and wine shop. As the lodge grew in popularity, new businesses were attracted to the area. The Wayside Inn or The Apopka House, a drug store, a dress shop, a printing shop and a livery stable were a few of the new business who that took advantage of the potential customers attracted to the lodge. The area grew and the lodge became the trading center for Northwest Orange County.

Time moved on and Apopka continued to grow. The town gradually spread to the west when the Florida Midline (Atlantic Coast Line) and Seaboard Railroads located their depots in that area. Wooden sidewalks were installed to connect "old Apopka" with the new.

About the same time as the widening of Hwy. 441 in 1952, the lower floor of the lodge was removed and replaced due to deterioration. The wood was cut away and replaced by cement blocks. While this work was going on, lodge members used a ladder to get to the lodge room.

And that majestic lodge still stands today, in the same spot where the slaves built it in 1859, with their wooden pins. Over the years, it may not have compared in appointments and comfort with those magnificent lodge rooms of some larger cities of today, but the brotherly love and affection emanating from this Masonic Shrine is tried and true. Within the four walls of the lodge room, many men have been raised to the Master Mason's Degree. May those same four walls continue to see many more.

Joseph G. Roberts

The story below was printed in *The Apopka Chief* on May 13, 1926. It was written by the editor, A.M. Hall. It is a very touching story of Joseph G. Roberts, an illegitimate mulatto son of plantation owner Major W.A. Delk. Roberts was an intelligent and prosperous person who tells about his life of being raised in and around Rock Springs. When Dr. Howard A. Kelly purchased Rock Springs, he expressed a desire to learn something of the early history of the locality and the springs itself. This request came to the attention of William Edwards.

Old house on Delk Plantation.

William Edwards first came to these parts from Chicago in 1889, to run Errol Farms and the Errol Cattle Co. He and his men from the cattle company often found themselves in the Rock Springs area when they needed a little rest and some refreshments. He remembered seeing a mulatto, a man who had been raised near the springs and was old at that time. Remembering Dr. Kelly's wishes, he looked for and found the man living in Mt. Dora. He arranged to have him brought to Rock Springs, to see again the place of his boyhood, refresh his recollection, and tell the story of the history of Rock Springs as he knew it. The old man was delighted to comply, and with his nearly 90 years resting lightly upon his broad shoulders, he was the happiest of the little party that went out to the springs. That small party included A. M. Hall, and William Edwards. Here is Hall's article:

"Arriving at the spot just above where the waters gush up through the gash in the lime rock, the old man got out of his machine and declared that he must first pay his respects to the old spring, the best friend of his boyhood. Standing close to the edge of the water, he reverently removed his hat and gazed long and earnestly into the water. Then with a trembling voice the old man said something like this:

Best Greetings, Mr. Rock,

Howdedo, Mrs. Springs!

Dr. Kelly at mouth of Rock Springs.

From whence you come, I do not know,

From whence you come in the beginning.

And whence do you flow, we do not know.

Blessings for years you have continued to bring.

Wherefore you are known as Old Rock Spring.

For, lo, many years did I hear remain,

This you may know, it is old friend Joe,

Who worked here so long, midst sorrow and woe.

Good night, old spring----Forever.

Placing his hat on his silvered head, the patriarch turned to the others of the party and announced he was ready to tell his story and points of interest. It was a sad story, and once or twice, the old chap was aroused to indignation as he recalled his life there and his treatment at the hands of the man he knew as his father and master.

"The first name I was known by was Joseph Delk. Wishing to get away from the name of my unnatural father, I took the name of Joseph G. Roberts. Today no one knows me by my other name—few know my history. My mother was a black Negro, and a good mother to me she was. My father was W.S. Delk, a white man, who was the first settler here at Rock Springs. That is why I am a mulatto. I was born over on the St. Johns River and my father—and master brought me here when I was a small boy."

W.S. Delk came from Liberty County, Georgia around 1840 and settled somewhere along the St. Johns River. After scouting out the area he finally found Rock Springs and moved here with all his belongings.

My mother and I were among his chattels. Things became somewhat complicated for my father in Florida, so he went away to Mississippi and was gone a year. After his return affairs settled down at the springs and he became prosperous. All our supplies were brought in by ox carts from a place called Hawkinsville (Crow's Bluff), 18 miles away on the St. Johns River. Back in those days there was not much to Apopka, and Orlando was a cotton patch---a little trading post, and I think the only one between Jacksonville and Tampa. There were only bridle paths through the forests---no roads, no railroads.

From 1854 until well along in the Civil War, we lived in comparative quiet, except for occasional outbreaks of family feuds, and now and then a killing. Our first house was a log cabin structure just north of the springs. In an effort to burn out fleas from underneath it, the house caught on fire and was destroyed. Another house was then built over on that hill on the south side and that is where Mr. Delk died in 1885. It was a miserable death and a pathetic funeral.

I was living at Sorrento, where I had homesteaded a piece of land. I came here and put the old man in a rough box, the best we could do, and the body was taken to Apopka and buried in a small cemetery there. But I am getting ahead of my story. Delk saw the possibility of the stream running from the big springs and we built a dam across it about fifty yards from the spring and set the water back in the basin to a height of about five feet. Then we built a flume that you see there and put a big bucket water wheel in it. This is on the right side as you face down the stream. The spillway was on the left. Adjoining the mill-wheel, we built a grist mill and the cotton gin and sawmill. All of these enterprises were successful.

Now, come up here to the top of the rock. Out there, where you see all those pine trees was a cotton plantation. There were also fields of sugar cane and rice. In that little depression was where we raised our garden stuff and we had to fence against deer and other animals that would come in and eat it up as fast as it would grow.

Things went on this way until we were well along in the Civil War. Then, trouble began. Delk was an old-line Whig, not a Secessionist. The story went out that he was organizing a company in here to fight for Lincoln, and a troop of cavalry was sent in here from Lake City to investigate. The story was wholly untrue. When the soldiers arrived they were hospitably treated and invited to supper. But Delk was arrested and the soldiers started out with him that evening.

In Sorrento, they camped for the night. Delk made his escape - took to the swamps and came back home. He told us slaves---there were nineteen of us---that we were free and to take care of ourselves. He then set out for St. Augustine, where there were federal forces.

The rest of us killed a beef cow, and taking what provisions we could carry, set out for Wekiwa Springs by ox team. At Wekiwa, we found an old boat and started down the river. Reaching the St. Johns without mishap, we were picked up by a federal gunboat and started north. Near St. Augustine, we were turned over to the Fifth Cavalry and taken into camp. Here, Delk later joined the party. I enlisted in the Union army and was sent to South Carolina, and there I did service until the close of the war.

The year of 1868 found me back at Rock Springs again, and that year I homesteaded a piece of land at Sorrento and lived there many years. Later I was able to acquire ten acres of land near Mt. Dora, and I am living my last days there with my niece."

This is his story of the early settlement of Rock Springs, leaving out many of the details. But I will ramble over the place with you and point out some features of interest. It only remains to be added that ownership of the property was lost by Delk through non-payment of taxes.

"The party walked over the place with the old mulatto. He showed the visitors several deep impressions north of the spring and said they used to be springs. One to the northwest was where they obtained water for the house. They imagined it was better water than flowed from Rock Springs, but it came from the same subterranean river that is the source of so many big springs in Central Florida. Ruins of the old house where Delk died was pointed out. One of the old log cabins still stands.

Save for the few evidences pointed out, like the old flume and the old cabin and an occasional sour orange tree, there is little now to indicate that man ever lived there. The forest has come back, and where the cotton and cane once thrived, only the old spring and the little river flows on as they did in those other days."

State Bank of Apopka

Main Street in Apopka

CHAPTER II - PIONEERS & COMMUNITIES

John Anderson

In 1870, John J. Anderson traveled a long way in order to realize his American dream. He left his home in Sweden and came to Piedmont, Florida, where he started farming in the citrus industry.

Luck evidently was not with him, because it was not long after he planted his groves that the citrus industry around Apopka began to decline due to the Depression. Florida also had the dreadful freezes of 1894-95 that put the final nail in his coffin as a citrus grower. After all this, many area grove owners left; but John J. Anderson remained. However, he did not replant his groves.

His American dream had led him to apply for U. S. citizenship in 1900; he was thirty-six years old and living alone, according to the Census.

On Easter Sunday, April 7, 1901, he married Rosa Hotz in the schoolhouse-church in the nearby community of Piedmont.

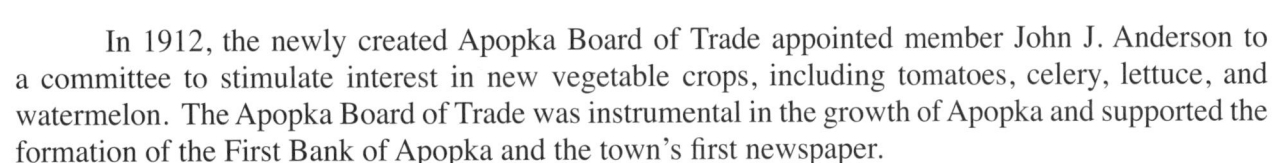

In 1912, the newly created Apopka Board of Trade appointed member John J. Anderson to a committee to stimulate interest in new vegetable crops, including tomatoes, celery, lettuce, and watermelon. The Apopka Board of Trade was instrumental in the growth of Apopka and supported the formation of the First Bank of Apopka and the town's first newspaper.

In 1923, he was one of several men who completed the construction of a parsonage and church for the Methodists, who had been holding their services at the town's Presbyterian Church.

Another one of Anderson's most notable contributions was donating the land which became Piedmont Park. The Apopka Historical Society is seeking to put a historic marker denoting this fact in Piedmont at the crossroads of Hwy. 441 and Wekiva Springs Road.

In the depression days of 1930, lawlessness and bootlegging were out of control in the Apopka area. Anderson became a member of the Citizens Protective League and was joined by several others who disliked the current mayor, John Jewell, and his handling of the disorder. Together, they hand-delivered a recall petition to the governor of Florida asking for the removal of Jewell. In 1931, Mayor Jewell resigned and left town.

John Anderson and his wife Rosa had four children: Otto, Mabel, Howard, and Raymond. His son Raymond later married Alice Green and they had John and Peter. John currently lives in Errol Estate and is an active member of the Apopka Historical Society.

Colorful History Of Lake Apopka

Let's go back in time and visit what we shall call Old Lake Apopka. We will fit this period in a little after the Timucua Indian Confederation and just after the War Between the States. Disillusioned from years of war, families fled the Deep South for a better life in an unspoiled Florida. The Armed Occupation Act of 1842 was offering 160 acres of land for those who would settle the land for a certain period of time. Many of these homesteaders chose to settle around the outer edges of Lake Apopka, where they could farm the "black gold" soils for vegetables and plant a little citrus on the higher grounds. In the beginning, the settlers grew the vegetables and fruits for their own consumption. Wild game was plentiful and there was an abundance of fish in the lake. Life during this period was good.

As time went on, they eventually started producing enough produce that they could start shipping outside the area. Seventeen boat landings sprang up, moving produce around the lake to the Oakland, West Apopka, Blue Point or the Lovell's Landing docks on the Apopka side. From Lovell's Landing, produce was loaded on oxcarts and transported to Clay Springs for shipment up the Wekiva River to Jacksonville and points beyond. W.A. Lovell owned Lovell's Landing, and also a wharf at Clay Springs for handling the shipping via the Wekiva River. He also was president of a company that operated a steamboat on the Wekiva. Lovell's Landing was located on the eastern shore of Lake Apopka, in the vicinity of where Magnolia Park and the Research Station are situated today.

Others hauled their produce by boat to Blue Point and reloaded them on wagons for the trip to Victoria, where they were transferred to the Tavares, Orlando and Atlantic Railroad for shipment by rail. Although the latter was looked upon as a temporary measure, a pattern was being formed.

Still thinking in terms of waterways as their principal commercial highways, Apopkans watched the activities on the Wekiva and began talking of a railroad which would serve as an adjunct to the stream, increasing the freight traffic through Apopka and Clay Springs, offering access to markets for growers along Lake Apopka. I wouldn't be surprised if William A. Lovell was not instrumental in building the Clay Springs-to-Apopka Railroad to connecting the two shipping points. However, at the initial organizational meeting in 1878, twenty-nine people subscribed to the eight-mile railroad. It was twelve years (1890) before they opened the initial six and a half miles.

While the Apopka-Clay Springs Railroad was attempting to connect the Lake Apopka Agricultural region with markets through Clay Springs, another ambitious drainage project was underway to connect Lake Apopka with the St. Johns River via the Oklawaha River and coming out north of Lake George. Chartered by the state in 1878 and capitalized at $20,000, the Apopka Canal Company was to be granted several thousand acres of sawgrass land north of Lake Apopka if it could complete a canal and drain the lands by January 1, 1881. The company promised to open canals between Lake Apopka, Lake Dora, and Lake Eustis, making the Oklawaha River navigable from Lake Apopka to the St. Johns River by steamboat with a draft of thirty inches and a beam of no less than twenty. The canals were to be wide enough for two such vessels to pass each other.

During the period of time that the Apopka-Clay Springs Railroad and the Apopka Canal Company were busy working on their projects, railroads were being built on all sides of Lake Apopka. These two projects were also dealt a severe blow when the Orange Belt Railroad, which connected Oakland with rail services in Jacksonville, Tampa, and the Key West Railroad at Longwood, launched the steamboat Ariel on Lake Apopka to draw the lake trade to its line. Ariel was a forty-eight foot vessel with a sixteen horsepower engine and was capable of carrying sixty passengers and over 200 cases of oranges or vegetables.

By 1925, interest in a canal connecting Lake Marshall with Lake Apopka was great enough that the legislature created the Apopka Navigable Canal District with the authority to issue bonds and levy taxes for their payment, subject to referendum. The voters approved it in July 1925, and R.J. Trimble of Tangerine and Mayor E.B. Morrey were named to plan the project. The project languished until 1929, when an engineer offered to build the canal and take payment in Canal District bonds. Before final arrangements were completed, the Depression destroyed any optimism of the 1920s. There was a flicker of interest in 1933 when the cross-state barge canal was begun, but nothing came of it. In the long run, it was trucks and not river vessels that superseded the railroads as common carriers.

****

A little "Historical Tidbits" as passed on by Owen B. "Sonny" Conner III: Sonny's grandfather started Oklawaha Nurseries west of Tangerine and developed it into probably the largest citrus nursery in the state. It was a very well-known nursery. When Sonny's father was fifteen years old, his father drove him to Jacksonville to board a train for a military school. While in Jacksonville, his father caught the flu and died. Later, Sonny's mother married R.J. Trimble of Tangerine. As time passed, Owen II grew into a six-foot, six-inch, 300-pound, hard-working citrus hand. One day, Mrs. Conner decided it was time for Owen II to take over the nursery. The first thing he did was change the sign on the door as to who was president. When Mr. Trimble returned, he went into a rage. Owen II proceeded to beat R.J. Trimble half to death. Mrs. Conner told Mr. Trimble that she was going to New Smyrna for three days and never expected to see his face again when she returned. And, according to Sonny, that is why the Marshall Lake-Lake Apopka Canal was never built.

****

There were four major ports on the lake. The southern port was Oakland, which was serviced by the Orange Belt Railroad that handled freight to Orlando, Jacksonville, Miami, and the Key West Railroad, which serviced communities all the way to Key West. The West Apopka port (Monteverde) was serviced by the Tavares-Apopka and Gulf Railroad that serviced Tampa and the west coast of Florida and north. The northern-most port was Blue Point, where products were loaded there onto oxcarts to Victoria to be serviced by the Tavares, Orlando and Atlantic Railroad for Orlando and all points north. The eastern-most port was Lovell's Landing, where products were hauled by oxcarts to Clay Springs for water shipment north. The Clay Springs-Apopka Railroad was designed to go overland to Clay Springs for shipment up the Wekiva River, but it was never finished. Whether the railroad would have connected with another rail system for shipments out is unknown.

The days of vegetables and citrus being transported out of the area via the waterways was gradually fading away, and the life and times of Old Lake Apopka was coming to an end. The railroads and trucking companies were laying the groundwork for days to come when the sawgrass lands of Lake Apopka would once again be reclaimed and managed by the formation of the Zellwood Drainage District in the early 1940s.

Do not shed any tears for Lake Apopka just yet, as it had many glorious days starting in the 1920s as a world-renowned sports fishing lake. In the early 1950s, there were fifteen fishing camps servicing the lake for sports fisherman.

Industrious Pioneers

We read a lot about the old pioneers who came to Florida in the 1800s and can't help but wonder about their daily lives and how they managed the essentials of life. I would suspect they were very ingenious.

For example, when Peter Buchan came to Florida, he took an Indian route (Wild Grass Trail) from Columbus, Georgia, to Palatka, Florida. From there, it is thought that he bought a large barge known as a "flat bottom." This was the method in which families moved entire farms by water in the 1800s. Such a boat was very large and had a house-type enclosure for the family and slaves or any other items the owner did not want exposed to the elements. The horses, cows, mules, oxen, and farm machinery were left outside. In Buchan's case, I believe that when he arrived at Clay Springs, he disassembled the barge and used the lumber to build his new home in Florida.

Those old early homesteads were generally crude log cabin structures that often had no more than a dirt floor. They were one-room structures with a fireplace at one end. This provided heat for the building and was also used for cooking. Usually, the cabin had two small windows and a door, and some had a floor that was made of split logs. This is pretty much how all the houses were started. The owners added more rooms as they went along. Light was furnished by homemade candles or possibly kerosene lanterns.

These versatile and industrious pioneers also made spinning wheels and looms; they fashioned beehives from hollow logs; and they made chairs, tables, bedsteads, side-tables, and other articles of furniture.

The settlers ranged their hogs and cattle in the woods; the hogs were fed on sweet potatoes, slaughtered, and smoked, and the lard was packed in containers made from large gourds. The cattle were also slaughtered, and their hair was removed from the hides by means of lye made from the ashes

~ 41 ~

of oak wood. The hides were tanned in "tan ooze" made from oak bark and fashioned into boots and shoes for common and Sunday wear, on lasts (mold for shoes) which were made from black gum. Deerskins were used for dress shoes.

Food was plain and wholesome. Vegetables were grown on the farm's garden that was always set aside from the main farm with a split-rail fence around it to protect the vegetables from the animals. In these fertilized plots were planted sweet potatoes, corn, beans, and other household crops. On the farm, one of the crops was sugar cane that was made into sugar and syrup. They sold the syrup for fifty cents a gallon and the drippings for twenty-five cents. The sugar went for ten cents a pound.

"Store-bought coffee" was practically unknown. They brewed their coffee from sweet potatoes cut into cubes, dried in the sun and then parched and ground up. When they went on hunting trips, they macerated bamboo roots in a hollow tree and put in a sack through which water was poured into a vessel underneath. The water was drained off and pone was made from the resulting flour. They lived chiefly and cheaply on pork, beef, grits, sweet potatoes, syrup, milk, and butter. Naturally, they distilled whiskey in considerable quantities from grits and corn. Salt and wheat flour was hauled in from the outside by ox teams. There was always plenty of fish in the area lakes and rivers. Some of the fish was dried, so it could be stored for consumption at a later date.

In addition, the pioneers made their own clothing, from the first process to the last. They planted cotton, stripped the bolls, ginned, carded, spun, reeled and warped the threads, and dyed them with indigo for blue. They used the bark of the blackjack oak for brown, the cotton bloom for yellow, and spinach or grass for green. They wove the cloth on handmade wooden looms. From these fabrics they made table cloths, sheets, pillow cases, quilts, suits, shirts, stockings, socks, gloves, and sunbonnets. Their hats were made of palmetto and grasses, and the carpets were knitted with large needles.

The children entertained themselves with rolling hoops, slingshots, stilts, stick horses, wooden tops, and Flying Jennies. (An activity like spinning a plate on a stick.)

Everybody wore long hair, which often harbored large and lively colonies of cooties. In order to rid their scalps of such critters, the pioneers would trim their hair. Then, after combing it with a fine-toothed comb, they put brimstone and lard on their heads for 12-14 hours.

There was the occasional dance or wedding when the string bands played for entertainment. They made the fiddles in the early days from gourds, with strings of catgut or, with that failing, of horsehair. The weddings were prolonged and festive occasions, with the guests coming many miles in oxcarts and wagons, as well as on horseback and on foot. The dancing sometimes went on for two days and nights, while guests feasted on barbecued beef, pork, and sweet potatoes--and whisky.

Pioneer Women

It is true that God created the heavens and the earth and also created man in his own image. However, I believe his supreme masterpiece was the creation of Eve. All of the old pioneers that we talk about who hitched their mules to a wagon and headed for the Promised Land certainly did not leave their most precious commodity behind. These creations of God stood by their men on their trip to Florida, worked in the fields with their men, and raised a house full of children. We need to talk about these pioneer women and the contributions they made in molding this society we live in now.

John and Susan Chapmen came in the 1880s with six children to homestead land in Plymouth. He had been a member of the Georgia Legislature and served three years in the War Between the States. They lived in a house on top of the hill east of Apopka until a home was ready west of the railroad and north of the depot in Plymouth. John taught school in Apopka the first year, while land was cleared and his orange grove was planted. Two more of their children were born in Florida.

With the coming of the TO&A Railroad (Tavares, Orlando and Atlantic) and regular delivery of mail by rail, the Chapmen home was closest to the depot. In 1887, Susan Chapmen was appointed postmaster by President Grover Cleveland. Receiving six more presidential appointments, she served until 1914. For twenty-seven years, it was her responsibility to bring the mailbags to the Post Office, which was the closed-in half of her porch. There is no way to count the thousands of items she handled as she faithfully carried out her official duties.

During this time, John T. Chapman served as a member of the Orange County Board of Commissioners and served for two years in the Florida Legislature. In addition to his own groves, he supervised eighteen others in the Plymouth area. He also was elected the first president of Plymouth Citrus Growers Association in 1911.

Many people, some of whom were interested local citizens and others who were professional teachers, taught in the schools of Northwest Orange County for at least a term. A few stood out for their length of service and the influence they had on their students. Two of John Chapman's daughters, E.G. and M.G. "Miss Mattie," taught at Plymouth, Lovell's Landing, and Apopka. "Miss Mattie" also taught the children of guests that were wintering at the Lake Standish Hotel. She taught for more than half a century after her first term in 1890, and became legendary among her numerous students. She retired in May of 1943.

****

Jenny Fudge, daughter-in-law of J.D. Fudge, Apopka's first mayor, was affectionately known as "Miss Jenny," because of her energy, good humor, and constant service to her church and community. She set an example in meeting hard times. From a prominent family in Jacksonville, Jenny Scarlett, born in 1862, was married in Apopka in 1881 to Anderson P. Fudge, who was born in 1859. During the five years before he was married, he had helped his father set out and care for a twenty-acre orange grove. After his marriage, he was determined to establish his own groves, and bought eighty acres from Mr. Wilkins of Plymouth.

Jenny and her new husband moved into a one-room log cabin with a stick-and-clay chimney that sagged a bit with each rainy spell. Three years later, after the grove was set, their cattle were raised, and their farm was established, they built a three-room home to accommodate their family of four.

With the groves prospering in 1890, the couple built a two-story house with columns for the front porch and a circular stairway inside. When the great freezes of 1894-95 hit, they lost almost fourteen years of work overnight. Although their groves froze to the ground, Jenny was determined to survive.

Jenny wrote to friends further north that she had her rooms partitioned for sleeping quarters and offered lodging to hunters who welcomed and paid for the Fudge hospitality, so the couple weathered the lean years and replanted. In 1920, she was still a catalyst at any meeting or frolic, and never lost her love of life and people.

Anderson Fudge died in 1935, and Jenny died in 1948.

Jenny had one daughter named Scarlett, who married a dentist, S. Akers. Dr. Akers was born in 1877. They built a home on the Old Dixie Highway about one block east of the Errol Estate entrance, on the south side of the road. In 1945, Dr. Akers committed suicide in the orange grove across the street from his home. Scarlett died one year later, in 1946. They had one son named Ernest.

May we offer a tribute to Jenny's courage in the face of adversity? "Miss Mattie" and Jenny exemplified why the Supreme Architect created Eve.

Mysterious Underground Waters

I will quite often come up with stories by Leslie S. Bray, who sent quite a few articles to the "Pioneer Florida" column of the *Tampa Tribune* back in the early 1900s. This is like someone speaking to us from over 100 years ago. Leslie lived a little south of Bayridge, on the Plymouth-Sorrento road in the late 1800s and early 1900s. I hope you enjoy his writings as much as I do.

"The absorbing history of Rock Springs published in the Pioneer series in the Tribune August 24 was doubly interesting to me, because our old homestead was only four miles to the west. The little settlement of Merrimack, two miles north of Plymouth, where my brother Everett and sister Edith and I went to school held its annual Sunday School picnic at Rock Springs in the early 1890s", said Leslie S. Bray, an esteemed collaborator.

As was pointed out in the Pioneer story, this spring was unique in that it flows out from under a rock bluff instead of boiling up from underground pressure. On one of these picnics two of the older boys wanted to learn what lay beyond the small opening through which the water came. Over the protests of their elders they lighted some pine knots and managed to get through the six inch space between the overflowing water and the overhanging rock. We smaller boys fairly held our breath while the voice of those two venturesome youths came to us in weird, echoing tones.

Not until the pine knots became too hot to handle did the explorers return to report their findings. Immediately inside the opening they found a large chamber, the roof beyond the reach of their hands, and the surrounding walls too distant to be revealed by the flickering torches. If my memory serves me correctly, these venturesome lads were the late John Haynes, for many years a resident of Tampa, and Warren Harshberger, now living in Oakland, California.

In regard to the lost spring which once supplied the Delk household with water, but disappeared so completely the mulatto was unable to recall the exact location, I'm offering a possible solution. On other picnics we used to go over to the Whispering Rocks, some 300 yards north of the springs. Between two prominent rocks was a slight depression. Dropping to our knees, we could plainly hear the sound of running water below.

Now, it seems very unlikely that anyone would discover this spot unless led there for some particular reason. To me it seems plausible that with plowed fields surrounding it, a deluge of rain could have washed the spring so full of sand that an underground channel was opened into a subterranean river, and the spring ceased to exist.

It also seems quite possible that years later someone looking for the spring discovered the sound of an underground river between the rocks, and while this information was passed on and kept alive by visitors to the spot, the lost spring was completely forgotten. At the time we held our picnics at Rock Springs, the Delk house had become a pile of rotting timbers, but sour orange trees still flourished about it.

One of the reasons Florida's underground rivers and sink holes appeal to our imagination is because they are so unpredictable. One day I met Chip Buchan, a fellow cattle hunter, who said, "I've just seen what I call Devil's Hole, and it sure gave me the creeps. There's a stray river pouring into a sinkhole that drinks it up without a ripple.

A few days later my curiosity led me to Devil's Hole in a valley north of Simpson Prairie, just off the Sorrento-Mt. Dora wagon road. A noisy stream of water some four feet wide and two feet deep was roaring over pine roots and heading toward the prairie. But suddenly it swerved across an old log road and headed for a sink hole some thirty feet in diameter. A lazy foam hung about the spot where the water poured in, but elsewhere the surface remained as calm as a lake.

I got off my horse and speared some long pine limbs beneath the water, but they bounced back immediately, showing there was no suction at the top. However, I agreed with Chip that it gave one a strange feeling to see all that water pour into a hole that never filled, but kept one guessing as to where it went. Some three weeks later I returned to find the stray river dry as a bone and the water level in the sinkhole unchanged.

Then there was the little pond about two miles north of our place, where Jake Anderson operated a sawmill. Jake had tapped a spring in a bay head on the hillside above the mill, and in a wooden trough brought the water down to a drinking box for his mules, where it spilled across the road and drained into the millpond to supply steam for the boilers.

When Jake eventually moved his mill to other parts, and our cattle drank at the pond while I was driving them homeward, I wondered if the pond would grow larger from the unused supply of water. Then one evening as my horse drank in the edge of the pond, I heard the sound of gurgling water. About five feet from my horse's head was a hole two inches in diameter, which the water was steadily pouring downward. The mystery of the millpond's unchanging water level was solved. But now I lost no time in urging my horse away from what easily might turn into a sink hole."

The English Colony Of Narcoossee

Back in the early 1800s, large land development companies bought land from the State of Florida or the large railroad corporations for one dollar per acre. These investors had agents in London, who put out fascinating advertisements in pamphlets and sporting papers, with information about the new Eldora. They particularly emphasized the orange industry, which promised an annual income of at least $10,000 after the groves had reached maturity. They described the beautiful outdoor life which might be enjoyed in this new land. Many responded to these allurements.

Somewhere around 1882, Fell, Davidson and Company brought a large colony of Englishmen to Apopka. They set out a citrus nursery and made plans to grow oranges in the area. However, E. Nelson Fell, a partner in the real estate firm, was also putting together an English Colony southeast of Orlando in a small town called Narcoossee, which means "bear" in the Seminole language. The upshot of this was that the Apopka Colony moved to Narcoossee to join their fellow Englishmen.

Now, moving to Narcoossee was not all that simple. Due to the remoteness of their new home, they had to remain in Kissimmee for five days before they could be transferred across Lake Tohopikaliga to Brack's Landing, and then travel on wagon roads eight miles to what would be known for the next few years as "The English Colony."

These Englishmen were divided into two groups. The elder section was made up largely of retired professional men and army officers, who came to Florida because of its climate and in some cases because of their limited incomes The younger section were sons of gentlemen mostly, just out of school and university, who were sent abroad by their parents for various reasons and supported by remittances from home – and were therefore known as "remittance men." They were sometimes used as common laborers or even as servants.

There were a lot of adjustments to be made by the young men from England. For example, upon returning one evening to their crowded hotel, the young men, running true to English form, placed their shoes outside the door to be polished. Much to their disgust, they found their shoes in the morning where they had left them, untouched, and were assured by the young English clerk that they were "jolly lucky" to find them at all.

These Englishmen were, as is the common and characteristic habit of Englishmen everywhere, devoted to sport. There were no game laws at the time, and the woods were full of deer, quail, and dove. A favorite sport in the fall of the year was to lie in wait for the vast flocks of doves, as they flew to the lakes for water before going to their roosting places for the night, and shoot them in great numbers. Saying there were no game laws might be the understatement of the year.

A retired army officer, General J. S. Swindler, formerly a colonel of the Dragoon Guards, who came to Florida in 1886, organized the polo team. The team attracted lovers of that sport to Orlando to watch them play against teams from all over the United States at the old fair grounds. Florida cow ponies were used in these games; their mettle can be judged by the fact that one of the players bought one of these tough and agile little beasts for forty dollars and sold it at a match in Camden, South

Carolina for $400. You could pretty well guess that these ponies were descended from the famous Florida Marsh Tackies brought to this country by Ponce De Leon around 1521. They were indeed wild little beasts.

The Englishmen organized a yacht club and held regattas on Lake Conway. They also formed the English Club and built a clubhouse on the northeast corner of Main and Pine Streets in Orlando.

In 1894-1895, a big freeze killed practically all the citrus trees of Orange County to the ground. It was characteristic of these lively young Englishmen that, during the three days of this freeze, they engaged in playing soccer and almost immediately afterwards, more than two hundred of them left together, abandoning groves, homes, and furniture, with tables set and dishes unwashed. It is reported that one of them sold a grove for which he had paid $40,000, for the price of a ticket to England. Those that returned to the old country or resettled in Australia, New Zealand, and South Africa prospered in many cases. Those who remained in Orange County have, for the most part, proven themselves useful citizens and contributed much to the community.

McDonald

McDonald Station, a little more than a mile west of Plymouth, grew into a community around a railroad depot which served the Merrimack community about two miles away. Its earliest settler was Andrew A. McDonald, who arrived there about 1873 from Virginia with his daughter and five sons – Matthew Gay, George N., John W., Percival, and Marion Fitzhugh. The eldest son Dr. M.G. McDonald practiced medicine around McDonald and Zellwood during the 1880s and afterward. Percival was also a graduate of medical school, but never practiced. Although all were interested in the grove business, only Marion Fitzhugh remained after the freezes of the mid-1890s. He became a major citrus grower and a charter member of the Plymouth Citrus Growers Association. An active member of that organization until his death in 1936, "Fitz" McDonald served as its vice president and spent several years on its board of directors. He was also on the Apopka School Board and the Democratic Central Committee.

Percival McDonald operated a general store, delivering groceries on order twice a week to local patrons. A local butcher also delivered meat in the same manner. A sawmill was operating there in the mid-1880s, shipping sawn timber and lumber on the railroad. J. Bray also shipped livestock from his stockyard at Merrimack. This was the father of Leslie S. Bray, whose articles we have occasionally printed. Percival McDonald opened a fruit packing house in partnership with S. W. Eldredge of Apopka.

At the height of the boom of the 1880s, everyone seemed interested in building towns, even when there were several already in existence nearby. McDonald was no different. With the railroad, depot, the store, the sawmill, and packing house, and a handful of residents, community leaders set about building the other social institutions required to become a full-fledged town. A Presbyterian congregation was started by the Rev. J.T. Leonard, and he became its pastor. A school was started and a building erected. Like most of the schools at the time, it was built and maintained without cost to the county. When improvements were needed, J.F. McDonald and others would hold fund raising events, including box suppers and dances. They also had theatrical productions that were enjoyed by citizens from most of the neighboring communities. The voting precinct was at Zellwood, but George N. McDonald often served as one of the election officials. With a population of about 100 in 1889, a post office was established and A.E. Fuller served as postmaster.

McDonald was seriously affected by the 1894-1895 freezes. Percival McDonald and S.W. Eldredge dissolved their partnership and closed their packinghouse after the freeze and a few days before the more devastating one in February. The McDonald brothers decided to look elsewhere for a place to live. John W. and George N. went to Tampico, Mexico, to investigate the possibilities of locating there. They reported it satisfactory and Percival soon joined them there, but not before he had married the daughter of Apopka druggist C.A. Boone, who accompanied him to Mexico.

Employed by the Smyth Orange Company at Tampico, Percival lived in Mexico for nearly twenty years, returning to the United States only after the birth of his daughter. George never returned to the United States, but John came back after a thirty-three-year residence in Mexico. He died at

Zellwood in 1946, and Percival died at Plymouth in 1937. H.R. Wilder, who had been turpentining on a small scale while he and his brother developed their groves, announced that he was expanding his turpentine operation and could furnish employment for several families on his turpentine farm. John B. Escott left for his native Kentucky, but came back in 1898 and spent the remainder of his life at McDonald. McDonald and a few others refused to give up and began rebuilding their groves immediately after the freeze. There was little activity at the McDonald Station for a while. When the agent resigned in 1896, the railroad company took several months in replacing him.

Consumers Veneer & Lumber Co.

Amos D. Starbird came to Orlando from Freemont, Maine, in 1885. One year later he went into the sawmill business with a rented mill in Apopka. By 1887, he was a major partner of Copeland, Starbird and Company, which owned its mill in Apopka.

In 1900, Austin C. and Percival L. Starbird organized the Starbird Lumber and Veneer Company as a partnership to manufacture lumber, boxes, barrels, and all kinds of crates. By 1903, they made arrangements for the incorporation of the company into The Consumers and Veneer Company, capitalizing it at $100,000.

The infusion of new funds enabled the Starbirds to expand their operation and make the firm a major part of the local economy. By 1904, the firm owned 25,000 acres of timber, employed fifty hands at the Apopka plant, and was turning out a carload of orange boxes per day.

A tram road was constructed between the Apopka mill and a logging camp on company timber land around the Rock Springs area in 1907. The tram road would be moved from time to time and additional locomotives would be added. Veneer Company was operating on a large scale by 1907-1908.

During the early years of the Consumers Lumber and Veneer Company, Percy Starbird also operated a shingle mill on the Rock Springs Road. It was destroyed by fire in 1914, but was rebuilt soon afterwards.

Austin Starbird was manager of the mill and president of the firm until 1922, when Bennett Land, Sr. succeeded Starbird. A civil engineer with a degree from North Carolina State, Land worked with SAL railroad as a division engineer. He was living in Plant City at the time and soon moved his family to Apopka. In the following years, his sons, Bennett, Jr., Henry W., and John H., would be involved in running the mill. When Bennett Land, Sr. died in 1936, Henry became president.

Employment remained fairly stable until the stock market crash in 1929. There was consequently a great deal of excitement in 1930, when citrus exchanges at Plymouth, Winter Park, South Apopka, and Winter Haven ordered 1,250,000 boxes. This meant a full year of employment for a slightly larger work force instead of the customary seasonal term at a time when employment was high.

When Henry Land became president and general manager of the company in 1936, it was employing 120 people and producing about 1,500,000 boxes and crates annually. By 1938, employment was up to 325, and production for boxes and crates was up to 3,000,000.

Severe freezes in early 1940 and again the following November, reduced demand somewhat, but a huge and unexpected war order was destined to make up the difference.

Actually, just two days before Pearl Harbor, Consumers received a government order for 500,000 wire-bound boxes. They were intended to hold gasoline cans as a part of a lend-lease shipment to British forces of North Africa. Before that order was filled, an additional 500,000 containers were ordered for use in the United States.

Even with the recent improvements to the mill, the firm was pushed to fill the orders.

All employees were soon working full time. However, there was a looming problem hanging over the company's head. Henry Land was a reserve military officer expecting a call at any minute. The company began to reorganize plant management. E. G. Roberts (the father of NASCAR driver Fireball Roberts), became the new plant superintendent, with full control over production and maintenance. W.A. Greenleaf was appointed the secretary-treasury and David Simpson took over as the sales and credit manager. Josephine Land became the first vice-president, and Robert T. Carlton, second vice-president.

In 1942, the Consumers Lumber and Veneer Company employees voted to have the CIO, Henry Land, represent them at the bargaining table. When Henry was home on leave in 1943, he had to spend some of his precious time at home negotiating the first union contract in company history.

With the supply of good timber diminishing in Florida, continued difficulties with organized labor rendered the profit margin unacceptable. The Lands were forced to close Consumers Lumber and Veneer in 1945. That was the end of an era in Apopka history.

Plymouth

During the 1800s, Plymouth was a beautiful area with hills, lakes, and miles of lovely pines where the cattle roamed on a free range. Settlers came from the New England states as well as from Alabama, Georgia, and South Carolina. Some came to make their fortunes in the golden citrus industry, while others came to the Sunshine State for their health.

This area of Plymouth has not changed much.

One of the earliest settlers was a gentleman named E.C. Swan, who developed a business tending the orange groves for out-of-state investors for $20 an acre. That seemed to be the going price. At any rate, he was instrumental in naming the little community Orange Heights, probably after the crops he tended. It was not until 1885 that Mr. Swan discovered that there already existed an Orange Heights, Florida, and decided to change the name of the community. At the urging of his neighbor, C. W. Smith, the name was changed to Plymouth. That is not too surprising, as a lot of the new residents in the area were from the New England states. (Just a little bit of historical tidbits: *Webb's History of Florida*, published in 1875, lists a community called Pennryn that was receiving its mail at the J.C. Stewart home on the corner of Lester-Schopke Road and the Old Dixie Highway. I cannot help but wonder if the area received its mail there until the Orange Heights Post Office opened in 1880.)

The post office opened in 1880, with Augustus Evans serving as the first postmaster. The community was quite isolated and received its supplies and written communication from the outside world through Mellonville on the St. Johns River. Sometimes this could take a long time to reach the settlers in Plymouth.

In 1886, the Tavares, Orlando and Atlantic Railroad was routed through Plymouth from Wildwood on its way to Orlando. They established a depot in Plymouth, although the McDonald Station Depot was just a few miles to the northwest.

Those beautiful pines in the area eventually caught the eye of turpentiners and sawmills. The pines were slashed for turpentine and cut for timber by the sawmills, answering the call for more timber for new homes and businesses coming into the area. New businesses did come, when an organ factory opened near the new depot in Plymouth. And it did not take long for the organ factory to be converted into a citrus packinghouse to handle the increased orange crops.

Two of Plymouth's earliest entrepreneurs, brothers C.W. and H.E. Smith, erected a hotel in 1887 on the south shores of Lake Standish on the Old Dixie Highway. They called it the Lake Standish Hotel or Lodge, and a lot of their guests were citrus grove owners who chose to spend the winters in Plymouth tending their groves and contracting with grove caretakers for the summer months. This seemed to be a good arrangement until the monster freezes of 1894-1895 virtually wiped out the Florida citrus industry. Fortunes were lost and the hotel suffered mightily. It wasn't until 1920 that B. H. Kinsman of Orlando bought the hotel and put it in back good repair by adding electricity, plumbing, hot and cold running water, and other amenities. Sadly, the hotel burned in 1940.

About this same period of time, Orange County surveyors set out from a point near the old T.O&A railroad depot to run a line for a proposed road to Sorrento about eight miles due north. This road would split the communities of Bayridge and Merrimack. With only a slight jog to the west around what is known today as the Ponkan intersection, the new road proceeded in a straight line to Sorrento. When the road was finished for automobile traffic, it was the only one in this part of the state to be hard-surfaced the entire distance over the original wheel ruts made by pioneers some forty years before.

The schools of Plymouth were always available during the season for winter visitors at the Lake Standish Hotel. J.T. Chapman taught in 1883 in Plymouth and, later, his daughter Mattie taught school in Plymouth, Apopka, and Lovell's Landing.

A community church was built and in 1893, it was organized into a Baptist church. Services were held when a preacher was available. There were two black churches, one Baptist and the other Methodist. There were schools for blacks through the eighth grade until 1950, when they were bused into Apopka.

From 1888 through the 1900s, the main area crop was citrus and the primary employer was the Plymouth Citrus Growers Association and Plymouth Co-op. Eventually, there was also Minute Maid and Citrus Central. Today, Coca Cola has a research department located in Plymouth.

Since Plymouth is unincorporated, it has been losing large tracts of property that have chosen to be annexed into the City of Apopka. For example, in 1970, the Pirie Estate became Errol Estate and was annexed into Apopka.

Now, most of the property south of Hwy. 441 in what we will call "Downtown Plymouth" is now in the City of Apopka. This is a little sad from a historical point of view.

Camp Wewa (Land of Many Waters) has been a haven for teen age kids since 1925, when it was first established as a Boy Scout Camp. It is surrounded by three beautiful lakes and has always been in a wilderness all of its own. In 1950, Wewa was purchased by the YMCA and still stands today much as it was in 1925.

Always remember that the first shipment of concentrated orange juice took place on April 15, 1946, from Plymouth, Florida. This was under the banner of the Vacuum Food Corporation that was to later be known as "Minute Maid." Most of us raised in the area can remember that in 1948, the Bing Crosby radio campaign, set Minute Maid on the road to national prominence. This was all accomplished in the beautiful community known to us as Plymouth.

Bayridge

Near the crossroads of the Plymouth-Sorrento and Kelly Park roads once stood the small community of Bay Ridge. From 1885-1886, a group of about thirty families, mostly from New England, moved into this area. Some of the early pioneers who settled in this area were the Pikes, Merrills, Hornes, Thompsons, Mayers, Andersons, Conroys, Stewarts, Harshbargers, Brays, Duggers, and Schopkes.

Nearly all of them started citrus groves, but in addition, several grew LeConte and Kieffer pears, scuppernong grapes, vegetables, and strawberries. Thompson and Mayer manufactured starch. John W. Anderson, who was from Indiana, had a saw and shingle mill. He also built and lived in an octagon house, a remarkable architectural style peculiar to upstate New York. E.S. and Wesley Poore operated the Bay Ridge Nursery, where seedling oranges, plums, and grapes could be purchased. There were two stores. C.K. Slonegar, the postmaster, offered general merchandise, as did Burley and Lyford. Joe Smith, Frank Walker, and W. Poore were carpenters. F. Wilson built cisterns and did plaster work. And F.S. Bray was a cattle dealer who also retailed milk.

One of these early settlers, John Henry Schopke, was born in 1845, in Henrietta, Texas. John, Emily, Ora Mae, and William all came to Bay Ridge in 1885. John Henry got into the citrus business, built a citrus packinghouse, developed the Schopke Mercantile, and was postmaster at Bay Ridge, thus becoming one of the early pioneers in that area. Two of the grandchildren, Myrtle Schopke Collins and Blanche Schopke Gaddis, left the following observations of their memories of those early days:

"The store, packinghouse, and Bay Ridge Post Office were maintained for a number of years, accommodating the numerous families that lived in the area. Supplies for the store came from Jacksonville by boat down the St. Johns River to Mellonville (now Sanford) and then taken by horse and wagon to the Bay Ridge store. Fruit was shipped to market on the return boat.

Bay Ridge was a voting precinct and elections were held in the store building for a number of years. Old timers took this day off (votin' day) to visit and politic. They came to the polls at sunup and stayed 'till sundown. Speculation on the election was great and the political comment was, "so goes Bay Ridge, so goes the election." My grandmother and her friends cooked dinner (noon) and carried the meal to the poll officials. Fried chicken, homemade pies and cakes were always abundant at this time.

Fresh eggs and homemade butter (the extra pinch of salt made it special) was sold in the store. John T. Pirie came to buy the special butter. Shoes were mended and half-soled in the store, also.

I remember hearing my Grandmother Schopke tell me that when she's heard the hens cackle after laying eggs she'd make a "B-line" to the nest to gather the eggs before that ole coach whip snake made it. He liked eggs too!

There was a one-room schoolhouse at Bay Ridge. Susie Pike and Jane Tatlow were among the teachers. This little schoolhouse was the home of many community Saturday night dances and parties.

George Conroy played merry tunes on his harmonica.

It saddens one to realize there are no visual landmarks left standing near the crossroads of Plymouth-Sorrento and Kelly Park roads. The love and memories remain in our hearts."

Mrs. Leonora (Lenna) Pike Schopke, one of John Henry's great grandchildren also passed on a few tidbits from her memories:

"I remember on Sunday mornings, when the weather was good, my father would host visits from Mr. Merrill, Mr. Jim Welch and Mr. Dave B. Stewart. After tying up their horses, they usually squatted in the shade of a big maple tree in the front yard. Topics of conversation were the price of cattle, the renewed interest in citrus after the big freeze of the late 1800s and politics."

The main entertainment center was Clay Springs (Wekiwa). Square dances in the open-air pavilion, tobogganing from the hilltop down into the springs, and swimming were the main sources of recreation. Many families would rent cottages or stay at the boarding house for several days at a time.

A big family gathering was always called for when it was time to have the "grinding." This was when home-grown sugarcane was squeezed into a large iron vat, with the juice-squeezing apparatus powered by a horse-driven rod. The fire heated the juice to a boiling temperature as the substance thickened to become syrup.

As the skim was removed from the top of the boiling syrup and thrown to the side, younger family members frolicked to get the first taste of the sweet treat."

Roy and William Horne told Belle Gilliam about coming to Bay Ridge with their father John Horne, in 1906. John Horne came to Central Florida to work in turpentine and with A.C. Starbird's crate mill in Apopka. They bought their homestead of forty-five acres that same year from George Conroy for $100.

Roy related to Belle a little story about his mother and a friend going to Orlando in 1916, to buy a year's supply of clothing and material. They went by wagon to Zellwood and caught the train to Orlando. During the shopping, his mother bought a trunk. When they got back to the depot in Orlando to catch the train to come home, the depot agent would not let her check the trunk because it was empty.

He told her if she would put some of her merchandise in the trunk and lock it, he could check it as baggage at no cost to her. This is what she did.

Merrimack

Traveling orange packing shed

Once upon a time in the tiny town of Merrimack, they built a school. Some say it was the crown jewel of its time. The local newspaper and surrounding communities called upon their schools to emulate the fine work done by the citizens of Merrimack. All this was done back in 1882, with $500 and donated labor. This school building was so fine that some families from Apopka, Plymouth, and Zellwood sent their children to school there.

Sometimes, it seems like reading a fairy tale to comprehend there ever existed a small community in our midst with a fine school, post office, a cattle stockyard and large citrus packing house that left no traces of existence.

The fact is true of Merrimack, Florida. Somewhere around 1875, James Campbell, his son George Campbell and Frederick Perry left their home in Manchester, New Hampshire, and homesteaded land north of Apopka. Each purchased 160 acres, and since they lived on the Merrimack River in New Hampshire, they called their settlement Merrimack. After they built their log cabins for their families, they immediately started clearing the land for citrus trees. It did not take long before others came to join them. W.L. Jamison moved from Apopka to join them in 1882, and Thomas Osborn and John H. Haynes arrived in 1884. Mr. Osborn served as Justice of the Peace in Merrimack during the late 1800s. C.D. Gregg and Dr. Henry Smith soon settled there, also.

John H. Hayes had the local store and post office. He was the postmaster from 1884, until he died in 1889. After Mr. Hayes, there was a succession of postmasters, including George C. Campbell, Dr. Henry Smith, and Hattie Smith, who was replaced by Gertrude Ridgeway in 1896. In 1902, they moved the post office to Plymouth where it still exists today. Merrimack had a Baptist Church.

However, it is unclear whether they had their own building or maybe met in the local school.

F.S. Bray continued in the cattle business and built his stockyard in Merrimack, and John Harshbarger handled a majority of the fruit in the area with his traveling packinghouse. Before the turn of the century and during the early teens, a packinghouse operation was set up in a tent that was moved around as needed. Fruit was hauled by oxcart (twenty-five boxes to a load) to the nearest railroad station, which would have been in Plymouth. More than likely, Mr. Harshbarger used the traveling packing house, as was the custom of the times.

Not all of the new settlers from New Hampshire followed Campbell's move to Merrimack. In 1885, Edward B. Wait and his wife Abbie settled in Apopka, where their son Leslie (Ted) was born. Of course, Ted went on to be an outstanding citizen in Apopka and served as its mayor during the Second World War. After Edward died, Abbie married a successful realtor in Apopka, Frank H. Davis. Abbie Davis was very active in community activities and played the organ in the Episcopal Church for many years.

According to Jerrell Shofner's book, *History of Apopka and Northwest Orange County,* Merrimack was located somewhere between Lester-Schopke and Ponkan roads, north of Errol Estate. *Plymouth Historical Trails* placed it near the intersection of Plymouth-Sorrento and Ponkan roads. An Orange County map of 1890 locates it just south of Wolf Lake, around sections 20-30. Merrimack had to cover a large area, as so many of their early settlers were homesteading 160 acres of land received through the Armed Occupation Act of 1842. I would not be surprised if the area did not go from the Plymouth-Sorrento Road to Vick Road and Lester-Schopke to Ponkan Road. The 1890 map pretty well substantiates that.

During this era, there were many small communities that were so totally dependent of citrus that when the freezes of 1894-1895 hit, many of the out-of-state and local investors never replanted. Communities such as Merrimack, Victoria, Grassmere, and Lakeville simply ceased to exist. These communities had post offices. Some had a train station and others had excellent schools and churches. Although these communities faded away, there were still residents who had diversified agricultural plantings and replanted citrus, which allowed them to prosper at a later date. These were the ones who hitched their oxen to a plow and lived happily ever after.

Frank H. Davis

This is a little "Historical Tidbit" from the files of the Orange County Historical Society concerning "The Early Settlers of Orange County." Frank Davis of Apopka was one of those early settlers. Frank followed his good friend Edward B. Waite (Ted Waite's father) to Florida around 1876. After Edward passed away, Frank married his widow, Abbie, and helped raise her young son, Ted. Ted went on to be the very popular two-term mayor of Apopka during World War II, and his stepfather Frank was a one-term mayor in 1915.

Frank Davis was born on April 5, 1854, in Manchester, New Hampshire. His father Dr. E. H. Davis was a physician and surgeon and practiced medicine in Manchester for more than thirty years. He was also a surgeon in the Fifth New Hampshire Regiment in the Civil War. Frank graduated from the Manchester High School in 1874. Being anxious to take up the business activities of life at once, he did not continue his studies as he was privileged to do, but went to Boston, where he secured a position in the counting room of a wholesale house on Summer Street. He remained there for about two years. His attention was first directed to Florida in 1876, through letters from a friend (Edward Waite), who had settled near Apopka. He came south in October of 1876 and joined his friend. For many years he lived the life of the average first settler by taking up a homestead and clearing land for an orange grove.

During those years, he occupied bachelors' quarters and roughed it with the rest of the boys. At that time Apopka had one mail delivery per week and that was on Saturdays. The one little store in town was the Mecca, toward which all steps were leading. With no mail boxes in those days, the mail was distributed directly from the mail bag. Sanford, or Mellonville, was the base of supplies, and mail and all goods were brought by team from that point.

Later, freight and passenger service was furnished via the Wekiva River. Apopka proper was early known as the Lodge, so-called from the old established Masonic Lodge. The Apopka district comprised all of the country around Lake Apopka and included present-day Oakland, Ocoee, Winter

Garden, and Apopka. Dr. Zelotes Mason, one of the very first settlers of Apopka, was the oracle of wisdom on all matters pertaining to fruit culture.

Judge Mills, who figures so prominently in land titles in this section, did the surveying. The Sims Grove on Lake Apopka was the best orange grove in the county, and Judge Speer, who lived in Oakland was quite prominent in county affairs.

The life of the early settler was filled with varied and trying experiences. Everything was crude and there were many deprivations.

At times, the one store in the settlement was without flour, butter, and other indispensables, but there were no fickle appetites, and hog and hominy were not frowned upon if the delectables were lacking. Social gatherings gave zest to life, and the first settlers always found time for fun. And then there was the old-fashioned camp meeting where all gathered once a year to be spoiled with the sweet potato pie and other interesting accessories.

The virgin pine forests, untouched by turpentine or mill men, were the special charm of Florida in the old days, and the roads and trails through them were well defined and easily followed. However, this would change. With the turpentining of the timber came obliteration of the old trails and consequent confusion as to roads and courses, and unfortunately, one of the most interesting features of the old Florida had left us forever.

The first railroad was built through Apopka in 1885, and it was around that time that Mr. Davis opened a real estate office, in addition to growing oranges. He later had trucking interests in Winter Garden, making a specialty of lettuce and cucumbers on sub-irrigated lands, using water from artesian wells.

He met with great reverses in 1895, along with so many others in Florida, and for a time it seemed that he might be compelled to make a change of base. However, he decided to stick it out and began getting a good share of his income from groves that were frozen during the Big Freeze.

Mr. Davis has been prominently identified with public affairs in Apopka. He served as a councilman many times, was active in the organization of the Apopka Board of Trade, and was the first president of the same, holding office for two terms. He took the oath of office as mayor of Apopka in January 1915.

The oldest real estate firm of the era ended with Frank Davis' death in 1916, but there were others that continued to contribute to the growth of Apopka."

Chapter III - Early Days Of Apopka

Four Early Disasters

William Fremont Blackman, Ph.D., LL.D., formerly Professor of Yale University and Rollins College wrote The History of Orange County in 1927. He wrote of four disasters that hit Orange County starting in the early 1870s. Three of them were caused by the blind and irresistible forces of nature, and the fourth by the greediness of man. These disasters were the great storm of 1871, the big freeze of 1894-95, the protracted drought of 1906-07, and the so-called boom of 1925-26.

"In August of 1871, an unprecedented storm of wind and rain occurred. For 48 hours, the tempest raged without intermission; then followed a week of calm weather; and then another 48 hours of storm, 'the rain descended and the floods came, and the winds blew.' Mr. A.J. Lovell, of Apopka, reported that a flour barrel standing on end was filled and overflowed by the rain, the Wekiva River was a mile wide, the Yowell-Drew corner in downtown Orlando was four feet or more under water, the ground in the flatwoods was saturated to such a depth that horses could not be driven over it, thousands of cattle were bogged down and drowned on the prairies, and that countless numbers of pine trees were prostrated. Fortunately, most of the houses at the time were built of heavy logs, and withstood the onset, but the property loss was great. No reference was made here to the hurricane which in September, 1926, devastated the lower East Coast of the state, insomuch as this did not reach to Orange County.

The second disaster was the reverse of the first in character---there was too little water rather than too much. In 1906-07, there occurred a severe and protracted drought. For more than a year, scarcely any rain fell. Crops of fruit, grain, and vegetables were destroyed; citrus and ornamental trees and shrubbery were injured; water courses and lakes were dried up, livestock suffered for want of both water and grass; and from ten to fifty percent of the pine trees in the state were killed, except on lower and moister lands, and many other varieties of forest trees were injured or destroyed. Naval store operators, lumber men and owners of timber lands suffered great losses.

The third disaster was the big freeze of 1894-95 that I have mentioned so many times in 'Historical Tidbits.' We won't go into this again with much detail however; Dr. Blackman wrote that at this time the state was mainly dependent on citrus fruits for its money income. Diversified farming, the growing of vegetables for the market, had not yet been developed, or hardly thought of. Many thousand people from the North and West had made their homes in Florida and invested all their scanty means in orange groves, which yielded them a comfortable support. And then, 'as a thief in the night,' the cold crept across the land with the northwest wind, bringing freezing temperatures and disaster.

One good result of this calamity was the diversification of agriculture and horticulture which followed. It was clearly seen that Florida could no longer be a one crop state. The growing of vegetables for the winter market was undertaken, staple crops were cultivated, and dairying, raising of poultry and developing new horticulture crops thus provided more varied, safer, and more helpful conditions of life.

The fourth of these disasters was the so called, boom of 1925-26. For this disaster, it should be said at once, the people of Florida were not primarily and chiefly accountable, though they cannot escape their share of responsibility for it. Also, it should be said that Orange County suffered less than many other portions of the state from its effects.

No attempt will be made here to analyze thoroughly the causes of this boom. It was no doubt brought about largely by the same traits of human nature, and the same economic forces and conditions, which have staged similar 'booms' periodically, in other parts of the country.

The mental unrest, and relative abundance of money which followed the world war, probably had an influence on the course of events. Also, the unique attractiveness of the Florida climate, the peculiar magic which the orange and its culture had long exercised on men's minds, the crowds of tourists who came to the state every winter and succumbed to its charms, the rapid growth of many of its cities and towns, the abundance of cheap lands which were available for exploration and the advantage which all these conditions provided for publicity and advertising campaigns, made, all together, a strong appeal to speculators in land, and subdivision promoters.

So the developers came in increasing throngs from all parts of the country, many of them shrewd and experienced in the business of land exploration, and set about the task of selling the country. No doubt many of these people were honest, both in intent and in methods of operation, and their work has been of permanent and inestimable value to the state; but a few were adventurers, intent only on making a quick 'kill' of 'skimming the cream'. Numberless subdivisions were laid out adjoining the cities and towns and extended far out into the country. Improvements were made, sometimes substantial and sometimes scanty; alluring promises of further improvements were given; more or less attractive. Often flimsy stucco gates were built, opening upon these developments; wide-stretching areas were laid off in lots and marked with white stakes like a cemetery; streets and walks were laid down; and lots were sold to eager purchasers at inflated prices, relatively small initial payments frequently being made, and obligations incurred which later turned out to be difficult or impossible of fulfillment.

For some reason, disaster number four had a familiar ring to it. You might notice there was no 'government bailouts' for the land exploiters. If there had been, we would still be paying off that debt just as our children and grandchildren will be paying off government bailouts of today."

Steamboats On Wekiva

Many people who came to settle in Central Florida reached Mellonville (Sanford) by steamer on the St. Johns River, and then traveled overland to homestead along the Wekiva River. The Wekiva in the 1870s was shallow and filled with brush. It was little more than a narrow stream through a swamp that led to the St. Johns River.

Still, captains of light draft steamers found they could navigate the Wekiva after clearing out the debris in the channel and dredging the bottom. Historian Jerrell H. Shofner said a pair of shop owners was among the first to bring steamers to the Wekiva.

To stock their general store at the Lodge (Apopka), William Mills and Matthew Stewart hauled supplies by wagon over a sandy road from Mellonville in the early 1870s. Not only did they recognize that using the Wekiva could make getting supplies to their store a lot easier, but Shofner said they also envisioned draining and selling swamp lands. Through their partnership, the Wekiva Steamboat Company, they signed a deal with the state—which was encouraging entrepreneurs to drain swamps—to keep two-thirds of the state lands they could drain within a year.

They didn't achieve all they set out to, but Mellonville steamboat lines were soon doing a thriving business supplying the community of Clay Springs. An 1847 government survey map noted the improvements farmer L.H. Clay had made to the springs. From just after the Civil War, Clay Springs had a wharf and warehouse for unloading and storing cargo that arrived on Wekiva River steamers.

In the 1870s, Captain E. R. Lewis' seventy-foot Mayflower, a side-wheeler with a draft of only fourteen inches, was making two trips a week between Mellonville and Clay Springs. An advertisement in the *Tallahassee Floridian* said the captain promised "fast day accommodations with a saloon below and an awning above with comfortable seats." Lewis later became a minor partner with Mills and Stewart in their steamboat company.

An 1888 newspaper described the Wekiva as a "narrow, tortuous and shallow stream," and said New York's Will L. Church had arrived in Altamonte with a boat he planned to add to the river's steam lines. Newspapers reported that Wekiva barges hauled cargo well into the 1880s, when railroad competition heated up and eventually overtook the steamers. Even after railroads replaced steamboat commerce, Clay Springs remained a popular bathing and picnic spot.

From the late 1870s, a steady stream of Northerners had bought land at Clay Springs. Land sales were brisk enough for four real estate companies. Henry Sanford, who had opened a branch of his Sanford general store in Clay Springs, was selling tracks of land along Lake Monroe and elsewhere. Some of Sanford's buyers included President Ulysses S. Grant and General William Sherman. It was not long until the settlers began looking for land in the interior, as well as land along the Wekiva. The area would vie with Apopka to become the political center of Orange County.

Clay Springs did succeed in getting its own polling place in the early 1870s. The county built a road from the Clay Springs wharf to the meeting point for roads from Sanford, Orlando, and the Lodge.

At the peak of optimism about Clay Springs' future, Shofner said, Iowa newspaperman J. D. Smith built a three-story, 100-room hotel and laid out a town near the springs. He named his town Sulphur Springs. Other people came to his town to buy home sites and open businesses, including a skating rink, which served as a church of Sundays. The rink was built on the site of citrus groves killed in the bitter back-to-back freezes of 1894-95. John Steinmetz, who had come from Pennsylvania in 1882, built the rink and later took over the lease on the hotel, opening what seems to have been the area's first amusement park. He added a bath house, a toboggan slide, and a dance pavilion.

Smith's choice of a name, Sulphur Springs, never caught on. The community and its post office remained in Clay Springs until 1906, when both became Wekiwa Springs. The post office closed in 1910.

Clay Springs/Apopka Railroad

By 1875, Clay Springs had developed into Northwest Orange County's port for receiving goods shipped down the St. John's River from Sanford, Jacksonville and above. It also handled outgoing goods to be shipped north on the St. Johns.

By 1877, Captain E. R. Lewis was making two trips a week between Sanford and Clay Springs in his Mayflower, a seventy-foot, double-ended vessel with a fourteen-foot beam, a side wheel, and a draft of only fourteen inches. Passengers were promised "fast day accommodations with a saloon below and an awning above, and oh yes, seats of comfort."

By 1884, barges on the Wekiva River were doing a thriving business delivering large amounts of freight in and out of Clay Springs. Apopkans watched the activities on the Wekiva and began to envision a railroad connecting Clay Springs to Lovell's Landing on Lake Apopka in order to connect the Lake Apopka agricultural region with markets in the north through Clay Springs.

Produce was being shipped overland through Apopka to Clay Springs by oxen, mules, etc. This was slow and expensive.

A meeting was held at Apopka in August of 1878 to raise funds for construction for the Clay Springs-Lovell's Landing Railroad, which was conceived as a tramway from Lovell's Landing through the town of Apopka and on to Clay Springs. The eight-mile line would be constructed of wooden stringers, thirty inches apart, and strapped with iron. Twenty-nine people subscribed to the company stock and hopes were high for its early completion. By early 1879, the right-of-way had been obtained and William Mills had agreed to furnish stringers from his mill at $8 per thousand feet. But in the late 19th century, it was always far easier to organize a railroad company than to finance and complete construction.

Ten years after its initial organization, the Apopka and Clay Springs railroad was just beginning construction. In March of 1889, grading was "progressing very satisfactory" and in April the *Apopka Advertiser* announced the arrival of "five carloads of rails and one load of spikes, consigned to the new Apopka and Clay Springs Railroad."

By 1890, they had only built six miles of it from Clay Springs through Apopka and about a mile to the south toward Lovell's Landing. It was standard gauge road with twenty-five-pound rails with switching connections to both the TO&A and the Florida Midland. Boosters thought that if the remaining two miles of the line were completed, "a very extensive territory would be opened up and a vast quantity of freight secured."

In July of 1890, the road was offering "Excursions to Clay Springs! Leaves Apopka every Wednesday and Saturday." The fare from Apopka was twenty-five cents; from East Apopka, it was fifteen cents.

This all reminded me of when I was a young fellow; I used to catch a ride on the old Atlantic Coastline from Apopka to Orlando. Passengers would have seats assigned in the train's caboose. The old coal-burning engine spewed its smoke into the caboose and the passengers spent their trip outside on the deck in the fresh air. I do not remember what the fare was, but whatever it was; the passengers got the short end of the stick.

This was about as far as that Clay Springs-Apopka Railroad got. Instead of completing the road, Auerbach traded it to Anna Dieter of New York for property she owned in Buffalo. During the depression of the 1890s and the 1894-95 freezes, the railroad was allowed to languish. The company paid no taxes after 1890, and when Orange County Tax Collector Seth Woodruff tried to collect in 1896, he discovered that the railroad had been taken up "and no property was found upon which to levy an execution."

Early Apopkans After Civil War

When Florida seceded from the Union in 1861, Orange County was pretty well divided on the issue. Whatever their sentiments were before secession, most Orange County residents accepted the situation and followed Florida into the Confederate States of America.

When the war ended in the spring of 1865, area residents soon resumed their peacetime pursuits. Continuing to grow cotton, corn, and sugar cane, they traded through Mellonville on Lake Monroe, either with a merchant there or directly with factors in Jacksonville or Savannah. William A Lovell resumed connections with John W. Anderson & Sons, a cotton firm in Savannah. When William Mills and Mathew Stewart opened their store at the Lodge in 1868, they also dealt with the Andersons. Cotton was still an important crop in the 1870s and Henry S. Sanford's store at the new town named for him on Lake Monroe catered to cotton farmers of the county. He even opened a branch store at Clay Springs, the better to reach the Apopka area trade. His stores did a considerable business supplying merchandise on credit to farmers who consigned their cotton to him. However, a change was already underway. Within a few years cotton would be replaced by citrus as the major agricultural enterprise of the Apopka area. During the intervening decade, however, times were different for the hardy pioneers of the Apopka area.

In the long run, the political and social disruptions of the Reconstruction years probably benefited Orange County. Because of their discouragement with political and social changes in North Florida, many residents of that part of the state, as well as Georgia, Alabama, and South Carolina moved to the Florida frontier to get away from affairs they could not control. Publicity focused on the state by Reconstruction activities brought other immigrants from the northern states who sought cheap land on the frontier in a desirable climate. With its small population and only a handful of freed slaves, the county was not directly affected by the political battles and social changes which devastated North Florida. President Andrew Johnson's proclamation of amnesty restored all former Confederates to United States citizenship except high-ranking military and civilian officials and all who had owned more than $20,000 worth of property in 1860. None of the residents of the Apopka area fell into these special categories and were covered by general amnesty. They were consequently free to resume their pre-war activities with all their property safe from the confiscation except the slaves, who had been freed. Still, the indirect effect was felt for several years.

Johnson's efforts to return Florida to the Union without upsetting social conditions failed after two turbulent years. In March 1867, Congress implemented its own Reconstruction program which required Negro suffrage as a condition of the state's restoration to the Union. In the meantime, the state was to be under the control of Major General John Pope, commander of the Third Military District. Supervised by the military commander, committees in each county were directed to register all adult males, regardless of their race, who desired to vote. At the time, Orange County's Third Precinct included the area from Clay Springs to Starke Lake between the Wekiva River and Lake Apopka. Fewer than fifty voters were registered, only ten of whom were black.

After the 1868 constitution was ratified and Harrison Reed was inaugurated, Republican administrations held office until early in 1877. There were several years of Ku Klux Klan violence, countered by United States military forces in the northern part of the state. In the meantime Orange County was consistently Democratic and just as anxious as the rest of the state to oust the Republican administrations and bring an end to Reconstruction. Much of their opposition was traditional. They had supported Florida in the Confederacy and lost to the people who were then in power, and some felt the Republicans were outsiders who should be ousted. But the opposition was also grounded in their belief that the economic adversity of the late 1860s and early 1870s was the result of Reconstruction difficulties. Both sides were partially correct.

With empty treasuries, both state and county governments issued scrip in lieu of currency for payment of their debts. The scrip fluctuated in value from as low as forty cents on the dollar to as much as ninety cents, before tax revenues improved enough to retire the scrip and place both governments on a cash basis. Such financial policies, coupled with uncertainties over the security of property during the turbulence of Reconstruction, made it difficult for Floridians to obtain credit at a reasonable rate.

Furthermore, the price of cotton was exceedingly unstable in the post-war years. Nor was the weather cooperative. Orange County was struck by a devastating hurricane in August 1871. It rained continuously for forty-eight hours. One observer claimed that nearly four feet of rain fell during that short period. Whether that was true or not, the rain and accompanying high winds partially destroyed much of the county's orange, sugar cane, and cotton crops. As if all this was not enough, the Panic of 1873 further diminished the prospects of local farmers.

There was a brighter side developing, however. Shortly after the war ended, new families such as the Raulersons, Princes, and McDonalds moved into the area, anxious to get away from the problems of Reconstruction and begin anew in a quieter section of the country. There was also a steady stream of Northerners buying land in the area for permanent settlement or for winter homes. Over the course of time, the economy settled down to its routine ups and downs, and the Apopka area put the war behind them and created a very desirable place to settle and raise a family.

Florida Cracker Horses

*This article was taken from the book **Cracker**, written by Dana Ste. Claire and copyrighted in 1998.*

"When Spanish explorer Juan Ponce De Leon sailed from Santo Domingo to St. Augustine in 1521, he carried with him six heifers and a single bull. From this original and modest stock, a vast Florida cattle population descended which today numbers in the millions. Cattle ranching has still held its place in Florida history, shaping the rural cultural landscape of the territory for over four and half centuries. But it was during the second quarter of the 1800s, especially after the Armed Occupation Act of 1842, when raising cattle as a way of life became attractive and widespread. With the surging industry, a unique breed of cracker cattlemen called cowhunters emerged.

The life of these early cowmen was lonely and hard, but well suited to the rugged existence crackers already knew well. Cattle drives lasting months meant rounding up herds in remote marshes and dense scrub forests, encounters with snakes and wolves, stampedes, torrential thunderstorms, searing heat, and swarms of mosquitoes. The evenings were spent around a campfire, drinking black coffee and telling stories, if they weren't too tired. Throughout the night, the crashing sounds of cattle tramping down palmetto patches would be heard.

Many crackers were attracted to the cowhunter lifestyle. Work as a ranch hand was easily found back when cattle ranged free of fences across endless miles of Florida swamps, palmetto prairies and scrub forests. The Cracker cattle they drove were direct descendants of Andalusian cattle introduced to Florida by the Spanish and of British Colonial breeds from the upper South. This hardy Florida stock, gaunt and mean, was bred to withstand tropical heat, insect bites, and sparse native forage. Their ponies, too, had bloodlines going back to the Andalusian breeds of the Spanish conquistadors. Called marshtackies, these small horses were favored by cowmen for their smooth ride, durability and quick maneuverability, and were well adapted to the Florida wilderness.

The cowmen seldom used a rope, as lariats were practically useless in the thick scrub. Instead, they used catchdogs which were trained to cut out and literally "catch" an errant cow and hold its ear or nose in its teeth until a cowman arrived.

They used 12-18-foot rawhide and buckskin whips called drags to drive their cattle. The whip's loud, rifle shot popping, audible for miles, moved cattle in a desired direction, with the whip barely touching the cow. Cracker cowmen were expert bullwhippers who could kill snakes or stop a herd of stampeding cattle with a pop from their drag. Florida cattleman and historian Doyle Conner Jr. explains that early cowhunter whips were made of tanned buckskin, and many of these were fabricated by Seminole Indians. After the 1930s, the drags were made with cowhide. Original 19th century buckskin whips are hard to come by and treasured by those cowmen who are fortunate to own one.

Aside from a good whip, the cowhunters carried few other things. Saddles were leftover Army issue McClellans that had no saddle horn. Coffee was cooked in tin cans, and firearms were mostly shotguns and pistols powerful enough to stop bears, mad Cracker bulls, and rustlers in their tracks. A leather 'wallet' stored clothes, if a change of clothing was needed. Very often the only extra clothes carried along would be a pair of pants with a hole cut in the crotch so that they could be carried on the saddle. To economize space, cowmen would sometimes store horse feed in the horned pants. In the early days, each Florida range-rider carried a distinctive hand-forged iron brand to mark his cattle. When the brands on the cow's flank became hard to see in the thick Florida scrub, cowhunters would cut notches in their stock's ear to identify them.

Cowmen slept through the night on the sandy ground, sometimes in heavy rainstorms, with little more than an old blanket to keep him warm. Food rations on the range were typically grits, hot biscuits, black coffee, and occasionally fresh meat, usually game. At times a fat steer was killed at the beginning of a long drive to feed a camp.

In many ways, the Florida range with its surly cowhunters, whip-popping cattle drives, feuds between ranches and shoot-outs in the scrub was wilder than the West.

An early cowman's meal on the range might consist of a frying pan full of bacon into which canned tomatoes were added, a pot of grits, baked sweet potatoes and buttermilk biscuits from the saddlebag, topped off by some very strong coffee. Huge batches of cornbread, biscuits and syrup cookies were usually baked up by the womenfolk to be taken out to the cowhands. On extended cattle drives the meat and sausage were fried and then packed into 5 gallon tins and then fat poured over it in order for the meat to keep. Being cattle country, a lot of beef was eaten. Many times in order for it to keep well, it was smoked, which also helped to tenderize it. This was a definite bonus when eating some of the early "scrub cattle," which were known to be a tough and stringy meal. A young recruit temporarily stationed in Florida before being shipped off to the Spanish American war wrote home to tell his mother not to worry about him getting shot because he figured he was fairly well bullet-proof after eating a lot of our local 'scrub cow' beef."

Lula Bowers

My wife and I were recently looking through some of her mother's (Gladys Bowers Stone Mahaffey) old papers, when we ran into an interview someone had with one of her relatives from the Low Country in South Carolina after the Civil War. We are speaking of Mrs. Lula Bowers, who was born on January 9, 1859. This interview was conducted on June 28, 1938, when she was eighty-seven years old. Mrs. Bowers is small and frail-looking. Though very deaf, she talks entertainingly. Her memory of dates and events is very good. Here is her side of the interview in full.

"We had parties in our day. We call'em Sociables - Sociables and Surprise Parties. They met in the homes. I've been to a many a one! Played games, cards and danced. But the church members weren't allowed to dance. If church members danced they'd turn them out. Didn't have any round-dances in that day. The girls would begin dancing by first dancing with their brothers and cousins. Then they would dance with everybody. I was a great dancer. And my husband was a fiddler. My father wouldn't let me dance the round dances. He didn't care how much I danced the other dances. There was a young man come up from Savannah. He was a great dancer. He danced all the dances. Then my son-in-law danced all the dances. Dixie Box, Jimmy Box, Nanny Box and Frank Warren were the biggest dancers around Estill. May Lawton was a great dancer – and Anna Sloane.

They'd have a big Quiltin' Party and dance. Didn't get much quiltin' out of 'em. They'd quilt all day and dance all night. I've been to a many a one! Nathalie Johnson was a perfect belle among 'em. She was a great dancer. Dr. Cleveland Johnson, Coy Johnson and Kruger Johnson were all great dancers. I had quilted out seven quilts when I married. My step-mother used'em. They were the old time Nine-patch and Seven Sisters. I have some of'em now. I have two quilts that were buried during the Civil War. My mother made them in 1857. One is the Open Rose. The other is the Album quilt, with the names of friends on it. They're good now! The Open Rose was a great quilt; and the Rose and Bud. My mother-in-law gave me a quilt in 1878. I've got it now. It's still good. I remember the home made blankets, too, made during the Confederate War. The wool was cut off my grandfather's sheep.

We had Spelling Bees in those days. I went to one up at Old Allendale near Martyn's Station. It was held at a Campbellite Church. I drove five in a buggy hitched to an old blind mule. That was September 1874. It was the first Campbellite Church I ever went to. Old Dr. Jim Erwin was the preacher. The poorest speller had to put a wreath on the hand of the best speller. Clarence Erwin was the best speller and Minnie Warren was the poorest. She crowned him with a wreath. Charlie Peeples knows all those people. He can tell you all about this. He and I danced many a dance together. My grandmother used to call it the frolicking church. They went to church and come back and danced till daylight. A fire in the woods burnt the church up. Not there now. Johnson People's mother was the greatest dancer ever was in this country – Catty Johnson! After the war when they first began making cotton and selling it for a good price, the husband's come in and ask the wives which they'd rather have – a silk frock, or a carpet to go on the floor. Some would want a silk frock, and some a carpet. They didn't have anything in their houses after the war.

We had Sewing Bees, too. I've been to many a one! We'd sew all day and dance all night. My aunt would take me to'em when I was a little child. They'd make clothes for the slaves. Make them out of homespun. My great-grand-mother had a loom, and they'd weave cloth on it. They'd give as a prize for the best sewer a bushel of potatoes, or some chickens or something like that. And they'd have beer made out of persimmons, and beer made out of sweet potatoes. They'd have all of them Sewing and Quilting. They'd have inspectors to overlook the sewing to see who'd win the prize. Generally have three (3). If someone made the most garments but weren't made the best, the judges would generally give the prize to the one that did the best sewing. But both counted. Had a regular button-hole worker. My old aunt worked the button-holes.

I've seen the Yankees come and burn down the houses. I saw two large houses burned to the ground. When they came to our house, I went out and sat in the Captain's lap and begged him not to burn our house. I was six years old. I hugged and kissed him and begged him not to burn our house. My mother was a widow. They didn't burn it. They came through several times. They'd keep coming through for two or three months. After the war we didn't have meat but once a day. Didn't have any meat for breakfast or supper. And flour was so scarce we didn't have biscuits but once a week. And then didn't have but one around – sometimes half a biscuit. I've had many a half – biscuit. I have a gold watch that my aunt had tied around her waist to keep the Yankees from getting it. My mother's grandmother gave it to her. I'm saving it for my grandchildren. That'll be five or six generations.

They'd have candy pulling, too. They had a lot of sorghum molasses. But they didn't have any nice cane syrup. But they had a lot of syrup and they'd have candy pullings. They'd sometimes put peanuts in the candy; but you can't pull it when you put nuts in it. They had a lot of cows and plenty of milk and butter.

I'll tell you another great thing they done. Made lye soap. They'd pour it through the ashes."

Zellwood

This is about the early pioneers of Zellwood. In *The History of Orange County Florida*, written by Dr. William F. Blackman in 1927, we get a real insight into who these people were and what their lives were like.

The first settlers in what is now Zellwood appear to have been Mr. Frank Gill, who located on Grasmere Lake; Mr. Frank Goolsby, whose home was also on Grasmere Lake; and a Mr. Neal. These pioneers cleared small areas of land and planted orange groves and gardens.

Colonel T. Elwood Zell, a Philadelphian who published *Zell's Cyclopedia* in 1868 and who will doubtless be remembered by some of the older readers (much older), discovered this lovely region of lakes and hills in 1875 or 1876,

Sydonie House

and for a time made his winter home here with his brother-in-law and business associate, Mr. John A. Williamson. The son of Mr. Williamson, Mr. A.D. Williamson, gave an account of the early days in an article by R. G. Grassfield in the *Orlando Morning Sentinel* of April 24, 1927:

"Mr. Williamson and his wife and three children left Philadelphia, going by way of steamer to Jacksonville, and then up the St. Johns River to Sanford and from there to their future home. They arrived at Zellwood on October 28, 1876. The thirty mile trip from Sanford to Zellwood took fifteen hours.

The Williamsons made their home with Daniel H. Fleming in the Neal home. Mr. Fleming had made arrangements with Mr. Neal to house the newcomers for a period of seven weeks. In the meantime, workmen were in the woods, hewing logs on three sides, and the new house had the roof on very quickly. At the end of the seven weeks the Williamson family moved into their new home. The house was without doors or windows, and the first cooking was done over a fire outside of the house. In this manner and under these circumstances, the pioneer life of the Williamsons began. I recall seeing deer grazing not far from the house. I was a boy of seven at the time.

Colonel Zell and Mr. Williamson married sisters, and when the Zells came, they made their home with the Williamsons. This continued for several winters. Colonel Zell subsequently built his home near the Williamson home and this house was one of the oldest dwellings in Zellwood. Colonel Zell adopted the name Zellwood for his home and this name was formally adopted by residents for the name of the community.

During the early part of 1876, R. G. Robinson, a native of Kentucky came to Zellwood and settled on the southeast corner of Lake Maggiore. The land he owned was at one time the property of President Zackary Taylor, from whom Mr. Robinson secured the piece. Mr. Robinson was a close relative of the former president. Mr. Robinson brought his family to Zellwood in November 1876 and thus, the Robinsons, the Williamsons and D. H. Fleming were the pioneer settlers of Zellwood. Another who came a little later to become a part of the community life and to engage with the others in the growing of citrus fruits was George C. Welby, the son of the poetess, Amelia Welby, of Louisville.

With the completion of the Williamson home, it became the social center of the community. Religious services, private theatricals and dances were here there. People from as far as Eustis and Apopka came to take part in the frequent entertainments.

With the founding of Zellwood there was no idea of establishing a community of retired army officers; however, Colonel George Foote and Captain D. A. Irwin bought property from Colonel Zell and lived in Zellwood up to 1895. Colonel Foote engaged in the growing of citrus fruit until he returned to Washington. Captain Charles Sellmer brought his family to Zellwood, coming there through the influence of Mr. Robinson. He engaged in the citrus growing industry and in the real estate business. Captain Sellmer was not retired from the army until a number of years after he came, but he returned to Zellwood upon his retirement and died in his Zellwood home.

During these years the small homes could not accommodate boarders, so the Williamson home became the place where those who came looking for a home site remained until they could erect homes of their own. Among those who made their home with the Williamson family while their new homes were under construction were the Laughlin's, Loraines, Footes, Irwins and a number of others. Not only the house but the barn and its loft also became the home of these early newcomers to Zellwood. The hospitality of the early pioneers was complete. The burden was shared by all, but upon these sturdy women of early Zellwood fell the greatest cares. Not one of them had known hardships, for they came from comfortable convenient northern homes into a new country, in order that the course of empire building might be broadened.

One of the early settlers was Mr. Davenport, an attorney and mayor of Kansas City and one of Theodore Roosevelt's trusted lieutenants in his campaign for the presidency. He built a home on Lake Maggiore, and was killed by a fall from the tower of his water-tank. His daughter, Edith Fairfax Davenport, was an artist of distinction; an exhibition of her paintings was given some years back, to the Albertson Public Library of Orlando.

R. G. Robinson was the first postmaster of Zellwood but held the office but a short time after the office was established. J. A. Williamson was given the appointment and he held the office for more than thirty years and until two weeks of his death in 1911.

There was, perhaps in all Florida, no more imposing and delightful estate than Sydonie, erected on the banks of Lake Maggiore by James Laughlin, Jr. of Pittsburgh. All that owner, architect, builder, decorator and landscape engineer and gardener could devise, at whatever expense, went to the fashioning of this perfect home and estate.

Mr. Laughlin was a member of the famous firm of Jones and Laughlin, iron masters of Pittsburgh, a graduate and trustee of Princeton University, a trustee and benefactor of Rollins College and a devoted member of the Presbyterian Church.

The estate was in the competent care of Mr. William Edwards who also had a charming home overlooking Lake Maggiore. Mr. Edwards came from Chicago originally to run the Pirie Estate in Plymouth and proved to be an excellent manager for both estates."

The Heritage House

Frances Rynerson of The Apopka Chief interviewed Miss Louise Claiborne Armstrong in April of 1966, concerning the history of the old Heritage House that stood on the corner of Main and McGee Streets, where Burger King is located today. During those years, I was Miss Armstrong's neighbor across the street on McGee. I found her to be as true a Southern Belle as anyone I have ever encountered. She also proved to be a most interesting person to talk to, especially if the subject was Confederate history. Here is the article Frances Rynerson wrote.

"The Heritage House, one of the oldest dwellings in continuous use in Apopka, is located just off Main Street on South McGee Ave. The original house was built in 1860 as a hunting lodge and was owned by Charles Percival, Earl of Egmont. From 1886 until 1950, the estate was owned by Miss Rewella McGee.

Miss Louise Claiborne Armstrong, niece of Miss Sally McGee, now lives in the house. Miss Armstrong moved into the house in 1934 to care for her aunt and uncle. The first member of her family to own the Heritage was her great-grandfather, James Watson. He purchased the property from Rev. Zander through a realtor named Frank Davis.

James Watson was originally from Louisville, Kentucky and had the first license to build inland water vessels. He used the lodge for about two months every year as a hunting and fishing base in Central Florida.

During the period in which Rev. Zander owned the house, he tried to add a room, but it fell down. He then had his church members try to build the room, but again it collapsed. The wall in the kitchen still sags as a result of the work that Rev. Zander tried to do.

The original design of the house had five porches, two of which are not enclosed. One is used as a sitting room and the other a jalousied porch, which is still used. The Heritage contains, besides the spacious porches, a living room, parlor, dining room, kitchen and three bedrooms.

Many of the furnishings of the old house are priceless and were brought over to this country many years ago. The draperies in the living room are made of Lyons velvet, which were imported from France and were brought here in 1865. Some of the chinaware and other services were also imported and were specially made for the owners of the place. Many of the items are of great value as antiques, but remain prized possessions of the owner.

James Watson, who was well over six feet tall, experienced trouble with the bathing facilities of the Heritage which, at that time, consisted of a small china bowl. He ordered a bathtub from Louisville and it took over three months for delivery. A zinc pipe from the well in the yard was converted into a large funnel and ran into the house. When bath time arrived the procedure was to dip the water from the outside well into the funnel and thence into the tub. Hot water was heated on the wood stove and added to the tub for comfort.

Miss Armstrong was educated in Saint Hearts Convent in Paris with a private tutor and in Rome and Verey, Switzerland. Later, she spent a winter studying in Aswan, Egypt, completing her formal education. She was married in Newport, R. I. in 1904 to Mr. Francis Upham after he received his lieutenant's bars from West Point. The ceremony took place in the Christ Church Cathedral. Miss Armstrong recalls that *The Apopka Chief* carried the story of their wedding. During World War I, Mr. Upham was called into service and sent to Paris, France, at which time Mrs. Upham accompanied him."

The Uphams were divorced in 1928 and she took back her maiden name of Armstrong. Miss Armstrong passed away in February of 1976.

Today, on the property of the old hunting lodge or the Heritage House, stands a Burger King. Manny Garcia of Davgar Restaurants, who had the distributorship for Burger King in the Central Florida area, took particular care to retain as much of the historical value of the property as possible. They maintained the theme as a hunting lodge and promised to decorate it as such. The wall around the house was constructed with brick from the first Orange County Courthouse, which was also used in part in the construction of the Burger King. They also maintained a 90-foot deep well, which was the first well dug in Apopka. They have also maintained a display case showing a model of the home."

"Early Days In Apopka"

Early days in Apopka was written in 1935 for *The Apopka Chief* by an unknown correspondent. Reading it, we get a chance to look back into the 1800s and catch a glimpse of who was who and what was what in very early Apopka.

"With the kind assistance of A. J. Lovell, a *Chief* reporter had a brief look back into those good old days of more than 50 years ago in Apopka (1885). The old town apparently has had the experience of a great many of us nestling contentedly on the eastern rim of its present limits, the junction of Alabama Avenue and Main Street. This was the principle corner of the city. The citizens went quietly about their business of raising oranges, gardening, fishing, swimming and attending dances at the Morgan Hotel or elsewhere in the community. All this added gaiety and zest to what might seem a modest or rather dull existence. But it wasn't. They also went to church more in those days than they do now, according to Mr. Lovell.

But the Florida Midland Railroad was built later; its station located approximately where the Atlantic Coastline station now stands (roughly across the street from the Catfish Place). This was a disturbing influence which tended to make the town spread westward, and later the Seaboard came in and built its station out in the woods (the present site), which caused the new town to be started up that way.

Mr. Lovell tells of being in charge of building of a clay road from the old town all the way up to the new town. Citizens would contribute a day or two a week, some bringing teams and wagons and the ladies bringing dinner, and before anyone knew it, they had a new clay surfaced road between the two communities, everybody had had a good time, and it had not cost a cent.

Financing of public road projects has taken on some complications since that time. The road followed the route of the present Fourth Street. But, at the very best, the railroads and new stations had the effect of scattering the objectives of the little community, as more recent changes have done to all of us.

The 'Old Town' was clustered around the Lodge for the Masonic order, which is still used by its various societies. It is a simple little two-story structure that one might come to town a lot of times and fail to notice at all. It is located at the corner of East Fourth and the old Orlando Highway (Alabama Avenue). Some remodeling has been done both inside and outside, but the original timbers put into it are of virgin Florida pine that has stood off all decaying influences since the '50s of last century. It is the oldest building in Orange County that Mr. Lovell can recall.

The business houses, at one time, included general stores belonging to W.A. Lovell and J.D. Fudge (W. A. Lovell was the father of A.J.) and J.J. Combs, S.M Love and others, a hardware store owned by E.R. Prince, and a drug store on the corner south of the Lodge owned by Dr. Jones. In the space immediately in front of the McGee home, there was a building used for school and a community church. Further east there was a printing office and a wine shop.

Were there any real estate dealers? There certainly were – Page McKinney & Frank Davis, and Hanley & Johnson among them.

There was a weekly paper published in Apopka by a Mr. Russell assisted by his son, M.C. Russell, afterwards he was the founder of the *Jacksonville Evening Journal*. Hood's restaurant was also in that block. On the site of Womble's filling station was a livery stable, first operated by Captain J.A. Johnson, later by W.C. and J.D. Lovell, (brothers of A.J.), then Jim Marshall and R.C. Waters. Here rigs were obtainable for pleasure rides over the sand roads on Sunday afternoons, usually to Clay Springs or Orlando or a lovely drive in the country.

The hotel for accommodation of visitors to the city was operated by Mrs. Morgan and situated across the street from the Lodge. There was also a tourist hotel, The Lake House, a half mile east on the Forest City road (SR 436) near the small lake seen on the left of the road going east after one gets well up on the hill. (I would guess this was the northeast corner of Sheeler Road and SR 436). The Lake House had a winter guest list running from 40-50 people. Some railroad superintendents and others lived there. In back of the Lake House, to the north on the railroad, was a large sawmill operated by Pierce and Torrey.

McKinney and John Bedford bought a steam boat, which operated on the Wekiva River from Clay Springs to a wharf on the St. Johns River. They brought in many kinds of merchandise and it would likely have been a thriving business if it had not been ruined in its early life by railroad competition. The road that now stops at the Atlantic Coast Line station (Tom Staley Park) continued out east to the town of Longwood, but earlier, a narrow gauged road had begun operation from Sanford to Orlando and wagons were hauling freight from Longwood to Apopka.

Of course, news traveled slowly, as did everything. It was not a fast moving world like we live in now. But men were men in those days. Mr. Lovell tells of James Mendham, who from the boat landing at Sanford to his place, about three miles east of Apopka, rolled a barrel of flour in a wheelbarrow."

Apopka Baseball

1926 Lake County-Orange County League Champs
Mascot: Leon Shepherd
Front: Mallory Welch, Pete Boswell, Leland Hawthorne, Oscar Cashwell, Robert Rencher
Middle: V.A. Stewart, Winifred Harris, Percy Starbird, Jimmy Thompson, R.G. Pitman
Back: Carl Jackson, R.A. Lasater, Toby Edwards, Paul Ustler, Ira Erickson.

Baseball has been popular in Apopka since the 1880s, and Apopkans have always played it well. After World War I, they played it well, indeed, with such players like Ted Waite (played for Rollins), Bucky Harris, Clem Womble, Mallory Welch, Bill Witherington, V. A. Stewart, and others who won many championships for the city. In those early days the local team traveled by horse and wagon to all of their out-of-town games, leaving early on game day with their lunches neatly packed in the usual brown paper bags. There were generally nine or ten to a wagon, all eagerly looking forward to the afternoon game. I am sure there were a few wagons of fans following the players and also barefooted little boys following the fans.

In 1922, Apopka joined with other cities in Lake and Orange County to form the Lake-Orange League. For nearly forty years, the men in these small towns of Lake and Orange County settled old feuds and started new ones on the baseball diamond. They were known as the Apopka Packers, Umatilla Umptums, Winter Park Crackers, Mount Dora Mountaineers, Winter Garden Gardeners, Tavares Travelers, Clermont Highlanders, and last but not least, the Zellwood Mudhens. If you think the Umptums was a rather strange name, don't worry, because one year later they changed the name to, "Umptatas."

By 1926, young Bob Pittman, Jr., known as "Pitt," was terrorizing the league with his .400+ batting averages. He was probably the best true hitter the league ever produced. Pitt went on to play baseball for the University of Florida, where he was Florida's first baseball All-American in 1933. After graduation he signed with the Boston Braves and began his baseball career in Harrisburg, Pennsylvania. In his first year he sustained a career-ending ankle injury. He returned home and had a very successful coaching career.

Vard "Junior" Hager of Ocoee tells an interesting story of one of his encounters with Pitt on the baseball diamond. "I was on third and Tiger Minor was pitching, and he called time to tell me that he had stolen the bunt sign that Bob was going to bunt," said Hager. "But Bob was a 400 hitter. He just did not bunt. But Tiger told me they were going to use the element of surprise this time." Hager, therefore, played up on the grass, preparing for the bunt Tiger promised was coming, and Pitman hit a line drive that hit Hager right in the stomach. "It knocked me out cold," Hager said. "I'd have sworn they were going to bunt," Tiger told him later.

In the middle 1930s, along came a young towhead named George A. "Jug" Anderson, the father of country singer, John Anderson. Jug was a fireballer who seemed to specialize in no-hitters. He has been known to pitch both ends of a double-header, pitching a no-hitter in each game. He earned the name of "Ironman." However, as might be expected, he threw his arm away early while pitching for the Jacksonville Tars.

The games were always played on Sunday and Thursday afternoons. On Thursday the local merchants closed up shop in order to attend. It was best not to get sick on game days because our local doctor, Tommy McBride, would be attending the game as close behind home plate as he could get. The old Edwards Field stadium, which had a roof in those days, would generally be filled to the brim.

During the Depression the Apopka Club and the Lake-Orange League had financial difficulties. The Apopka Baseball Club had leased Edwards Field from the city and was unable to pay the lease because of the hard times. The citizens of Apopka wanted lights at Edwards Field, so they could have their Thursday games at night instead of closing the stores in the afternoon. During those hard times the merchants could not afford to close on Thursdays anymore. The City worked out an agreement with the WPA to improve Edwards Field. They spent $14,000 on the project. With the support of the Apopka Sportsman's Club, the Apopka Club reorganized and continued to play. Good baseball was alive and well for the time being.

December 7, 1941, changed it all. Most of the ballplayers were drafted or volunteered for service during World War II. With the outlook of fielding a baseball team being very slim, Apopkans consented to leasing Edwards Field to the Army for the duration of the war. The 351st Coast Artillery Search Light Battalion, with about 250 men, changed the field into an army base. They had searchlights scattered around the area. I recall two searchlights, one being somewhere around Buchan's Pond and another toward Lake Apopka. I am sure there were plenty more.

Ray Goolsby returned after the war and continued his baseball career. Ray was with the Washington Senators farm system in Chattanooga, Tennessee. Washington had their spring training in Orlando at the time and Ray had an extremely good spring and was moved up to the Senators. He was another product of the Lake-Orange League to make it to the majors.

And, of course, we had our left-handed wonder Jim Mahaffey, who always claimed, "I won more games than any other pitcher we ever had." He forgot to add that he also lost more games than any other pitcher, because he pitched in more games. Jim was not known as a humble soul.

As the boys returned home from the service, baseball was restored and Apopka continued its winning ways. Crowds in the thousands turned out for the games.

In *Sport Magazine*, Bill Oswski reported that "At a quickly called 'Hot Stove League' session held at former mayor Ted Waite's home recently, no fewer than nine veterans of the Apopka teams turned up. The youngest began playing semi-pro baseball in 1931, and three were members of the 1915 entry into the Lake-Orange League."

Besides Waite, there were several leading merchants of the town, an All-American college player, and a barnstorming pitcher who picked Apopka to settle down in.

After some preliminary rhubarbs about whose generation had the best team, the meeting got down to some serious yarn-spinning.

Mallory Welch, a peppy veteran of the 1915 contingent, remembered the time the Apopka nine ventured down to the wilds of Fort Meade for what was supposed to be an afternoon's recreation.

It seems that the Fort Meade batters were having a devil of a time hitting the Apopka pitcher's deliveries, mainly due to the fact that they were being served nothing but the Apopka man's favorite pitch, the emory ball. (Now, for the females and those who chew gum instead of tobacco, the emory ball is one that gets an extra dip on it after the pitcher scruffs up the horsehide with a piece of emory board he's concealed somewhere in his uniform. It's not illegal, unless you get caught throwing it.)

So the first seven innings went by, with the Fort Meade batters having no luck touching the jumping ball.

As Welch remembers it, the umpire was fairly well into his cups by this stage, so he never did check to see if there were any illegal pitches being thrown. He simply threw baseball after baseball out of play, because they all got scuffed and dirty in such a hurry.

"Now I'd seen a pistol beside their second baseman's glove before the game," Welch recalled. "So I didn't think we should take those crackers too lightly."

After the befogged umpire had gone through about two dozen balls, the home team started to get restless. Not only were they being whitewashed, the umpire was using up their season's supply of baseballs.

At this point, the Fort Meade manager stormed onto the field, making clear his suspicions that this affair was not being played strictly according to Abner Doubleday.

Hastily calling a strategy conference, the Apopka manager summoned his pitcher into the dugout. While he conferred with the pitcher, the manager made a great display of anger, shouting and throwing his baseball shoes around the dugout. (It turned out that this show was just to cover up for the manager's desire to change out of his spiked shoes, in case his crew was forced to make a run for it.)

The field where the game was being played was little more than a clearing, and the edges of the playing area were lined with wagons of the local fans from the little mining community. When the rhubarb started on the field, the Fort Meade rooters began to sense that this could develop into some real fun.

"Those crackers reached back into their wagons," Welch said, "and before you knew it, there were 30.30 rifles pulled out all around us."

Thus persuaded by logic that could defeat the emery ball, the Apopka players convinced their pitcher to ease up a little. "We told him to let them hit the ball," Welch said.

From then on, the Fort Meade hitters satisfactorily pounded the Apopka pitcher's offerings and scored enough runs to make the day a success. Nevertheless, the Orange County nine beat a hasty retreat out of the phosphate country that evening and there is no record of a rematch.

By the late 1950s, you could watch major league baseball on television, visit the beaches by way of the new roads that were available or spend your leisure time in the new shopping centers springing up in the area. Attendance for local baseball slowly faded away. The Lake-Orange League was abandoned and baseball as we knew it in the good old days was gone.

Apopka's Early History

In 1883, before Lake and Osceola Counties split off from Orange County, the Orange County commissioners asked Sherman Adams to come up with a description of the topography, climate, soil, productions, resources, advantages, opportunities, prospects, and general characteristics of Orange County, Florida. This report was called "Orangeland."

Since these reports were rather lengthy, I would like to highlight some of the observations Mr. Adams had about Apopka at that time in history. I do not necessarily agree with some of the dates and conclusions in his report; however, I will pass his words on.

"In 1854, an old couple named Rodgers settled upon a portion of the land now embraced in Apopka City. In 1855, J. L. Stewart and sons and Peter Buchan and his sons moved from Georgia and cleared a considerable body of land. About 1860, Orange Lodge #36 F. & A. M., built a hall, and for many years, the place was known as the Lodge. For several years, from 1868 to about 1870, the neighbors took turns to go weekly to Mellonville, 22 miles distance, for the mail.

In 1868, the topography of the Apopka region attracted the attention of a physician, (more than likely Dr. Zelotes Mason) who desired to locate upon high, rolling land as far removed as possible from the swamps and other causes of disease.

This gentleman was so well pleased with the location that he made it his home, and though "three score years and ten," is living today in better health than when he came, full of activity and enterprise, a monument to the wonderful climate and locality. All representation to the contrary, Apopka is one of the highest, if not the highest, locations in the state of Florida. It is situated in township 21 south, of range 28 east. It is three miles south of the celebrated Clay Springs, which is the source of the Wekiva River, navigable for steamboats to the St. Johns River (a distance of 18 miles), and is about the same distance west to the great Lake Apopka. Next to Okeechobee, it is the largest body of water in the state.

The present population of Apopka and the immediate vicinity is about 800, an increase of 400 in the past two years. The rich hammocks and pine lands are being utilized rapidly for vegetable growing. The shipments last year aggregated several thousand crates, which realized fabulous prices in the northern markets.

Cucumbers, beans, onions, potatoes and tomatoes are the principle varieties raised. The number of orange trees in grove form within the corporate limits is nearly 11,000 and including the surrounding neighborhood, about double that number. These comprise groves in all stages of advancement, and count among the number some of the largest and most profitable in the county. There are, of course, many lemon and lime trees, and a constantly increasing variety of other fruits. Strawberry culture has not yet been attempted beyond domestic needs. Pineapples are attracting attention as a crop that can be realized in a short time, and their cultivation bids fair to rival that of the orange and other fruits.

The country around Apopka is high and rolling, covered with a heavy growth of yellow and pitch pine. The timber is simply magnificent. The whole region is interspersed with beautiful and clear water lakes, full of the finest fish, affording the rarest sport and an excellent diet. The quality of the land is not surpassed by any other section of the famed Orange County. Almost every foot of it is suitable for orange culture, and many orange groves in the bearing stage have been made without the use of fertilizers. Besides the pine lands, there are a number of tracts on high hammocks, of the richest quality of soil, covered with hickory, oak, magnolia, sweet gum, bay, wild orange and palmetto. This grade of land is unsurpassed in the United States for natural fertility and adaptability to gardening purposes, besides the growth of the orange, which it frequently brings into bearing in five to seven years from the seed. The great hammocks along the eastern shore of Lake Apopka alone ensure the future prosperity of this section comprised of hundreds of acres of the finest vegetable land in the world, protected from damaging frost from the north and west by 150 square miles of water never at a lower temperature than sixty degrees F, over which cold winds must pass to get them.

Apopka is located directly on the line of the Orlando, Tavares and Atlantic Railroad, which connects with the Transit railroad at Leesburg, forming a direct all-rail route with the north. This road will prove the most formidable competition to the St. Johns River has yet had in securing the carrying trade of South Florida. Work has been going on actively for several months in grading from Tavares toward Orlando, and Apopka, being midway between these points, will probably have been reached by the graders and ironers when these pages come from the press. It is expected that the whole line will be in operation by the first of January 1884.

Independently of railroad communication, Apopka enjoys the advantage of water transportation on the Wekiva River. For years past, this river has been navigated by steamboats and barges up to its source at Clay Springs. These springs, within three miles of Apopka, are destined to become famous as a resort for invalids and pleasure seekers from all parts. The waters are strongly, though not repugnantly; impregnated with sulfur and other medicinals, and have a reputation for effecting remarkable cures of scrofulous diseases.

A candid comprehension of the advantages offered by the Apopka region must inevitably lead to the conclusion that, all things considered, it is one of the most favored sections of South Florida, and that therefore; the home seeker, health seeker or the tourist will find it both profitable and pleasant to pay it a visit. The hospitable character of its inhabitants, from all parts of the Union, warmed up with the prospects of a brilliant future, will ensure them a kind hearted greeting and outstretched hands."

Midget Grill

Apopka City Hall

Chapter IV - The William Edwards Era

Piedmont Wineries

When you are thinking of the beautiful vineyards of the world, your mind might stray to the Bordeaux regions in France, the rolling hills of Napa Valley in California or possibly the Piedmont area in Italy. However, would your mind dare to imagine beautiful vineyards in Piedmont, Florida?

Absolutely; because there were three vineyards and wineries in Orange County in the 19th century, and probably the best of the three was operated by Gust Jackson and Jonas and Olaf Larsson in Piedmont, Florida. In 1989, they were the first to produce grape wine in Central Florida, and did so until about the 1900s. They were more than likely growing the traditional muscadine or scuppernongs, which were the first grapes made into wine in the United States. French Huguenot settlers around Jacksonville had the first winery in this country. They operated from 1562 until 1564. The Vitas Vinifera varieties as grown in Europe and California did not grow well in the South, due to bacteria, black rot, mildews, Anthracnose, and more. These diseases are prevalent around the country, but in Florida, with its extended humid weather, they are almost impossible to control. That is true even to this day.

The Piedmont Winery was built near a small stream which was boxed in with timber to provide a steady water supply. This created a pond that was known as "the box." They produced a very fine orange, lemon, grapefruit, and mulberry wine. In the early 1890s, they were shipping wine as far away as Wakefield, Nebraska. According to the Agricultural Census of 1889, they produced 3,360 gallons of wine and sold it for $8,572. At that time there were 149 acres of grape wine in production in Orange County.

By 1891, grape culture was expanding in Orange County and, as the *Tallahassee Floridian* wrote, "Grapes promise to become a vigorous rival to the orange." The Florida Star Wine company opened a winery near Orlando that same year, and the next year the Orlando Grape and Fruit Company set out 220,000 Niagara grape vines. At the time, there were 494 acres in production. Although both companies grew and sold fresh grapes, neither produced wine for more than two years. Anyone who grew anything other than the muscadine and scuppernongs seldom made it more than a couple of years.

The 1895 Agricultural Census showed slightly over 100,000 pounds of grapes selling at $13,297, but only 955 gallons of wine, at a value of $740. The value of the wine had declined precipitately since 1889, but the Piedmont Winery was still in business. It was awarded a medal for the excellent quality of its orange wine at the 1895 Atlanta Exposition. By 1897, it produced only 400 gallons of wine and sold it for one dollar a gallon. Keep in mind the 1894-95 freezes virtually wiped out citrus production, and curtailed the wine production in Central Florida. After a few years of small scale production, the Jacksons and the Larssons gave up the wine business to concentrate on rebuilding their citrus interests.

A little farther north of Piedmont was the small river port on the Wekiva River known as Clay Springs. This area was quite often compared with the Mediterranean grape growing areas because of the pleasant weather. Grapes may have been the rage during this period of time but there were those who thought otherwise.

Amos M. Schultz of Norristown, Pennsylvania, was a winter resident of Clay Springs who had planted a few acres of orange groves there. In 1887, he organized the Clay Springs Wine Company to make wine from oranges. With fifteen employees, he projected using 2.5 million oranges to produce 2,000 barrels of wine. The oranges that he could not produce himself were purchased for $8 per 10,000 and arrangements were made for immediate payment at a bank in Apopka. In 1887-88, the company did not reach its goal. However, it did buy 1.5 million oranges and produce more than 1,000 barrels of orange wine. Schultz continued his operation until the mid-1890s. These dates also coincide with the big freezes and ended Mr. Schultz's dream of 2,000 barrels of citrus wine per year.

Over 100 years after the heyday of the Piedmont Wineries, the Institute of Food and Agricultural Services in Florida developed grapes suitable to compete on an international scale with other wine regions. One Central Florida Winery took top honors for its Blanc Du Bois at an International Wine Competition in 1998. Then-Florida Commissioner of Agriculture Bob Crawford said, "It demonstrates that the wines produced in Florida can compete with the best from around the world."

Mr. Crawford's statement might have been a bit overly optimistic, but the fact remains that Florida is slowly developing grapes that are more suitable to the humid climate of this state.

Orange - Lake Boundaries

Apopka area residents were active in county and state affairs in the 1880s. David B. Stewart served as county commissioner in the early part of the decade and Charles W. Smith of Plymouth followed him. R. G. Robinson of Zellwood served in the state legislature from 1885 to 1889.

As the county became more populous, there were demands that it be divided into more manageable political units. A public meeting was called at Fort Mason in early 1887, to discuss the formation of a new county called West Orange (now Lake County).

The group seemed agreeable regarding the new county, but a vigorous struggle developed over the exact boundaries it should have. According to one observer, every town in the proposed new county wanted the boundaries drawn so that it would be in the center and, therefore, be the logical choice for the county seat. Although there was sentiment for including the Zellwood district in the new county, R. G. Robinson led a successful fight to prevent that. The 1887 legislature formed Osceola County from what had been the southern parts of Orange County and Lake County, separating it from portions of northwest Orange County and eastern Sumter County. After that, Robinson was able to have the Orange-Lake border established at the line between Ranges 26 and 27 as it presently exists, with Orange County including Tangerine and the area up to the southern edge of the city of Mt. Dora.

The establishment of new county boundaries set off another heated struggle over relocation of the county seat. A petition for an election to decide the question received the requisite number of signatures by the fall of 1889, and the county commissioners called an election for December 18 of that year. Apopka joined Sanford, Longwood, and Orlando in vying for the designation as county seat. Orlando won easily, receiving 1,907 of the 2,968 votes cast. Apopka received 188 votes.

There was a rumor at the time that Judge John G. Speer of Orlando invited some United States Army personnel over to Orlando from Sumter County for free drinks and a fine barbeque to help celebrate Election Day. The law stated that these soldiers could vote at any location within the state, whether they were county residents or not.

Keep in mind that the hard freeze of January 1886 had just occurred and the citrus industry was still struggling. There was more bad weather in 1888, but the yellow fever epidemic which brought Jacksonville and the St. Johns River traffic to a standstill during most of the year was even more disruptive.

The threat of yellow fever created a dilemma for Apopka Mayor Horatio S. Brewer, and a political confrontation for Orange County. One of the last things that community boosters wanted was a yellow fever scare which would cause people to stay away. On the other hand, as a medical doctor, Brewer was concerned about public health. Acting upon his medical feelings but in his official capacity as mayor, on August 14, 1888, Brewer quarantined Apopka against visitors from all points and ordered City Marshal J. D. Lovell to enforce the quarantine. The proclamation was published in the *Apopka Advertiser*. Orange County officials and promoters were enraged and fearful that Brewer's action would cause a yellow fever scare and a boycott of the county. The *Orlando Reporter* declared that "Dr. H.S. Brewer of Apopka is crazy." E. J. Reel, chairman of the county board of health, argued that Brewer had no authority to issue his proclamation, that only the county board had such authority. An argument between the board and the mayor culminated in Reel's instructions that Brewer "call in your proclamation of the 14th….or be arrested." The mayor recanted, but the damage was already done.

The Road That Was Straight

This is another article by one of our local authors, from somewhere back in the late 1800s. Leslie S. Bray's family was one of the early pioneers of Bay Ridge and Merrimack. He called this article "The Road that was Straight." Hope you enjoy it.

"Many readers of pioneer Florida can recall the wagon roads that twisted and turned around the pines, sink holes, ponds and lakes to arrive at their destination with the least inconvenience to the traveler.

They may also remember that a large fallen tree across the well-worn trail bothered no one. They made a new road around it.

But something happened back in the early 1880 that was considered an achievement bordering on the impossible. Surveyors set out from a point near the old Tavares, Orlando & Atlantic railroad (now Seaboard) depot at Plymouth, to run a line for a proposed county road to Sorrento, some eight miles due north.

The land between these towns was high and rolling, heavily timbered, and dotted with ponds, a few sinkholes and bayheads and a mile stretch of scrub. The settlements of Merrimac and Bay Ridge, composed mostly of scattered homesteads, were on the route.

To carry out their plan the surveyors found it necessary to make a slight jog to the west about two and one-half miles north of Plymouth (Ponkan intersection).

They then proceeded on a straight line cut through the center of John Harshberger's young orange grove and divided my father's homestead into two 80-acre tracts. The line missed a sink hole on the Harshberger property by 10 feet on one side of the road and a pond on our land by 50 yards on the other side.

While I was too young to remember the trail-blazers, I never heard that anyone complained of sacrificing land for the right of way.

When the pines were felled and the stumps dug up this was claimed to be the longest straight-away public road in the county.

The names of the surveyors are lost with discarded files once housed in the old Orlando courthouse but they have an unusual monument left to their memory.

When this road was prepared for automobile travel it was the only one in that part of the state to be hard surfaced the entire distance over the original wheel ruts made by the pioneers some 40 years before.

This old highway brought many travelers, and our place proved to be a convenient overnight stop for many of them. But one of the most exciting events was when the circus went by. It was a one-ring affair that traveled through the country by wagon.

It had played at Apopka three miles east of Plymouth and was now headed for Sorrento to show the next day.

My brother and sister and I were already excited by the prospect of seeing the circus at Sorrento when in the dead of night our dog began barking furiously and then we heard the shouts of the drivers urging their horses up the slight but sandy rise past our house. As we leaned out of the upstairs windows we could see out there in the dim light of the stars, long wagons loaded with mysterious circus things, each wagon drawn by four horses. We learned the names of the horses as their drivers called to them to do their part.

The sound of clanking chains, squeaking leather and the groan of wagon wheels finally died away along with the men's voices.

But that was not all. About 10 o'clock the next morning I saw an odd looking vehicle drawn by four white horses coming up the road. The front and back sloped down towards the center with seats facing the middle. There were about a dozen men aboard and from the billboard pictures we had seen I recognized the band wagon.

I was standing by the front fence beside mother's Marechai Nell rosebush and as the wagon drew opposite (I suppose) the band master, a handsome young man, called to the driver to stop. With a friendly smile he stepped down and said, "Sonny, may I have one of those beautiful roses?"

As I handed him a choice bud which he placed in his coat lapel, he thanked me and asked me if he would see me at the circus. By now I felt that I was practically a member of the outfit and fervently assured him that I would be there.

To describe the thrills of seeing ones first circus is impossible but one small boy was doubly thrilled that day back in 1890, for he had received the bandmaster's smile and his gracious thanks for a beautiful rose."

Lake Standish Hotel

It stood in the rolling hills of Plymouth, Florida, on the south side of Lake Standish, adjacent to the Old Dixie Highway. To the east were the unspoiled lands of what is now known as Errol Estate. The Lake Standish Hotel, sometimes called Lake Standish Lodge, was erected in 1887 by two of Plymouth's earliest entrepreneurs, brothers, C. W. and H. E. Smith. It was a seasonal hotel, opening the first of December and closing the last of April. There were large parties given at the December opening and generally a picnic at Clay Springs (Wekiwa Springs) to close the season. All during the season there was periodic dining, dancing and other types of activities for the guests.

A large portion of the guests were Boston residents who had investments in citrus groves in the area. They spent their winters in Plymouth, looking after their groves and when they left, they turned the groves over to caretakers who charged about $20 an acre to care for the trees for the next six or seven months.

It is believed that cooks, maids, housekeepers, and other personnel were brought from Massachusetts to serve the distinguished clientele who visited the hotel.

During the winter of 1894-95, the freeze of the century hit Florida with temperatures in the area of sixteen degrees that lasted for many hours. This pretty well wiped out the citrus industry in Florida for some time. Some people reset and others did not. After that, the winter guests of the hotel began to decrease each year, and the hotel fell upon hard times for about the next twenty-five years.

It was not until 1920 that B. H. Kinsman of Orlando bought the hotel and put it into good repair by adding electricity, plumbing, hot and cold water, etc. He then reopened it for business in 1921.

The hotel's grand opening was a December holiday event that was spectacular in every way. The highlight of the evening was a dinner-dance with music provided by the Vincent Orchestra, who did an excellent job of entertaining as the guests danced until one 1 o'clock in the morning. The holiday decorations consisted of local evergreens and brilliant crepe paper banners.

John H. Pirie of Lake Forest, Illinois, board chairman of the Chicago dry goods firm Carson, Pirie, Scott and Co., spent his first two winters in Florida at the Lake Standish Hotel.

The experience proved so beneficial to his wife's health that he bought a large tract of land to the east of the hotel and established Errol Farms, later known as the Errol Estate, and even later developed into what is now Errol Estate subdivision.

Pirie varied from the usual Plymouth visitor in that he was from Chicago. He may have been influenced to come to Plymouth in the first place by an old friend of his, Henry W. Norwell, a fellow merchant prince of the last century, whose business was in Boston. Norwell and his family were frequent visitors to the Lake Standish Hotel. Both Pirie and Norwell had immigrated to the United States from the Scottish village of Errol, located on the Firth and Fourth.

The hotel never really recuperated from the freezes of 1894-95, nor did the Mr. Kinsman's renovations help for any length of time, so the building was eventually turned into a boarding house. The relatives of L. R. Brown of Plymouth were living in the boarding house toward the end of its existence, and they said the lobby and dining rooms had two fireplaces each. It was also noted that a lot of expensive china imported from England was still in evidence when the hotel burned in 1940.

Tangerine

A few years back, the City of Apopka officially designated the Museum of the Apopkans to create and maintain a Northwest Orange County Register of Historic Places. In looking at the number of homes listed from the 1800s, it's amazing how many are in Tangerine. The citizens there are to be commended. This might be a good time to take a look at our neighbors to the north and their history.

In 1887, a majority of the citizens of Orange County felt that the county was becoming too populous and wanted to divide it up into more manageable political units. They called for a public meeting in Fort Mason (on the north side of Lake Eustis) to discuss breaking off the northwestern part of the county to form a portion of what is known today as Lake County.

There seemed to be a general agreement on forming a new county but, as you might expect, the devil was in the detail. It seems everybody wanted the boundaries drawn so that their town was in the center and, therefore, the logical choice for county seat. There was a move to have the eastern boundaries of the new county include Zellwood. However, R. G. Robinson from Zellwood, a state legislator from 1885-1889, led a successful fight to prevent that. He was able to have the Orange-Lake border established as it is today, with Tangerine and areas at the southern edge of Mt. Dora remaining in Orange County.

The community of Tangerine is just west of Zellwood, between Lakes Ola and Beauclair, in the extreme northwest corner of Orange County. Tangerine was originally called Olaville, after Lake Ola. The name of this lake supposedly comes from the name of the daughter of an Indian Chief who had camped there years before the coming of the white man.

In 1874, J. E. Dudley was one of the first to homestead in Tangerine. The following year, Dudley W. Adams and his family, who were from Massachusetts, settled there, because he was seeking relief for his bronchial troubles.

Lewis Marot came with his brother from St. Louis in a covered wagon drawn by a pair of mules, in 1879. He set up business in Tangerine's first store, which was built by Holland Williams. Then, on a weekly basis, Marot drove his mules and wagon to the nearest store in Mellonville (Sanford), twenty-five miles away, to bring supplies and mail back to the village. He was the community's first postmaster, serving from 1879 until 1902.

Tangerine and Zellwood were so closely connected that many of their early settlers were claimed by both communities. They were shocked when the popular Marot was beaten to death at McDonald Station (where he had recently moved) by axe-wielding H. A. Blocker, who was aided by Hunter Fudge and Alex Walker. The county commission offered a $200 reward for apprehension of the criminals and the three were ultimately indicted by a grand jury and sent to jail.

Across Lake Ola, William Morton homesteaded a tract in 1874 that was eventually bought by Orwin Sadler in 1885. After 1900, his son S. S. Sadler became a longtime leader in Tangerine and Orange County. David Simpson, from Jefferson County, Florida, settled at Tangerine and engaged in the lumber business, operating sawmills in Zellwood and Gainesboro (south of Lake Ola) for several years. Bessie Huestis settled on 160 acres in 1879, and is credited with changing the name of the place from Olaville to Tangerine. It is said that Bessie had a tangerine tree at the doorsteps of her home that inspired her campaign to change the name of the town.

The first hotel was the Bourland House, built in 1883 by J. M. Bourland. The name was soon changed to the Acme Hotel, and it was operated by Mr. Riddick. In 1884, William H. Earl bought the hotel and renamed it the Wauchusett House. Being the social center of the town, it hosted various groups, such as the Saturday Afternoon Leisure Club and the Literary Society. It burned down in 1888, and after being rebuilt, was known as the Lake Ola Lodge.

About 250 people picked up their mail at the Tangerine post office in 1885. Tangerine was governed by the Tangerine Development Society, which was organized in 1880.

Disaster struck Tangerine in June 1898, when a fire broke out in A. C. Bennett's barn. A brisk wind carried it to the store nearby. Despite the valiant efforts of a bucket brigade, the fire consumed the barn, the store, the Wauchusett House, and three homes. Tangerine was rebuilt after the fire, but despite a hardy group of permanent residents and a well-developed citrus industry, Tangerine's population continued to consist of mostly winter residents.

The Wauchusett House, rebuilt after the fire by Charles Bennett, enjoyed capacity crowds each winter, from 1905 until 1913. It was then sold to Doctor Benedict Lust, publisher of a New York health magazine and owner of Jungborn, a New Jersey sanitarium, which emphasized natural cures for the afflicted. He opened Jungborn of Tangerine, also called Qui-Si-Sana ("to be young again"), in 1914. Despite its exotic name, it was popularly referred to as the Lust Sanitarium, and was a focal point in the Tangerine community until it burned in 1943.

Dr. Lust, who had arrived here from Germany, remained loyal to his native country during World War II. On his property was a tall tree in which he installed a radio transmitter he used it communicate with German submarines in the Atlantic Ocean, until the federal government discovered it and put a stop to the transmissions.

The Tangerine post office in Layton's store was robbed twice, once in late 1913 and once in 1914. In the latter incident, the thieves made off with $6,350 from the post office and $40 from the store.

With quiet, winding streets canopied by gigantic spreading oaks, and surrounded by the beautiful lakes Beauclair and Ola, Tangerine is today one of the most desirable residential communities in Central Florida. Take a little time from your busy schedule and visit.

Fred Marden

This is a story by Leslie S. Bray about his dear friend, Fred Marden. It was mailed to D. B. McKay of the *Tampa Tribune,* who wrote an article called, "Pioneer Florida." It was published many years ago; however, I thought you would enjoy it.

"In the early 1880s Calvin Marden moved to Florida from New York State, and homesteaded about a mile east of Lovell's Landing on the shores of Lake Apopka. Before the railroads came, a small steamboat carried mail and passengers across the lake to the little town of West Apopka (Montverde).

There were five boys and two girls in the Marden family and, as the saying went in those days, there wasn't a lazy bone in any of them. Fred, the oldest of the children, was a hunchback, but in spite of his handicap, which limited his strength, he developed one of the finest apiaries in the county". He bought books on bee culture and became an authority on it. But he did not confine his reading to this subject—he subscribed to many magazines and newspapers, and was well posted on current events and scientific discoveries.

It was often amusing when two of his brothers got into a heated argument on some subject, one would exclaim, "I know I am right, Fred said he read it in such and such magazine and it said so and so." Immediately the other brother would calm down with, "well, if Fred said so, of course he is right". What Paul Barber is in *One Man's Family,* (a popular radio program of the time), Fred was to the Marden family.

As the number of hives increased, Fred built a little home of his own on the homestead land and moved his bees close by. In order to get a distinct flavor and color Fred moved his bees from time to time. With the help of one of his brothers, the hives were placed on a wagon after dark. A long "reach" permitted heavy planks to replace the wagon body, and the hives were loaded and unloaded without disturbing the sleeping bees.

When goldenrod was in bloom, Fred took his bees to McDonald Station, not far from the north end of Lake Apopka, where in those days hundreds of acres were yellow with bloom in season. When the swamp palmettos were blossoming he took his hives to Clay Springs, and around February his bees found themselves surrounded by sweetly scented orange groves.

Returning to the family home over the weekend, he would often invite my brother, Everett and me to go with him. They were a good hospitable family, set a good table supplied with dairy products and vegetables but with one outstanding feature—honey was used instead of sugar in cooking and on the table. This gave the visitor a firm conviction that this was a land flowing with milk and honey. Over at Fred's house we were welcomed with jovial cordially, for he loved to joke, and could see the humorous side of most every situation. His house was neat as a pin, every book and magazine neatly stacked.

One of the most popular events in our neighborhood during the 1890s was the dance held at the Bay Ridge school house, which was about halfway between Plymouth and Sorrento. Young folks, and older, for miles around came to square dance, waltz, two step, schottische or just look on. Arthur Budgen with his violin, Joe Smith with the banjo, and Dr. Bliss with the bass viol, furnished the music.

George Marden called for the square dancing, and sometimes Fred would come up to look on. He knew every pretty girl from 8 to 80 years of age, and between dances he was the center of a laughing group of young folks being teased and highly amused by his wit. With his head sunk between his shoulders, making it necessary for him to turn his body to face those he addressed, no one seemed to notice his affliction for there was something in his spirit that everybody admired.

After his parents died and one of his brothers took over the homestead, Fred, with his usual independent spirit, moved to a new location.

One day a neighbor passed by and Fred was not out working with his bees. He went back the next day, and when Fred did not answer his call, he went into the house. The misshapen body lay on the bed, but like the bees that he loved, his spirit had flown to a flowery kingdom free from earthly handicap.

Fred Marden, the hunchback, was gone but he left behind countless friends, the memory of a courageous man whose smiling face outshone a crippled body, and whose tireless energy was a shining example for those more fortunate."

William Edwards

When John Pirie began developing his Errol Farms in 1889, he brought in a fellow Scotsman from Chicago, William Edwards, to manage the farm. Edwards had demonstrated his managerial skills in Chicago while working with the local YMCA and the Dwight L. Moody Evangelistic Crusades. Immediately upon his arrival, he started stocking Errol with blooded livestock, including a herd of Devon cattle. He later started managing the McLaughlin Estate in Zellwood. Together, the two farms totaled over 7,000 acres.

Even with the improved breeding stock, better hay crops, and other improvements, Errol Cattle Company also ran cattle on the open range. Around 1910, the range cattle became so infested with ticks that the threat of an epidemic of tick fever began making out-of-state buyers reluctant to purchase cattle from Florida. It was William Edwards who traveled around the county convincing cattlemen of the merits of a new tick control measure and ways to get the federal government to assist in building vats for dipping. In the 1918 election, Orange County approved dipping the cattle. There was only one vote against it in Northwest Orange County. It took a few years to eliminate the ticks; however, the problem was largely solved in the Apopka area when they closed the open ranges in 1924.

One of William Edwards's finer achievements in 1911 was to help organize and manage the Plymouth Citrus Fruit Growers Association. He was on the original board of directors and soon became the president. He retained that position for many years. During his presidency they always maintained a close affiliation with the Florida Citrus Exchange, constantly pushed for national advertising, and in 1915 adopted the trademark Seald Sweet.

In 1912, Edwards was one of the founders of the Apopka Board of Trade, the mission of which was to encourage development in the Apopka area. They pushed for a newspaper, a bank, hotel accommodations, available electricity and water, adequate rail and highway transportation, and a city government friendly to new business.

It was William Edwards who convinced local businessmen of the value of having a local bank. This project was accomplished in 1912, when the Apopka State Bank opened and Edwards was elected to the board of directors. C. P. McCall was the first board president. In 1921, Edwards was elected president. When he took office, the bank's deposits were averaging around $275,000. By 1925, they had increased to $600,000.

During World War I (1917), Edwards served on the Orange County Council of Defense. At the same time, he was on the Orange County Branch of Herbert Hoover's Food Administration.

The Apopka Board of Trade was instrumental in encouraging the formation of the Apopka Hotel Corporation. Its objective was to pursue the construction of a suitable hotel for Apopka. They began by offering shares of stock to the residents in denominations of $100. They hoped to capitalize for $150,000; however, in their final drive in April of 1926, they raised $163,000, and that made their dream a reality. After demolishing the old city Hall at the northeast corner of Fourth and Central, they started construction. After a lively contest, the citizens of Apopka chose to name the hotel the William Edwards Hotel.

At the same time that all of this was going on, Edwards had teamed up with his brother Stewart, W. D. Rogers, and H. Carl Dann to purchase over 5,000 acres to the north of Apopka in Mt. Plymouth. They planned to develop a "playground city," with four golf courses, a hotel, and an airport, as well as commercial and residential areas. They actually put in eighteen holes of golf, a 150-room hotel, an airport, and a few houses before the depression of 1929 hit.

During the fern industries co-op days, William Edwards negotiated the various differences among the growers and drew up a charter for the Orange County Fern Clearing House Association. With packing houses in both Apopka and Zellwood, they hired John Masek as manager. They soon controlled ninety-five percent of the fern production.

Apopka was fascinated with baseball as far back as the late 1800s. At some point, Apopka residents bought roughly a city block (east of the Kit Land Park) to build a baseball field and wooden bleachers. They sold stock to the public to raise the necessary funds. William Edwards spearheaded this drive and purchased a considerable amount of stock to ensure its success. The field to this day is known as Edwards Field.

Edwards passed away in 1934. There have not been many citizens in Apopka's history who answered the call for leadership as well as William Edwards. We should forever be grateful to him.

Turpentining In The Apopka Area

With its immense stands of long-leaf pines, Florida was most attractive to the naval store firms and individual farmers who had been moving south and west from North Carolina since the Civil War. Although there were a few small turpentine stills in Central Florida a little earlier, it was about 1895 before the industry entered the pinelands in northwest Orange County. Having preceded the turpentine farmers by nearly two decades, the sawmill and logging camp operators had cut a considerable amount of timber, but immense stands of virgin pines remained.

DIPPING AND SCRAPING PINE TREES, TURPENTINE INDUSTRY IN FLORIDA

During the next quarter century, turpentine farmers and sawmill operators made the forest industries a major part of the local economy. Some firms bought the land, farmed it for turpentine for several years, and then cut the remaining saw logs or cross-ties themselves. Others bought the land, turpentined it, and sold the remainder to lumber companies. But much of the timber was leased by the turpentine companies and then returned to the owners at the end of a specified term. A few small-scale operators turpentined their own trees and sold the gum to a company, which operated a still.

Extracting the gum from the pines and converting it into spirits of turpentine and rosin was a difficult, dirty job for the laborers who worked the trees and manned the stills. It was a risky business for the operators---or farmers, as they were called---who tried to earn a profit in an industry controlled by a small number of firms---naval stores factors---which furnished the credit necessary for the operators, graded the quality of the products by their own standards, and kept rigid control of the prices.

Depending upon the size of the operation, a turpentine farmer had to have $10,000 or more in liquid capital to lease or buy the land, build quarters for the work force, construct a still, and sustain operations until receipts began. Each crop consisted of 10,500 trees---about 200 acres, depending upon the size and density of the trees. During the winter the trees were boxed or cupped, with the receptacle being fixed to the tree about ten inches above its base. A V-shaped indention was cut above the receptacle. Beginning around March 1 and continuing for thirty-four weeks, the laborers who worked the crop visited each tree, chipping a new cut just above the last one, to keep the sap flowing. By the end of the season, a face about two feet in size had been cut into the tree.

The still was simply a huge copper kettle capable of being heated to boil the gum. It was connected to a coil which ran through a tank of water. As the gum boiled in the kettle, steam and vapor rose through the coil, cooled into water and spirits of turpentine, and was drained off into a large tank.

The spirits of turpentine rose to the top and was drawn off into barrels for shipping to market. The rosin remaining in the kettle was drained off through a coarse wire cloth, then a finer brass wire cloth, and, finally, through a layer of cotton batting and into a trough. It was then dipped into 500-pound barrels and allowed to congeal; then it was ready for market.

Each crop of trees was turpentined for three, four or five years, depending upon the terms of the lease or the operator's preference. A good crop yielded about fifty barrels of turpentine and 160 barrels of rosin the first year, about forty barrels of turpentine and 135 of rosin the second year, about thirty barrels of turpentine and 115 of rosin the third year, and proportionately less over subsequent years. The quality produced by a turpentine farmer depended upon the number of crops he farmed each year.

Many turpentine men preferred to work the trees for three years, then allow them a year or two of rest before cutting back faces on the trees and starting over. If the trees were very large, they might be worked three times before the face of the tree was too scarred to allow further turpentining. The cup method was not as hard on the trees as the box, because it did not require as deep a cut. Large trees withstood either method better than small trees, but if workers were not careful, many smaller trees were killed or so badly weakened that high winds broke them off. A sizeable number of trees were lost, but there was much timber left after a stand had been turpentined. The saw-logs or cross-ties were taken out by the turpentine firm or sold to a lumber firm. Cut-over land was often left abandoned in those days, when it was so abundant. This changed in later years.

The great freezes of 1894-95 hastened development of the turpentine industry in Orange County, as some grove owners looked for other pursuits while they awaited the recovery of their trees. But outside turpentine interests were already moving into the area at about that time. In early 1885, it was announced that W.B. McKeithan and Company had leased 60,000 acres of pine land and was establishing a turpentine still in Apopka which would employ about fifty people. Coming within weeks after the two freezes, this was welcome news for the community. H.R. Wilder of McDonald, who had been turpentining on a small scale while he and his brother developed their groves, announced that he was expanding his turpentine operation and could furnish employment for several families on his turpentine farm. In partnership with J. B. Norman, Wilder turpentined some of his own land and expanded into leased property during the next several years. In one case, he leased land and then his crew entered the wrong property. By the time the mistake was discovered, several crops of trees had been notched for turpentining. L.G. Johns of Skillman, Georgia, who owned the land, was a reasonable man and agreed to allow Wilder and Norman to work the trees and pay him one dollar per hundred for the boxes which had already been cut on his land.

The Great Freezes Of 1894-95

I have written many lines about the so-called "Great Freeze" of 1894-95 and how it touched the lives of so many people. I do not want to leave the impression that these freezes had the lowest temperatures in the history of Florida. This is simply not the case. Other freezes have had lower temperatures and others equaled it; but in terms of combination of factors, including the havoc it created, the Great Freeze no doubt will be remembered as the most damaging of all the major freezes.

When the area's first settlers arrived, they found many orange trees growing in the pine forests. These trees probably were planted by the Seminoles, or even the Acuera tribes, who obtained seeds from the sour oranges brought to Florida by the Spaniards in the 16th century. Many of these early settlers cultivated those oranges and eventually developed them into much sweeter varieties. Even with the development of better varieties, citrus production and sales did not develop until about 1880, when the first railroad enabled growers to get the product to the market faster.

Many of our ancestors and out-of-state investors came to the Apopka area with visions of wealth derived from owning an orange grove. Articles in out-of-state newspapers and magazines (generally written by Florida real estate developers) told of how people of modest means could prosper from a few acres of citrus—if they could afford to wait five to seven years for the trees to bear fruit. Of course, that was not the whole story.

A little over 112 years ago, the first round of the most devastating one-two punch ever to hit Orange County citrus industry flattened growers. What came to be known as the Great Freeze destroyed Florida's citrus crop in the winter of 1894-95, and killed more than ninety percent of Orange County's fruit trees. It would take fifteen years for the industry to recover to the point that the county could ship as much citrus as it had previously.

The Great Freeze was actually two freezes, with one occurring on December 29, 1894, and the other occurring on February 7, 1895. At the time, the freezes were the most dramatic and devastating blow in the history of Orange County's namesake industry, which has endured numerous ups and downs over the past 130 years.

The days leading up to the first of the freezes gave no indication of the disaster that was to come. Christmas Day of 1894 was sunny and beautiful with temperatures in the eighties. Three days later, a cold front from the northwest pushed a strong rainstorm with high winds through the area. By the next morning, December 29, the temperature had settled in to the point at which pumps were frozen, water pipes began to burst, and foliage blackened and died. The temperature dropped to sixteen degrees and stayed there long enough to kill the entire citrus crop while most of it still hung on the trees.

Karl Abbott, who was a youth at the time of the freeze, recorded his recollections of citrus growers and buyers gathering in the lobby of the downtown Orlando San Juan Hotel, which his parents ran, as the temperature dropped on the day of the first freeze. By 2 p.m., the San Juan was in an uproar. Prices had dropped to "no sale." Commission merchants were frantically trying to get out of options and heated debates and fistfights started in the lobby. About 9 p.m., a fine-looking, grey-haired man in a black frock coat and Stetson hat walked up the street in front of the hotel, looked at the thermometer, groaned, "Oh my God!" and shot himself in the head.

For three more days, the icy winds blew over a dead world. The gloom in the San Juan was something you could almost feel. It was Florida's worst freeze since 1835, historians say, and by far the worst in the generation during which citrus had been cultivated here on a large scale. A number of mom-and-pop growers who had come to Orange County and invested all their savings in groves moved back up North totally discouraged. Most, however, dug in their heels and hoped the next year would be better. But just six weeks later, things only got worse.

During a January that brought unusually warm, wet weather, the orange trees produced new growth. The layer of woody tissue just under the bark filled with sap as the wounded trees struggled to recover. The presence of so much liquid in the trees made them far more vulnerable to the second freeze. When the temperature dropped to seventeen degrees and held on February 7, more than ninety percent of the remaining fruit trees were killed, although some with large root systems would survive once the dead wood was cut away. Witnesses said they heard what sounded like pistol shots when the sap froze and blew out the tree bark.

Land values plummeted, and growers with mortgages were forced to sell at a loss. Because it took several years for new trees to mature and bear fruit, people with money were able to scoop up large tracts at bargain prices from those who could not afford to wait. It was sort of like the lyrics from one of the old hymns, "You could only hope for the sunshine tomorrow after the shower is gone".... and so it was. By 1905, the showers had passed and the rolling hills once again gave off the smell of sweet orange blossoms.

Grace Richmond

Zellwood, which lies north of Apopka on Hwy. 441, has an amazing number of famous names associated with it. These associations date back to the late 1800s, and include a president of the United States who owned land along the shore sparkling Lake Maggiore.

There was also the president of the Grand Rapids and Indiana Railroad, W.O. Hughart, who had his private car backed into a siding at Zellwood, where it stayed during the winters as he whiled away his time with his cronies. Of course, there was Col. T. Elwood Zell, for whom the community was named, and J.W. Paul, who had made a fortune in tool manufacturing in Verona, Pennsylvania. There was the widow of Ethelbert Nevin, composer of "The Rosary" and "Mighty Like a Rose," and Charles Baker, one of the pioneer railroaders in Pennsylvania. Another land owner, James Laughlin, Jr., head of the Jones-Laughlin Steel Corp. in Pittsburgh, was best known for building the fabulous Sydonie house at Lake Maggiore.

R.G. Robinson of Zellwood was a state legislator for Orange County in the late 1800s, and was instrumental in setting the boundaries of Orange and Lake counties. In his effort to save Zellwood as a part of Orange County, he included Tangerine into Orange County. Robinson was a near relative and acquaintance of Zachary Taylor, 12th president of the United States. A native of Kentucky, Robinson had been left a spot of land on the southeast corner of Lake Maggiore by Taylor.

I do not know how many of you have read the books by Grace S. Richmond, a 20th century American writer most noted for her Red Pepper Burns series of novels. She wrote twenty-seven novels, including *Strawberry Acres* and *The Twenty-Fourth of June*. The following is an article she wrote about passing through Zellwood on the way to Mt. Dora. She called it, "One Who Has Not Merely Passed Through."

"The mile-annihilating motorist who dashes past a sign marked Zellwood, twenty-two miles above Orlando on the smooth pavement of the road to Mt. Dora and Eustis often fails to note that he has passed anything at all except a railroad station. But he who knows his Zellwood knows that the place has no Main Street upon which are to be found most of the buildings and all of the interest, and that the beauties collected under its name are mostly well-hidden from the indifferent traveler.

Not that the tiny hamlet, with its churches, post office and general store, its few pleasant homes and well-known Inn close by, are not of interest. To the eye that notes and the ear that listens, Zellwood's little center is by no means negligible. It's not asleep under the warm sun. If you came to the post-office at mail time, twice a day, you would discover that many letters and newspapers come to Zellwood, and that the people who look and speak as though they had many contacts with the world outside are there to receive them.

But, it is when one begins to explore the outlying lands that one sees what may be had for the trouble of looking. The writer has never forgotten a certain small English Inn, in Devonshire, typical of many other rural hostelries abroad – as of many lives and communities. It was old, grimy and forbidden, standing almost in the narrow street, without a sign of attractiveness to lure the passing traveler. But once within its heavy door, there was everything of interest and charm.

The long, open windows of its coffee room, at the back of the house, gave upon one of the most beautiful of all the gardens of rural England, and sitting there, one seemed to be far away from the dusty streets and raucous noises outside as though one were in the heart of the deep country.

So it is that striking away from the motor road that passes Zellwood, and following certain sandy roads and lanes, one comes upon concealed delights. Perhaps these inconspicuous roads lead to the real Zellwood – they certainly lead to the lands that were acquired years ago by a famous army officer who had been a great traveler. In the two connecting lakes far away behind the pines and palms and live oaks, he found a resemblance of those lakes of Italy, Maggiore and Minore, and he so named them.

About them, a few attractive homes were built, and these, and others more imposing, which have taken their places, stand upon the well-kept lawns that slope down to the lovely lakes. These grounds are not open to the public, but in their secluded beauty, they are, to the writer, suggestive of some of Florida's greatest assets – the possibilities that lie outside the cities in this land of – no, we will not say 'land of sunshine.' That phrase is a trifle radio-and-advertising-worn – rather call it this land where life may be renewed.

Florida's cities are interesting, stimulating, and full of engaging life. To this writer, it happens that a place of five acres in the country, with a blue lake sparkling at its borders, a real home back among the trees, no matter how small, surrounded by such planting as only a semi-tropical region knows, is worth more than the costliest city residence, in the most exclusive locality. Near Zellwood, and everywhere in Orange County, high among its hills and lakes, are to be found such places for homemaking.

In spite of the apparent evidence of these last sentences, this writer is neither a buyer nor seller, has nothing to exploit, and certainly nothing to gain by exploiting. After two winters in Florida, while constantly extending observation of what is to be found here, she has been sorry, and even indignant, over many an article in newspapers and magazines published all over these sometimes-not-too-United States, crying cynically that there are only vultures and unscrupulous money-getters in Florida; that her charms of land and climate are heavily exaggerated; that to venture within her gates is to be fleeced; and that a newly made friend south of Georgia is only a newly made intriguer against one's prosperity and happiness. It is not so, except in occasional instances, as in other parts of the country. It is nature which paints the skies and sinks the blue into the lakes down here, and makes the air balmy and life giving; and though it is true as ever, anywhere, that 'only heaven may be had for the asking,'" something not far from Heaven may now be had in Florida at no extortioner's terms.

Zellwood has made winter a perfect thing for some of us from the North this year, living inside a gateway covered with flame vine, looking through the trees at the lake shining below a terraced slope, walking miles in the evening through pathways lighted for half of each month by such a Southern moon as never seems to show its face half so brilliantly in the North. Zellwood is now to us a name to conjure with. We, like everybody in it, including the fine police dog we met at the little post-office at the heels of its master, and who, though he gives us scant attention, we not being on his list of personal friends, seems somehow to be saying to the public generally, by his air of contentment: "A pretty good country, eh?"

We agree.

Waite Davis House

The Waite-Davis House is located on the corner of Orange St. and Central Ave.

When you are driving east on the Old Dixie Highway and come upon Central Avenue, you can't help but notice the old Waite-Davis house on the right. This historic old home is listed on the National Register of Historic Places by the United States Department of the Interior. It is a Folk Victorian I-House with a rearward extension, built by Edward Waite in 1886.

In 1874, there were only nine homes and a store in what was to become Apopka; but by 1882, enough people had moved into the area for the Town of Apopka City to be incorporated. In 1876, Frank H. Davis, a native of Manchester, New Hampshire, moved to the Apopka area where he set out an orange grove. In 1885, Mr. Davis opened his own real estate office while continuing with his groves. Also in 1885, Edward B. Waite, a retired merchant from Manchester and a friend of Mr. Davis, along with his wife Abbie, purchased two lots and immediately built their new home in what was known as "Yankee Town." It was so named to distinguish it from "Old Town," which was the area around the Masonic Lodge.

After Edward Waite's death, his widow married Frank Davis, who lived until 1916. Mr.

Davis was one of three promoters responsible for the early development of Apopka. He was a leader in organizing the Congregational Church in Apopka in 1886, and in that year formed the Town Improvement Association to deal with the emergency brought on by the freezes of December 1894 and February 1895. He served many times as a city councilman and was elected mayor in 1914.

Leslie P. "Ted" Waite lived in the Waite-Davis House all his life, having been born there in 1892. He was a leader in city government and economic development for over thirty years, from 1916 to 1947 as a city councilman and as mayor from 1941 to 1946. He was one of the first to go into the foliage plant business in a big way.

Interviewed in 1969, Ted Waite told of an ornate watering trough located in the center of the intersection of present Main Street and Central Avenue. Travelers watered their horses, mules or oxen there. It was also used by wild cattle roaming at large. These cattle would sometimes go by the grocery store and eat from the rack of vegetables outside on display. Because the sand got deep in dry weather and walking was laborious, there was also a boardwalk that ran from present uptown all the way to the municipal swimming pool and recreation area at the foot of Central Avenue on Dream Lake. It was to accommodate foot traffic and contained ten thousand board feet of fine-grained lumber.

When built, the Waite-Davis house was in the middle of a pine forest, which through the years, had been cleared to build homes and businesses. It is one of the fourteen surviving homes built in Apopka's earlier years. Only the Waite-Davis House retains most of its original gingerbread trim. It is constructed primarily of heart pine lumber, some if not all of which was cut and planed in Apopka mills. Cut nails were used throughout, except for brass wire nails used on the picture molding in the living room and study.

Orange Street (Old Dixie Highway) was constructed in 1914-15 as part of the western route of the Dixie Highway. Central Avenue was paved with brick by the City in 1921. It was at the corner of Central and Orange that house numbers for the city of Apopka started, the Waite-Davis House being number 5, the lowest number.

The exterior of the house is essentially the same as it was in 1915, when the complete porch was added. Bathrooms were added in the 1920s or 1930s.

In 1976, by David and Andrea Harden began working to return the house to its 1915 appearance. They worked for twelve years restoring the home. For the first two years, they could not live in the house at all because of major work being done. Then they moved into the small back room, which is now the laundry room, to sleep, and had pieces of board nailed over window openings and doors. During the restoration, they found antique chandeliers in the old barn out back and bought Victorian hinges, etc. from old Victorian homes in San Francisco and other places to replace those that were missing. David Harden was city manager for Winter Park. He accepted a similar position in another city, and they left having just completed their restoration project.

In 1991, the house was bought by Henry "Buddy" Stone and his wife Evelyn. Henry had just retired from IBM and the couple moved here from Los Angeles, California. Since that time they have continued working on the house by adding a garage and a new roof. Inside, they have been redecorating in a Country Victorian motif.

A gentle breeze moves through the Spanish moss as you pass this old Victorian house on Central Avenue and if you look closely you can still see "Ted" Waite and his good pal "Doc" Standard sitting on the porch reminiscing about their golden days in Apopka.

Eldredge House
(The Old McBride House)

In 1854, Matthew A. Stewart became one of the first settlers in the Apopka area by receiving permits to homestead 165 acres under authority of the Armed Occupation Act of 1842, signed by President Franklin Pierce.

In 1903, Samuel W. Eldredge and his wife Mary M. (Stewart) Eldredge, purchased a portion of this beautiful property to build their dream home that they would call "Eldorado." It was a 4,000-square-foot Queen Anne revival style home with a wide veranda around the main house.

Mr. Eldredge was born in 1864, in Malden, Maine, and was educated in his native state. He first came to Orange County as a visitor around 1880, and moved permanently to Apopka in 1883, where he first engaged in the grain business. In the 1880s-90s, S.W. Eldredge operated a livery stable that also sold grain and fertilizer. He dealt extensively in real estate and construction, erecting the second brick building in town, the post office building.

He owned orange groves and operated with a partner one of the first orange packing houses established in Orlando. Around 1900, he opened a grocery store on the southwest corner of Park and Hwy. 441 (now a pawn shop). He was a member of the city council in 1895, as well as a member of the school board of Apopka. He also served as postmaster during the administration of Woodrow Wilson in 1914, after he resigned his Orange County Commission post. He was a member of the First Baptist Church, the Masons, and the Knights of Pythias, and ever-active and influential in the good works of his community. In 1919, Samuel W. Eldredge passed away.

Mary Eldredge continued to live in their beloved Eldorado until 1926, when she sold the homestead to Fred and Ida A. Chamberlin. The Chamberlins lived there for nineteen years and in 1945, they sold the house to Dr. Thomas McBride and his wife, Helen.

After Helen passed away, Doc Tommy continued to live there until his death in 1978, at the age of eighty-two.

In the meantime, Doc Tommy's son Robin took over the medical practice in the office next door, on Park Avenue and Fourth Street. He and his wife (and best friend) Jackie built their beautiful home on the Eldridge property next to the old home, "Eldorado." Robin passed away in 1997, and soon afterward, Jackie moved to Errol Estate where she resides today.

In the l980s, Jackie McBride donated the old Eldridge-McBride house to the City of Apopka. In April of 1987, the City sold the house to Clay Townsend for $10, to move it to its present location on the fifteen acres at the intersection of Hwy. 441 and SR 436, or as it is known, Martin's Pond-Meade's Bottom area.

The cost of moving was estimated at between $35,000-$40,000, and another $2,000,000 was spent on renovations and upgrades.

The copper turret on the house had its original copper sheath roofing in place. Originally, the entire roof was copper, but a large portion of it was replaced during refurbishing. The house was built of heart-pine timber, and most of the wood in the house is original. The walls were plaster on wooden lath strips. These were damaged and had to be replaced and re-supported. The Townsends also upgraded the house by adding a sprinkler system, a fire system, and a burglar alarm.

Much of the antique furniture was purchased in 1987 by the Townsends from the historic Ormond Beach Hotel, which was made famous by the long residency of the Rockefeller family.

Townsend's Plantation was opened in 1987, when the population of Apopka stood at 8,800. They remained open for ten years and were especially well known for the Civil War re-enactments they held on the grounds annually.

The Plantation was closed to the public in 1997. However, they did host occasional banquets and the home was sometimes used as a haunted house attraction at Halloween.

In 2005, Don Green, a Silicon Valley entrepreneur, bought Townsend's Plantation and spent over $3 million on the house and grounds in opening The Captain and the Cowboy restaurant. This venture did not last very long, and in 2006, the City of Apopka bought the restaurant and twenty-three acres back for $9.5 million.

In 2008, the Trust Hotels and Resorts entered into a fifteen-year contract with the City of Apopka to lease the old restaurant. After a massive restoration of the building to preserve the history of the structure, it was opened on February 27, 2009, under the new name of Highland Manor.

The Apopka Chief

It would be remiss for me to not mention one of the most important entities that molded Apopka through the years. The newspaper in any town has always been a powerful mover and pusher in the community and, throughout the years, *The Apopka Chief* has filled that duty.

The Apopka News did not survive the 1918 Tornado, so the Board of Trade, a group of men from the community, banded together to encourage development of those modern facilities which could stimulate economic growth. They worked to create a newspaper, a bank, hotel accommodations, a city government friendly to business, available electricity and water, adequate rail and highway transportation, and assistance in acquiring sites for new firms. The committee was composed of Henry Witherington, A.C. and A.M. Starbird, Frank H. Davis, W.G. Talton, Dr. C.H. Morrison, Francis E. Zepp, John J. Anderson and J. R. Womble, Gust Jackson, William Edwards, and Nathaniel Cogswell. This is the group that took the initiative in securing a newspaper for Apopka.

William Edwards headed a committee that worked nearly two years, finally arranging with Albert M. Hall to publish *The Apopka Chief.* With Hall as editor and G. Ellwood Kalbach as business manager, the paper issued its first issue on April 20, 1923. Strong support from the local business community made it a vigorous advocate of town interests. It also undertook aggressive subscription campaigns, such as the one in 1928. Prize winners in the contest were Wallace Champneys of Apopka and T.D. McGraw of Zellwood, who won new Chevrolets for securing the most new subscribers.

The Apopka Chief was sold in 1929 to Josiah Ferris and Son, who published it until 1933. It was then acquired by John C. Robinson.

Like many small town newspapers across the nations, *The Apopka Chief* suffered a marked decline in the 1940s, followed by a strong revival in the following years. J.C. Robinson edited the paper until 1949, when it was sold to Eldon Johns who published it from Winter Garden. From 1949 until mid-1951, the paper was managed by Mrs. B. P. (Kit) Nelson and edited by Mrs. Joe (Janet) Connelly. The two young women were partners in the Fern Nook Gift Shop near Sheppard's Drug Store, and the paper was a part-time enterprise for them. They were succeeded briefly by Jack Mixson, who soon left for a job in New York. Mrs. W. D. Millitzer, the former Virginia Colbert, became editor in late 1951.

In 1964, Johns sold the paper to John W. Rynerson who became publisher and editor. Rynerson kept the newspaper just five years, selling it in 1969 to W.R. and Delores McGuffin, who had begun a competing newspaper, *The Planter*, in 1964,.

With W.R. as publisher and Delores as business manager, they ran *The Apopka Chief* for nearly a decade before their son, Patrick J. McGuffin, took over as publisher.

Soon after, the newspaper was sold to Foliage Enterprises, Inc. John Ricketson, president of Foliage Enterprises, named Patrick McGuffin to run the newspaper, and he did until 1982, when John Shore took over for a short period as interim publisher.

In August 1982, John Ricketson became and remains the publisher. His wife Eileen Ricketson has no title, but works side-by-side with him.

Neoma DeGard Knox is the newspaper's general manager in a semi-retired manner, and she is the paper's reigning employee as far as longevity goes. She was hired by the McGuffins in 1965 as a columnist for the Lockhart and Forest City areas, and has been an integral part of the paper since.

John Peery, who began as a sports writer and circulation clerk in April 1978, is now the editor of *The Apopka Chief*. He noted the 20th anniversary of his original hiring a few years ago.

Through the years, the various owners have reported on the good, the bad, and the ugly in Apopka. On the business side of the newspaper, there have been good and not-so-good years.

Recently, John Ricketson said, "We have endeavored to maintain the high standards of coverage about the great Apopka area. Our product is a reflection of our community. Our niche is local news, sports, city and county government, and the people of our coverage area. The local newspaper belongs to the people it serves and we, the current owners/management, are temporarily in charge. If we do our job right, then long after we are gone, local newspapers will be here as a viable product that has been and is important to the growth of the greater Apopka area.

"The goal when I took on the awesome responsibility of management was to maintain the integrity of this area's newspaper and to leave it in better condition that it was when I came. That has been and continues to be the long-range goal."

But through it all, no matter who has owned it and how much they may have made or lost, the bottom line for *The Apopka Chief* is that it really belongs to the community.

The Apopka Chief, since its inception, has always been a community institution with Apopka's best interest at heart.

Chapter V - The Train Wreck / Tornado Hits Apopka

The Great Train Wreck Of '05

It was a rolling, thunderous boom that rattled the Plymouth-Zellwood countryside on that chilly December morning ninety years ago.

A thirteen-year-old boy perched in the window of his home in Grassmere, (Zellwood Station) a mile away, knew what was coming. These days, boys want to become astronauts, but Chauncey Daniel knew he wanted to be a railroad man. He had studied the movement of trains through McDonald and knew the schedules as well as the men who operated them.

His mother did not believe him when he told her the two Seaboard Airline Railway trains were going to collide at the McDonald curve (where the Orlando North Airport is today) on their Orlando-Wildwood run. On this day, Chauncey knew a train wreck was imminent from the sounds he heard coming from the now defunct McDonald Depot.

For the rest of his life, he remembered the wreck that left wooden train cars toppled and splintered, two steam engines twisted, and three men dead. When he heard the "big boom," he knew the Orlando-bound freight and passenger train had not pulled off at a siding as it usually did to let the northbound passenger train by.

He ran the one mile to the wreck site, between Plymouth and Zellwood. Chauncey was the second person to arrive at the wreck. "The first thing I saw was the back end of a Pullman coach on the mixed, (passenger-freight) train and the porter was outside and wanted to know, what happened," said Chauncey. However, he kept running.

A few passengers were carrying seat cushions to the side of the rails to lay the scalded engineers on. A beam had pinned the railway mail clerk to the floor of the car. Jeff Goss, who had been working the groves nearby, was hacking at the beam with an emergency ax to rescue the clerk, who later recovered. But a boxcar had overturned and crushed two firemen who stoked the engine fires. "I was so young that there was nothing that I could do," said Daniels.

Mrs. Cora Starbird and her daughter, now Mrs. Mable Raulerson of Apopka, were on the passenger train and still have memories of that fateful day.

"The southbound train had been pulling twelve to fifteen freight cars and several passenger cars on the rear. The northbound train had three passenger coaches," Daniels said. They met at the bend in the tracks where the orange grove obstructed the view. Luckily, most passengers were merely bruised.

Daniel said that he heard later that as a one-car train sped from Orlando to pick up the injured, the dying engineer's wife was pacing up and down her long front porch in Orlando waiting for her husband to come home. He died as the rescue train reached Orlando. Daniels added, "The passenger train engineer recovered but was never the same."

"There has been nothing since in the area to even compare to the great wreck of '05." said Daniels who signed on with the railroad himself in 1912. "Either the southbound train did not have time to clear the track or its engineer was trying to reach Plymouth before the northbound train," he added, then summed up the accident as "just human error."

Chauncey S. Daniel, whose father, Fernando Daniel, was postmaster at Grassmere, went on to become postmaster himself and mayor of Tavares, our beautiful neighbor to the north.

Apopka Water, Light & Ice Co.

In 1905, the Apopka City Council authorized the incorporation of the Apopka Water, Light and Ice Company. The incorporators were Mayor Joseph D. Mitchell, Councilmen A.C. and A.M. Starbird; his brother, Charles Converse and Henry Witherington. They had the power "to use and occupy public streets, lanes and alleys to lay pipe for water, erect poles for wires," for a term of fifty years. A.M. Starbird was appointed manager and reported back to the city council.

Before there was ever any agreement, A.M. Starbird had a deep well in his back yard with a gasoline pump and water tank that he used to irrigate his grapefruit grove. He supplied his father with water and later extended the service to his neighbors. During this period, there was an ever-growing demand for water and electrical services.

Up to that time, water had been carried or hauled from a spring on the edge of Dream Lake. It was the same spring that Peter Buchan and his family had used when they first settled on Dream Lake in the 1840s.

Deciding that Apopka should be on par with other communities in the area, the Citizens of Apopka group took two very important steps toward that goal. First, it obtained from the state Legislatures of 1913 and 1915 the authority to levy taxes on all real and personal property. Then, in a mid-1914 election, the voters approved two bond issues, $6,000 for a city hall and $9,000 for an electric lighting system. As president of the newly formed franchised electric light and water company, Delbert Starbird contracted with International Harvester Corporation for construction of an electrical generating plant.

The electricity was turned on in Apopka on February 10, 1915. At first, the plant only operated from dusk to 11:30 p.m. William Clark, who recently arrived from Detroit, celebrated the occasion by opening his new motion picture theatre with two shows, one for the white and one for the colored.

Starbird continued stringing wires until the Consumers Lumber Company and the Marshall Packing House had electricity in late 1915. In early 1916, he received authority from the county to erect a line along the highway to Plymouth and to the Pirie Estate.

A deep well was pumping water to a 17,000-gallon tower that stood fifty-three feet above the town. Fire plugs were installed in June and with the arrival of necessary equipment shortly afterward, the business portion of town had fire protection.

In 1921, J.G. Grossenbacher headed a board of trade committee to negotiate with A.M. Starbird for both a larger water supply and twenty-four-hour electricity. In the meantime, William Edwards was installing an electric-generating plant at Plymouth to supply that community and Zellwood with electricity. They called the company the Plymouth Fruit and Electric Company. They were operating by April of 1922. The company agreed to sell power to Starbird, so twenty-four-hour electric service came to Apopka later the same year.

A controversy evolved over whether the town should buy Starbird's company and operate its own utility. At the same time, the Florida Public Service Corporation was buying up most of the private utilities. At a public meeting in early 1924, Apopkans instructed the council to purchase the water and light plant, but a month later Edwards sold his plant to the Public Service Corporation, and in 1925, Starbird did the same.

The FPSC's electric service proved satisfactory; however, the water supply was a different matter. Apopka was growing rapidly and the company refused to extend service to the new dwellings, despite its new construction of a new 50,000-gallon water tank atop a ninety--foot tower. After a suit reached the Florida Supreme Court, the company and town settled their differences by arbitration in a manner that satisfied both parties.

In 1927, the deep well began falling short of increased demand and a pump station was installed in Dream Lake, from which the city obtained its water after July of that year. By 1935, the Florida Public Service Corp. dug a 363-foot well to replace Dream Lake.

In 1940, FPSC sold its ice plants to the Atlantic Company. Florida Power Corporation took over the power in 1943, and that same year, Florida Utilities took over the responsibility of supplying the city's water. It was a very eventful period from the formation of the Apopka Water, Light and Ice Co. in 1905, to the eventual split up of the services in 1943.

Plymouth Citrus Growers

In the early 1900s, two of Northwest Orange County's largest and most stable employers were the Consumers Lumber and Veneer and the Plymouth Citrus Growers Association. We have written about Consumers Lumber and Veneer in past articles, so let's take a look at how Plymouth Citrus Growers Association became a reality.

After the devastating freezes of 1894-95, the Florida Fruit Exchange closed its doors. This was the marketing arm of Florida's citrus industry. The growers continued to hold their so-called annual convention in Tampa to discuss their problems and prospects for the coming year. From discussions in 1908, it was decided to send a delegation to California to study their success with marketing their citrus crops, especially using the trade name of "Sun-Kist." After returning with their observations and holding many stormy sessions in 1909, the growers finally formed The Florida Citrus Exchange. It was to be a federated arrangement with local organizations joining if they wished. While many growers determined to continue on their own, a number of Apopka area citrus men supported the idea of cooperation. That same year, the Plymouth Citrus Fruit Growers Association was organized.

John E. Merrell, John A. Smith, and John B. Steinmetz had been operating a fruit packing house near the Seaboard Airline tracks at Plymouth. In 1910, the newly formed association rented the packing house for the 1910-1911 packing season. Then, in April 1911, with John T. Chapman of Plymouth as its first president, the Plymouth Citrus Fruit Growers Association purchased the packing house from the three former owners. For a tract 100 feet wide adjacent to the railroad and a twenty-foot right-of-way to the nearby clay road, "including the packing house and the equipment of every kind," the association paid $825. Additional land adjacent to the packing house was purchased for $925. The association was given three years to pay the total of $1,750.

William Edwards of Zellwood, one of the area's most vigorous developmental leaders, was also one of the driving forces behind the new cooperative organization and soon replaced Chapman as its president, a position he retained for many years. Membership in the exchange and its affiliation with the state organization was beneficial to the Apopka area growers. A national advertising program was accompanied by efforts to protect the reputation of the product handled by the organization. The trade name "Seald-Sweet" was adopted in 1915. The same year, the exchange first began to improve the grading practices of its constituent member packing houses and to prevent the shipment of green fruit. Wishing to reduce the costs of supplies, the exchange board organized the Exchange Supply Service to purchase in bulk for resale to members at better prices. Despite sizeable losses from another severe freeze in 1917, the citrus growers who had survived the disasters of the 1890s and others who had joined them since were enjoying much more stability in the fruit industry than had existed in the past.

There was also increased cooperation in dealing with diseases and pests that threatened the citrus. When white flies threatened the groves in 1904, the county commission lamented the lack of adequate power to deal with the pest and called on the state Legislature to pass local legislation "giving our people power to deal with the white fly." During the next few years, assistance was made available. By 1915, D.W. Grimes was serving as state tree inspector to prevent the spread of citrus canker and other diseases. W.W. Yothers, as head of the Tropical and Sub-Tropical Fruit Insect Investigation Service, addressed the members of the Plymouth Citrus Exchange and other groups on improved spraying methods, which he believed would increase yields by a fourth.

Under a new United States government program in 1914, John Henry Baker of Zellwood became the county's first agricultural agent. At a farmers institute in Apopka in 1916, he reported on the activities of his office during the first two years of existence, which his listeners agreed had been beneficial to them. W.W. Yothers also addressed the meeting, along with J.G. Grossenbacher of the Florida Department of Agriculture. Grossenbacher had been sent by his department on a brief mission to Apopka, but ended up settling there.

The state also provided a solution for another problem. Growers had experienced considerable difficulty in pricing because of varying sizes in boxes in which fruit was picked. After conferring with the Apopka growers in 1915, Representative S.S. Griffin introduced a bill calling for uniform field boxes for fruit packing.

Although the Plymouth Citrus Exchange was shipping nearly 100,000 boxes per year by 1913, numerous growers preferred to continue handling their fruit independently. Robert W. Nix, a representative of John Nix and Co. of New York, and several others were still buying large quantities of fruit, much of it on the trees, from Apopka growers. W.B. Davis of Southern Growers' Company opened a packing house for both citrus and vegetables in Apopka in early 1915. The facility was taken over by A.C. Marshall in the fall of that year. By December, the Marshall packing house was shipping three cars of fruit per day and providing employment for numerous Apopkans. The volume of fruit being shipped by Marshall was large enough that the Seaboard Airline Railroad built a siding to the packing house late in 1915.

Sawgrass Jones

Around 1908, James W. Jones heard glowing reports of the fabulous new farmland being developed from the Apopka marshland near Zellwood, Florida. These reports, put out by the Guarantee State Bank of Dallas, Texas, described the Apopka marshland soils as being like black gold just waiting for farming prospectors to develop them into the richest farmland in America. In 1909, Jones traveled to Zellwood to see this area firsthand. He was impressed with its great potential and became its most ardent supporter. As a result, Jones was nicknamed "Sawgrass."

Jones wrote Arthur King, his young friend in Tennessee and advised him to come down right away. In the meantime, he returned to Texas to get his family and to tell his Tennessee friends in Texas about this fabulous new frontier.

Arthur King arrived in December of 1909 and, being single and only twenty-four at the time, was eager to start farming. King said that, compared to the farmland he had just left in Tennessee, the area looked like one big manure pile just waiting to be farmed.

Sawgrass Jones and his family arrived from Texas in early 1910. Jones' enthusiasm got him the non-paying position of soliciting his friends to buy tracts in the new farm frontier. Arthur King bought ten acres of the recently opened marshland for $100 an acre, and started his first farming operation in 1910.

Jones and King both advised their Tennessee friends in Texas to join them in this Promised Land, which offered so much more than Texas. Before bringing their families, Tom Morton and Jones Vincent came to see for themselves. They returned to Texas convinced of the correctness of their friends' appraisal of the area. Upon their return to Texas, the two men convinced John Morton and Harry and Lee Gregory to come to Zellwood. In late 1911, several Texas families—Tom Morton, his wife and two children; his brother John Morton with his wife and five children; Jones Vincent with his wife and seven children; and Henry and Lee Gregory, chartered a Pullman car for the trip to Florida. They rented a freight car to transport their farm equipment and assorted livestock. George Vincent, son of Jones Vincent, was selected to ride the freight car with the equipment and livestock.

The Pullman car carrying the Texas families arrived in Zellwood on December 1, 1911, and George Vincent arrived the following day with the livestock and equipment.

Before long, this group convinced other Tennessee friends and relatives to join them. The Fieldings, Flys, Holts, and Letsingers were among the later settlers to follow. George Vincent remembered that the promoters had constructed a tower so new arrivals could climb up and get a good view of the tremendous expanse of the marshland.

However, of all these families, only Arthur King bought some of the Apopka marshland and attempted to farm it. The others became involved in citrus and other activities in the area, but none participated in the vegetable-growing venture.

The black gold prospectors soon found that farming the marshland was next to impossible. The low-lying land located on the north side of the lake was subject to frosts early in the fall and late spring. The cold hazard was difficult to plan around, because a cropping schedule for the area had not been worked out at that time. However, the major problem was the lack of water control. As a result, the area was so soggy that work with horses was next to impossible, even when they were equipped with special muck shoes. Rain and breaking dikes were an ever-present problem. However, as one disgusted group left, another group of enthusiastic newcomers would arrive fully expecting to succeed in this area. The rapid coming and going of farm prospectors gave rise to their being called "suitcase" farmers.

Mr. King remembered particularly the problems of trying to store potatoes grown on these mucky peat soils. For some unknown reason, potatoes grown in these soils rotted quickly. King remembered that this condition was thought to result from the low potash and phosphorus content of the soils. He ordered sulphate of potash and superphosphate from the Wilson-Toomer Fertilizer Company in Jacksonville to correct the condition. He believed that the storage life of the potato was improved after that.

Since this experiment was conducted in 1912, it may have been the first organic soil field demonstration in Florida.

Around 1914, King decided that the cold and water problems were too much for him and that his "promised land" had disappeared. As a result, he ended his peat soil farming and started a citrus nursery on high, sandy land in the Zellwood area.

By 1917, the few remaining individuals accepted King's estimate of the Apopka marshland and got into other agricultural endeavors. The Zellwood farm area was abandoned and Lake Apopka was allowed to "recapture" the mucky peat area once again.

T. J. Smith

Let me tell you a story about a railroad man, T. J. Smith. This man could have told you something about the old railroad days. He came to Apopka in 1909 to run the Atlantic Coast Line daily mixed train from Apopka to Kissimmee. It consisted of a baggage coach, one or two passenger coaches, and a number of freight cars.

The depot was located at Main Street and Forest Avenues. On the way to Kissimmee, the train gave passenger and freight service to the cities of Ocoee, Minorville, Windermere, Zantee, Orange Center, and Shingle Creek.

Products hauled were fruit, especially fruit crates from the big crate mill here in Apopka. Other items included vegetables and forest products such as turpentine, rosin, and lumber, as well as fertilizer and furniture, plus all kinds of merchandise.

In a period just emerging from the log wagon, the mule team, the horse and buggy, and the sand roads over which these vehicles traveled, the railroad was the best way of getting around.

To give you some idea of how dependent people were on railroads, there was a disastrous fire starting in an important Southern city. Other cities, notified by telegraph and wanting to help, loaded fire-fighting equipment on flat cars and shipped it by rail. Some of it got there in time to help bring the fire under control. It was the only practical way.

A weekend visit to Oakland, for instance, could be accomplished by going to Toronto (where the overhead bridge used to be located on old Hwy. 441) and changing trains for the balance of the journey. Winter Park was reached by taking the Seaboard to Orlando and changing for Winter Park.

There was a lot of timber left in the country. The big veneer and crate manufacturing plant was located south of Eighth Street, between Park and Forest Avenues. The Coast Line, which Smith ran, crossed the Seaboard tracks at that point.

So dependent were large manufacturing plants, wholesale houses, and such enterprises on railroads, that they were always located alongside the tracks or where sidetrack facilities could be extended to them. The manufacturers' products had to be shipped by rail.

Smith, himself, in later years built one of Apopka's first ice plants. It was a ten-ton-per-day operation. It was operated by steam and was on the Coast Line track near the crate mill.

The dependence of manufacturing and important merchandising on the railroads caused numerous branches to be built from the main line.

The road from Apopka to Kissimmee originally took off from the main line at Longwood, came through Apopka and the communities mentioned above, and rejoined the main line at Kissimmee.

Very early and before Smith's time, the track from Apopka to Longwood was taken up.

A turntable was put in just north of Third Street (Tommy Staley Park), where the engine could be turned around at night and be ready for the trip back the next morning.

Wagons and buggies were used strictly for local hauling. They plowed through the sand to assemble the products at railroad stations for the trains to take to the big markets.

T. J. Smith's train left Apopka around 7 a.m. and had a layover in Kissimmee, so the round trip took about twelve hours. For the day, the brakeman got $1.08, and the baggage and express men each got $1. Engineers in those days got fantastic wages. Smith drew $4.40 for the day.

Some of the economists say trucks have taken over too much of the long-distance hauling. It is said long haul can be done more economically by rail.

The changes from that time to this seem tremendous. There are many grown people today who have never taken a ride on a train; however, there are still a lot of the older people who agree that the train is the best way to travel. If our battles with the bullet trains and commuter rail continue in Central Florida, we will have a lot of young people who may never ride the rails.

Apopka Roads Improved

The Apopka Chief recently ran an article by one of the old local pioneer writers, Leslie Bray, entitled "The Road That Was Straight." As much a miracle as that road was, we also have a disaster in "The Road That Was Not Straight." Without giving it much thought, we realize that would be the road from Rock Springs to Mt. Plymouth.

They say that all these roads started as Indian trails and later became military trails that made way for the carts pulled by oxen or horses. If that particular road was an Indian trail, then some young brave had been drinking too much Kick-a-Poo Joy Juice. Maybe a storm came through and knocked a lot of trees over the trail and our pioneer friends took the easy way out and made a new road around. Back when it was a trail, it had to be a much safer road. Today, any speed above fifteen mph would be declared unsafe.

Generally speaking, these old trails have gradually improved over the years as the population has grown. As they moved supplies inland from Mellonville and Clay Springs, and with the addition of postal service, people needed more than the customary trails. Over the course of time, the automobile was beginning to show up on the scene. The old Model Ts, etc. started digging deep ruts into Central Florida's sugar sand. They were getting stuck.

The local governments began to cover their roads with pine straw. This was sufficient for a few years but in the early 1900s, Apopka and Orange County were changing to clay and some limestone. This change did not last too long as far as primary roads were concerned, because the clay and limestone were running out and those surfaces were too expensive to maintain. Secondary roads used clay up until recent years.

In 1911, the county board concluded that all funds available for the construction of hard-surface primary roads would be spent on brick. They called for an election to approve a one-million-dollar bond issue to build brick roads, theorizing that the greater initial cost would be more than compensated for by the reduced cost of upkeep. After more than a two-year debate it was decided to sell $600,000 worth of bonds, $500,000 to be used to build brick roads and the balance for clay roads. This was approved by the county voters in 1913. This was the largest bond issue by a county for public improvement in the history of the state at the time.

By 1915, bricks were in place from Orlando through Apopka and Plymouth. Apopka joined Orlando and other Central Florida communities in an effort to have this road designated as part of the Dixie Highway as advocated by Carl Fisher. The Old Dixie Highway system was nine feet wide. The locals were disappointed, but not defeated, when the Dixie Highway Association chose routes down the east coast. Further lobbying resulted in the designation of an eastern and western route. The western route would go through Gainesville, Ocala, Leesburg, Tavares, Apopka, and Orlando, and then head south. Apopka citizens were ecstatic to have their town on the western route.

The citizens of Apopka had also fallen in love with brick streets. In 1920-21, they approved a $50,000 bond issue for laying bricks on Central Avenue and Fourth Street and down the Wekiwa Road to the city limits. Work was hardly completed on this project when, in 1922, the citizens approved another $82,000 for brick extensions. They proudly proclaimed they had come from sand trails to paved streets. Some of these brick streets are still functional today and they are some of Apopka's most treasured assets. The more heavily traveled ones have been asphalted. We should treasure these old brick streets in the same manner that you would treasure our oldest homes. It probably would not be a bad idea to try to get the remaining part of the old Dixie Highway that is still bricked included in the National Register of Historic Places.

Dr. Charles McCall

As hard as it is to believe, there actually were doctors in Apopka before Dr. Tommy McBride. Sixteen years before Dr. Tommy established his practice in Apopka, Dr. Charles P. McCall moved here from Lamont, Florida. This was the same town from which Apopka's lifelong pharmacists, the Sheppard family came. And it also was the same town where his successor, Dr. Cole, was born.

Dr. McCall's practice goes back into that period when young men and women, community social leaders, staged rubber-tire buggy races on what is now Main Street.

Or the period when young men made ice cream in hand-operated ice cream churns, using crushed ice and salt. And the girls brought cakes they had made for the ice cream supper. There were also candy-pulling events.

Dr. Charles McCall brought with him his younger brother Winborn, who was a pharmacist. Dr. Winborn McCall later married the woman who assisted him in the drug store, Mattie Lovell.

Dr. McCall, a graduate of Emory University, was well respected by his colleagues. He was praised by the medical fraternity on his diagnosis of a case of Hodgkin's disease here in Apopka. His patient, a young woman, was transported to Atlanta for treatment.

For his diagnosing and curing of a case of pellagra, he was asked to submit a paper at a meeting of the American Medical Association.

Like his successor Dr. Cole, Dr. McCall was unmarried during the ten years that he practiced here (1910 until 1920). He later married an Apopka woman named Nellie Wilson. She was the daughter of a former postmaster and station agent, William T. Wilson.

Dr. McCall and his brother, the pharmacist, lived upstairs in the drug store building and, as usual, took their meals with Mrs. Williford at the Wayside Inn that was later to become the Swanner residence, on Park Avenue off Fourth Street.

Although the doctor had an office in the rear of the drugstore, there were no office calls, according to Lee Lovell. He said Dr. McCall was on the go all the time, and on-call day and night.

Lovell, a brother of Mrs. Winborn McCall, worked around the drugstore and drove Dr. McCall's car for him. It was a Buick Pug Roadster. Lovell thought it was the first car in Apopka.

He did not remember any cars coming through Apopka at that time on cross-country trips. He thought Dr. McCall must have sold the car when he left here for Reidsville, Georgia. He lived there the rest of his life.

Lovell recalled hard times getting the car over the sand trails that were roads, making calls to Plymouth, Zellwood, Piedmont, and points between. The experience included patching inner tubes and pumping them up to sixty pounds of pressure with a hand pump. Three thousand miles was a good, long life for a tire.

One night, cruising at perhaps ten to twelve miles per hour, they made a sharp turn on an old country road and ran the car up on top of a cow that was lying in the road. Lovell said as the cow breathed, the little red car went up and down. The tail pipe exhaust was burning the cow and there was odor of scorched hair.

He could not remember how the two of them managed to get the car off the cow. But he said that when they did, the cow went running off through the woods.

The McCalls, according to the doctor's sister-in-law, tended to take up "the pill bag or the Bible." One brother, Moses, served forty-three years as a missionary to Cuba and was decorated by the Cuban government.

John Grossenbacher, Sr.

I have said many times that Apopka was very fortunate to have had outstanding leadership during the early 1900s. John G. Grossenbacher was one of those leaders. John was born in Bern, Switzerland, on April 11, 1875, and was brought to this country at the age of five. He was the son of Jacob Grossenbacher and Anna Gasser Grossenbacher, who had settled in California, Missouri, in 1880.

John received his B.A. degree at the University of Missouri and his Ph.D. at the University of Wisconsin. He did post-graduate work at Harvard University, majoring in plant pathology and citrus diseases. In 1908, he married Isadore Smoot, who had A.B. and A. M. degrees from the University of Missouri. They had one daughter and four sons. After graduation, John went to work for the U.S. Department of Agriculture in Washington, D.C., and was sent to Apopka in 1913 to open the first Orange County Department of Agriculture office .

By 1915, John had fallen in love with the northwest Orange County area with its budding citrus, foliage, and vegetable industries, and he decided to stay. He immediately started to work on putting together the Florida Insecticide Company, which manufactured and distributed insecticides for the agricultural industry.

With M.L. Lee as his assistant, Grossenbacher developed FICO-60, the demand for which was so large that another plant was established in Haines City in 1921. His Apopka plant burned that same year, but it was rebuilt on a larger scale in less than sixty days.

A proponent of preventive maintenance, he wrote and spoke about the proper use of insecticides and frequently gave demonstrations with improved sprayers, which he also sold. With an apparent sense of humor, he once announced a demonstration under the heading, Spraying for Pleasure and Profit.

Grossenbacher achieved wide recognition as an expert on the diseases and insects affecting citrus groves. He published a number of papers on diseases of trees and plants (such as "It Pays to Control Rust Mites" in 1921), and had a number of discoveries along these lines, which have not been published.

A nationally recognized pomologist, Grossenbacher published the *Citrus Leaf*, a monthly journal with a circulation of 5,000, from which many of his articles were reprinted in scientific journals.

He became prominent in the Plymouth Citrus Exchange, the Orange County Sub-Exchange, and the Florida Citrus Exchange, and was named to the citrus growers Committee of 50.

John was very active in civic affairs in Apopka and Orlando. He was active in the Apopka Board of Trade, where he helped to establish the Central Savings and Loan Association of Apopka and chaired a committee to raise the funds to build a suitable hotel in downtown Apopka in 1927.

Mr. Grossenbacher also served on the Plymouth Citrus Exchange board and was president of the Florida Citrus Exchange, as well as a director of the Orange County Chamber of Commerce. He served on the Orlando Committee of 100. He was also a member of the Central Florida Harvard Club and the University Club of Winter Park.

The tornado that hit Apopka in 1918 completely demolished the Florida Insecticide Co. that was located on the northeast corner of Forest Avenue and Third Street. Mr. Grossenbacher rebuilt his building on a much larger scale and expanded sales and services of his FICO brands.

The Florida Insecticide Company was incorporated in 1926, with a $200,000 capitalization. Richard Whitney, president of the New York Stock Exchange and member of an influential New York family, bought it in 1931, and William B. Goding became general manager. V. W. Haygood was in charge of the Apopka office and M. L. Lee remained manager of the mixing plant. FICO's capacity was enlarged in 1933 and again in 1936, by which time it had been merged with Stauffer Chemicals of Texas. Whitney sold a two-thirds interest to the Texas firm, and the Florida company thereafter distributed Stauffer products, in addition to the FICO brand.

Old Spring Place

This is an interview with Peter E. Buchan on March 24, 1964. It was written at the two-story frame dwelling that he built at Buchan's Landing at Englewood in 1916. He was ninety-two at the time of this interview. The interviewer is unknown.

"Peter E. Buchan was the grandson of the original Peter who came to Apopka in 1830.

Young Peter was born February 22, 1872 at the Old Spring Place, on Rock Springs Road in Apopka, the homestead of Thomas Charles Buchan, father to Peter, Chip, Malissa and two other girls.

Thomas had two brothers. Joe Buchan, who was killed in the battle of Gettysburg and John Buchan who died at home soon after returning from service in the Confederate Army. (Peter thinks John was tubercular.)

Joe was not so badly wounded in the battle. He sent home some trinkets in a little tin box. He could have been saved, but doctors were busy with others more badly wounded. He died some three days after the battle. He had started a letter, which was finished by his commanding officer and sent to his people here in Apopka. He was a graduate of a school in LaGrange, Georgia, which offered about the best and highest educational courses in this section.

Tom was "the best man in Orange County," Peter said. He was also a graduate of the same school as Joe in LaGrange. He wrote letters and legal documents for people. Much of his work was filed in the courthouse. "He could do anything he wanted to do," Peter said. But he indicated Tom would not do anything that did not appeal to him. Tom and his wife Mallissa tanned hides and made harnesses and shoes for soldiers during the war.

Peter worked on the Pirie Estate with a Scotsman who had been brought over from the "old country." This old Scot told Peter that Peter's grandfather, the father of Thomas, Joe and John, that the Buchans, Cummings, and Stewarts were the families best known in that part of Scotland. The grandfather Peter was a silversmith. He made for his grandson Peter a small sword of gold, which was part of the Buchans' emblem. (It may have been their coat of arms.) The coat of arms bore the slogan, "I make sure." The elder Peter, who came from Scotland, according to the Pirie gardener, was not of the ruling class, but very close to it. He was "bound out" to learn a trade at seven. He got married soon after finishing his apprenticeship and came to America.

He settled in LaGrange, Georgia, bought land, mules, plows, and slaves and set himself up as a cotton farmer. Nobody seems to know, according to Peter, why the elder Peter came to Florida. "There were no neighbors, as far as we knew, for miles around. What the devil he would want to bring his family into this wilderness is a mystery to me."

Old Peter and his slaves helped build the Masonic Temple in 1856.

Twenty years later he died. His slaves were still with him. His nephews moved him to Mellonville during his last illness, which extended for more than a year. The slaves finally left when Peter was taken away.

As a silversmith, the elder Peter made silver spurs, spoons, and many other trinkets and devices. People brought him silver dollars in twice the weight of the device to be made. When he died, he had a box about 6" by 8" by 6" full of silver dollars. Young Peter remembers seeing this sitting around unattended in many places, and remarked how times have changed."

About Apopka Young Peter remembers:

"Beverly W. Hull delivering the mail between Clay Springs to Apopka with her mail cart being pulled by a cow.

Further concerning his father Charles Thomas Buchan, he said he had no talent or liking for making money. He never had to since his father had plenty, and things went hard for him after the grandfather Peter died. He believes his mother came from the east coast somewhere in the vicinity of Merritt Island and thinks her maiden name was Mallissa Hendricks.

He remembers seeing William S. Delk in his groves. He said Delk was a tough employer and charged a picker a nickel if he dropped an orange and damaged it. Charles Thomas Buchan and Delk were great friends. He could not remember Delk having a mill at Rock Springs.

He says the Stewarts had a mill, which he thinks was run by steam power that cut lumber and ground meal. Their saw worked up and down, like a cross-cut and not a circular."

Oaks Hotel

I would only guess that Nicholas W. Prince had a cotton plantation somewhere near Tuscaloosa, Alabama. He was able to educate his children with a degree from the University of Alabama. One of his sons became a dentist. After the Civil War, he was in financial ruin and wanted to locate somewhere in Florida and start anew. He had heard glowing reports on the land in Central Florida for growing cotton; so in 1867, he and his three sons Rufus, James, and Oliver drove a covered wagon down to and settled in Apopka. He chose Apopka because he wanted to be near the Masonic Lodge, where later he served for many years. He served on the school board in 1870, and was county superintendent of schools in 1872.

When the father and sons got themselves established in Apopka, the mother and daughters came down, traveling by way of steamboat from Jacksonville to Lake Monroe. There were no railroads in the area at that time. The residence of the elder Prince was west of town somewhere near Bradshaw Road.

Dr. Edmund Rufus Prince, the son who became a dentist, built his fourteen-room home in 1879, at the corner of Main Street and Edgewood Drive, where Bank First now stands. This was only one block west of Apopka's main corner, which was called "Old Town." At the original main intersection was the Masonic Temple on the northeast corner, the Morgan house and a hotel on the northwest corner, a livery stable on the southwest corner, and an apothecary and other shops on the southeast corner.

The Prince home was converted into the Oaks Hotel, where the Johansens operated their famous dining room in 1916. Their slogan was that their table was supplied "from our own dairy, garden and poultry." For only $12.00 per week, guests could stay "at the highest point in Florida." The Rotary Club met there for years, after they left the Wekiwa Springs Hotel.

In 1935, Mr. and Mrs. G.A. Bryant purchased the hotel and operated it for the rest of their lives. One of their daughters, Mrs. Alice Coleman, kept it open as an apartment house until 1963.

When the Tavares, Orlando and Atlantic railroad opened in Apopka in 1885, it drew the center of town westward from its original location in "Old Town." The citizens of Apopka covered the road with clay, connecting the Lodge to Central Avenue. This became the first hard-top road in town. A wooden sidewalk was built along the side of the road to accommodate pedestrians.

Also in 1885, Mr. Prince opened the Bank of Apopka, the first bank in town, somewhere around Forest Avenue and Main St. They offered regular banking, bought and sold exchanges, made collections, and loaned money on time. They had corresponding banks in Orlando, Jacksonville, and New York.

The bank failed after a very short run, due to the freeze of 1885. Mr. Prince sold his house, his groves, and other property in order to pay his losses. He moved to Tampa, where he later died.

Think about the tricks that history plays. The old building on the corner of Main and Edgewood was the home of Apopka's first banker. Today it is the home of Bank First, where Bill Arrowsmith is the manager. There are plans in the works to move Apopka's downtown district back to where it came from. I guess the city was feeling the effects of growing old and wanted to go home to "Old Town." As they say, "What goes around comes around."

1918 Tornado In Apopka

On a chilly evening on January 11, 1918, as Apopka residents were settling down to an evening meal, a light yellow cloud was forming over Lake Apopka. Observers said the cloud looked as though it had fire in it. Fire, indeed, as a vicious tornado was coming off of Lake Apopka and mowing down a half-mile path on its way to the center of Apopka.

Newell and Ustler Fernery

It hit downtown about 9 p.m., with brilliant lightning bolts lighting up the sky. Apopkans said the wind was not a whirlwind but a steady wall of power crushing everything in its path.

Homes collapsed like cardboard boxes. Joists weighing hundreds of pounds were picked up like toothpicks and hurled through the air. Pine trees were bent nearly double and others cracked in two like matches. Railroad cars were overturned. Iron roofing from Eldredge's livery stable was found by hunters miles away wrapped around trees in the Wekiwa swamp.

The Orlando Sentinel said, "Many of the residences are wrecked and most of the business houses are completely destroyed." Actually, twenty-five buildings were completely destroyed and others seriously damaged. Some of those that were completely destroyed were Consumers Lumber, the S.A.L. Depot, Apopka High School, Leslie Waite's Dry Goods Store, and the Apopka Publishing

Company. Observers said the Newell and Ustler Fernery "lay flat as if it had been rolled out like a pancake." Two carloads of fertilizer on the Seaboard tracks were overturned and the warehouse near the station was badly damaged.

Eldredge's warehouse was completely destroyed and his store badly damaged. Heavily damaged were the Apopka Drug Company Store, the citrus packing house, the Apopka Telephone Company, and the electric light plant. There were serious injuries; however, nobody was killed.

Many magnificent oaks were blown down or uprooted. W. G. Harris, a real estate man at the time, said Theodore Anderson used ropes and teams of mules to pull the trees back to an upright position.

With the high school went a sycamore tree which had been planted on Arbor Day, 1904, by P. D. Shepherd. Its mate, a gigantic tree which is still standing, was marked a few years later by the Apopka Garden Club with a plaque honoring Shepherd. It stands today on what was a corner of the old frame school building that went down that day in 1918.

Like all tornadoes, this one did some unusual things. W. T. Champney was lying on a sofa in his living room when the storm struck. When it was over, he was still on the sofa but it was out in the yard. Wilson's store was completely wrecked, but there were still several shelves left intact with the goods standing in place. Harry Ustler's family was around the table having a late dinner. The storm took the house away and left them sitting there no worse for the experience. Elwood Ustler was in the kitchen with his mother. When the storm hit they got under the kitchen table. The tornado took the top story of a two-story house and Elwood and his mother were unharmed. In the Roy White's family house, a baby was sleeping in a crib on the second floor, according to the story; after the storm passed, the baby was found unharmed in his crib on the first floor.

Neighboring towns responded with a great deal of compassion. Orlando Mayor James L. Giles, Zellwood-born and a former Apopka resident, appealed to his constituents to, "assist our sister city." *The Orlando Sentinel* acted as a depository for a relief fund. Apopkans held dances to raise funds for those in need.

Although B. F. Wilson, after losing his home and business, moved to Miami to start anew, most Apopkans remained to rebuild. Only three months after the storm, they set a record for the most money raised in a single day on Liberty Bonds Day. You would have to tip your hat to the Apopka pioneers of 1918; they persevered after the storm.

Chapter VI - Apopka's Illustrious Residents

Mallory Welch

This is an interview by Torrey Paulson of the Orlando Sentinel with Mallory Welch in 1978. Mallory reminisces about being raised in Apopka and believes that he has lived in the best times there's ever been.

"He remembers the time about 1919 when electrical lights in the Apopka area came on at 5 p.m. and went off promptly at 11 p.m. every night.

He remembers when the telephone exchange shut down at 9 p.m. Several party-line families could distinguish which hand-cranked phone was being rung, by the number of long and short rings. Three long rings and a short for one family, two shorts for another, he recalls.

The eighty-year-old former nurseryman who's lived in the Apopka area all his life remembers when the ice man came and when meat wagons carrying freshly butchered meat for sale traveled through the community.

He remembers the wooden sidewalks along Apopka's Central Avenue, only a clay street at that time.

He's seen the times when, as a growing-up youngster he helped the family grind its own corn meal and grits. The family had to buy sugar and salt, and flour could be obtained by the half or whole barrel.

An alert man who played baseball for years around the area, and who's still an avid listener to the radio-broadcast games, he recalls entering the third grade as his first experience with school. His parents couldn't take him to school, so he didn't attend until he could ride a pony the approximate three-mile distance, he said.

His mother taught him at home until then. He attended the Apopka School, which used to stand beside the current city hall before the school was destroyed in a 1918 tornado, he recalls. The school then had about 100 students in the first through 12th grades, he said.

When he was about fifteen in 1912, he 'didn't know too much' about bicycling so he decided to take an adventure by renting a bike in Orlando. Very few children in the Apopka area then had bikes, and there was no place in the Apopka area where they could be rented, he said. He set out, and before long, he and a grocery delivery boy on a bike collided. "Grits and sugar spilled everywhere," he said. He said he was so upset he immediately "rode back to the rental place and turned the bike in."

The man who now lives in a quiet Central Avenue home grew up on "the homestead," which was located on Welch Road about one-half mile south of Rock Springs Road. Welch Road was named for Mallory's father James O. Welch, after he donated his portion of the road to the county, Mallory said.

Mallory's grandfather built the two-story home at the homestead; the home has since burned. The home, at first, only had four large rooms without a kitchen or dining room, so the family temporarily used the fireplace in a nearby log house originally built on the property by Welch's great-grandfather.

On the farm, the family grew velvet beans to fatten cattle, plus corn, potatoes, sweet potatoes, and tomatoes. One year, the family even raised wheat and ground its own flour. Several other area farmers, including his family, would ship their home grown tomatoes to Chicago, Illinois for sale, he said.

Welch remembers the time when area residents owned cattle, which roamed freely across Orange, Seminole and Lake Counties. The cattle were marked on their ears and branded on their sides. He remembers area residents periodically held large gatherings and a dinner so neighbors could help brand between 150 and 200 calves. The calves' owners were easily identified, because the calves would remain by their branded mothers.

From 1923 to 1962, Welch was in the slat shed and greenhouse business. He remembers when he retired that Orange County Extension Agent Henry Swanson said Welch had grown the Boston Fern longer than anyone else in the county. Welch still owns some citrus trees. He began that business about 1928.

Welch also worked with the Florida Game and Freshwater Fish Commission for fourteen years, working to ensure that hunters didn't illegally shoot game and that fishermen didn't illegally use nets instead of the legal trotline."

Ryan Brothers

Mark and Nat Ryan are the older and younger sons of Edward J. Ryan, who for years devoted himself to the development of the lumber and building supply business in Apopka, and served our community and Orange County in many ways. Mark and Nat Ryan also prominently identified themselves with activities that have aided the growth of the area. They were the owners of Ryan and Company of Apopka, started in 1920, which would make it the oldest continuous family owned business in Apopka.

Nat Ryan, Mark Ryan and Mark Ryan, Sr.

The firm handles a complete line of hardware, paints, building materials, and electrical appliances. They also operate a retail lumber yard. Both men took a leading role in civic affairs, and Mark Ryan was a veteran of World War I.

Their father Edward J. Ryan was one of Central Florida's outstanding citizens. Born in Plattsburg, New York, on July 10, 1867, the son of James and Elizabeth (Riley) Ryan came to Florida with his widowed mother when he was thirteen years old, and lived in this state until his death in 1935. He was educated at Merrimack, Florida, and began his business career as an associate of A.C. Starbird in the sawmill business.

Mr. Starbird's business became Consumer Lumber and Supply Company of Apopka and Edward Ryan continued with that firm until 1920, when he established Ryan and Company with a sawmill of his own.

Edward J. Ryan married Emma Yocum in Apopka, in the latter part of the nineteenth century, and they had three children, Mark, Nat, and Minnie May. Minnie became the wife of William Stewart, who ran a general store he founded and operated in Plymouth, Florida.

The following year he added a crate-manufacturing mill. He operated these two mills until 1924, at a location which is a block from the present location of the Ryan Brothers store. In 1924, he bought a building on a 150' by 180' lot facing the highway. (That area was later known as Stokes Hardware and, later still, Dunkin Donuts.) This structure had previously housed a Ford automobile display room and garage.

Mr. Ryan virtually rebuilt the building and launched the building supply business Ryan and Company. He continued his retail lumber yard on Fifth Street, behind the building supply establishment. The business flourished mightily, and had his personal supervision until his death in 1935, when it was taken over by his sons Mark and Nat.

His older son Mark was born in Apopka in 1895, and was educated in the elementary and high schools of Apopka. Following his high school graduation, he joined his father in the administration of Ryan and Company, but had barely begun his business career when the United States entered World War I in 1917. He left home and business and entered the Army, in which he served seven months. Upon his return home, he resumed his place in the family business and was closely associated with it, assuming full management in association with his brother when his father died. Mark Ryan was active in community affairs and a member of various organizations.

Mark Ryan married Dorothy Vaden of Apopka, and they had two children, Mark Jr. and Janet.

Nat Ryan was born on June 25, 1900, in Apopka. He was a graduate of the city's elementary and high schools and like his brother, went into the family business after graduation. Like his brother, he was also a member of the Masonic fraternity.

Nat Ryan married Josephine Griffin, the daughter of J.J. and Maud (McCollum) Griffin of Kissimmee, Florida. They have two daughters, Kathy and Nancy.

In 2011, Ryan Brothers, Inc. is still offering the town the same old fashioned service and still being run by members of the Ryan family.

Edward Ryan left a legacy of more than a business to his children. He left a tradition of public service in his business field, in the municipality, and in his church. He served on the Apopka City Commission for quite a few years, and at the time of his death was mayor of the City of Apopka. He was a leader in the Masonic Order and in the Knights of Pythias in Orange County and was a man of tremendous influence and wisdom. His wife was also active and well regarded.

Moonshine In Apopka

When the subject of moonshining comes up, we often think of the hills of North Carolina or maybe the entire Appalachian range. The truth is that there is not a state in the Union that has not had its share of citizens making their liquor illegally. This practice would date back to the Revolutionary War.

In the early 1900s, states began passing laws that banned alcohol sales and consumption. In 1920, nationwide prohibition went into effect. It was the greatest thing that moonshiners could have asked for.

Suddenly, there was no legal alcohol available. The demand for moonshine shot up like a rocket. Moonshiners couldn't keep up with the demand and were determined to keep the government out of their business, and thusly, paid no taxes. The profits were good and the number of stills increased.

Taken from an old newspaper clipping, this picture shows 103 gallons of illicit alcohol. Shown with the haul are, (l-r) Constable Fred Risner, Police Chief W. J. Dunaway and State Beverage Inspectors Bill Peacock and Fred Kiser.

At the same time, the Federal Prohibition Bureau was formulated in order to see that the Volstead Act was enforced. As good as the idea sounded, Prohibition was far easier to proclaim than to enforce.

Illicit liquor stills had been repeatedly discovered and destroyed since the Volstead Act passed, but the issue excited Apopkans in 1924, when a dinner party at the home of John L. York ended in a shootout. After Deputy Sheriff John Urquhart completed his investigation, *The Apopka Chief* reported that "moonshine liquor" was the cause of "one dead, two wounded, two in jail, and others trembling." All the churches pledged cooperation with the sheriff to improve law enforcement and stamp out "the traffic in moonshine liquor."

In a sermon entitled "Shall we keep Florida Christian?" A.M. Hall said Christians would be to blame if gamblers and bootleggers had their way. With Alfred E. Smith, a New York City "wet" and member of the Catholic Church, which had not condemned evolution, running as the Democratic candidate for president against Republican Herbert Hoover, the issue became prominent in the 1928 presidential election. Bishop Cannon returned to campaign against Smith and was joined by John Stratton and the Bible Crusaders. Smith lost Florida, with Northwest Orange County joining the rest of the state to vote for Hoover.

Shortly after the elections, Apopkans were shocked when they discovered one of the reasons why their battle against illegal liquor was not succeeding. Orange County Sheriff Karel had found that, when his men raided stills and bootleggers in Apopka without the knowledge of town Marshall H. D. Miley, they had much greater success than when the marshal was involved. One Monday morning in late November, Miley was sent on a mission into the countryside. While he was gone the sheriff's force, some Orlando traffic officers, and two U.S. Revenue agents raided several locations in both white and black sections of Apopka, finding liquor and its owners in all of them. They were especially successful at a house on Highland Avenue, just a block from the Baptist Church, where Dale Metzger was running a still which filled an entire room, the sides of which were lined with eight full barrels of mash. Marshall Miley was removed and J. S. Parrish replaced him in early 1929. Arrests of distillers and bootleggers continued. Marshal Fred Risener was still finding stills and arresting liquor dealers when probation ended. After that, Apopkans were confronted with a different kind of liquor problem, the "jooks" and roadhouses.

Several bars opened in town and along the highways, causing Chief of Police Fred Risener and the sheriff much difficulty. Licenses were required if there was dancing, but noise and frequent violence were major problems. Buster's Place, operated by Bob Partin, was a frequent cause of complaint, and after numerous citizens in South Apopka complained and two serious brawls occurred there, Mayor Ryan threatened to "close them up tight." Under existing laws, that was most difficult to accomplish. When Joe Patterson, a former prize fighter and "jook" operator at Zellwood, killed Roy Channel in a fist fight, local residents were stirred to action. They found, however, that their only avenue of action was a nuisance abatement suit at their own expense. Although they proceeded with the action, a second-degree murder charge was more effective in the Patterson case.

Police Chief Fred Risener was also constable for Orange County's sixth district, involving him in law enforcement over a large area. He investigated robberies at Clarcona, at SAL Station Agent Frank Weaver's office in Plymouth, at Robert Williams store in South Apopka, and at Nolle's service station on Fourth Street., among others. A series of robberies in late 1938 culminated with the high-noon plundering of Apopka City Hall and Western Union. Then, in early 1941, Police Chief Fred Risener and Deputy D. L. Hudson surprised two safecrackers at the Standard Oil Plant, and Hudson was killed in a resulting gun battle. The killer was never caught. To my knowledge, this was the only time an Apopka law enforcement officer was killed in the line of duty. I see no monuments in his honor or streets bearing his name, but the memory of a man who gave his all will always remain.

****

A little more than seventy years after his death, the Apopka Police Department honored the memory of Officer Denson Hudson. The ceremony was held Sunday, May 15, 2011, at the First Baptist Church of Apopka in connection with National Law Enforcement Month. Police Chief Rob Manley presented a plaque to Hudson's daughter Clemmie Hicks.

Mabel Raulerson

Jan Dunn was on the Apopka Chief staff a few years back and managed to come up with some very good interviews in her "Who's Apopka" series. This week, we will reprint a portion of her interview with Mabel Raulerson in the time frame that she wrote it.

"Mabel Raulerson is practically a walking history of Apopka.

A member of the pioneer Starbird family, who migrated here from Maine in the late 1800s and became business and industrial leaders, Raulerson witnessed and took part in some of Apopka's most memorable events. And though she admits to "never being good at dates," Raulerson recalls events like the great train wreck of 1905, the infamous tornado of 1918 (HT-Dec. 7, 2007), the introduction of electricity to the area in 1915 (HT-Nov. 30, 2007) and her uncle Austin's train, which served commuters in the outlying rural areas of north Orange County and transported picnickers to Clay Springs.

Three generations of Mabel Starbird Raulerson's family enjoy an outing circa 1910 in their family automobile, one of the first in Apopka. Seated in the rear of the car are grandparents Mary Jane and Amos D. Starbird, parents Adelbert and Julia Starbird in front, and standing, left to right, are sisters Lillian and Mabel.

Mabel Starbird Raulerson is the daughter of Adelbert M. Starbird. He was one of eight children of Mary Jane and Amos Starbird whose clan built a logging and sawmill empire and extensive accompanying interests that were to be the commercial backbone of Apopka in the early 20th century. Her husband, Wesley B. Raulerson, was also a pioneer Apopka family, a descendent of W. H. Raulerson, who came to the area from Georgia after the War Between the States.

Born in 1902, she was raised with her three sisters in their family's home on the corner of Lake and First streets during Apopka's infancy. Although she didn't finish high school, the young Miss Starbird helped her father establish the city's first utilities company, Apopka Water and Light, managing the office and keeping the books, she said.

"I remember when they put up the first power pole in Apopka," Raulerson stated.

The utilities business apparently came about more by accident than by purpose. According to accounts, Starbird had installed a well machine to water groves of grapefruit trees surrounding his home, and brought in a gasoline engine to pump the water, which apparently was better quality than the water drawn and carried in buckets from Dream Lake, according to Raulerson. Starbird piped the water into his home, and later extended the pipes to neighboring houses. The idea apparently caught on and demand eventually exceeded supply. So Starbird later installed a larger well, with a larger tank, and set up an electric power plant. The utilities were later expanded to Plymouth, and to the Pirie Estate, which would later become Errol Estate.

Mabel Starbird and Wesley Raulerson were wed in 1923, and their family eventually included three sons; Merton, (Mert) Samuel, (Sammy) and Adelbert (Delbert). She also now claims seven (7) grandchildren, and six great-grandchildren.

Her husband went to work for her father at Apopka Water and Light, and continued with the company even after the senior Starbird sold the company in 1925 to Florida Power Corporation, reportedly due to failing health. He was offered opportunities to advance with the power company, Raulerson said, but due to the travel required he rejected the offers. "He always said that it wasn't worth being away from his family," she explained.

That strong family loyalty was apparently shared by the couple, as Raulerson came to relish her role as mother, and eventually grandmother. Grade school trips as home room mother and family outings highlight her memories.

"We had a big old station wagon," Raulerson recalled, "and we'd pile in all of the kids and go on picnics to the beach," she remembered.

For most of her life, Raulerson was content with her role as mother and home-maker. "All I've ever done is raise children," she quipped, including her own children as well as her grandchildren.

But the death of her husband forced Raulerson to find a means of support. She began to sell plants grown on the five acres of land surrounding her home on Highland Avenue, which even now is abundant in flowering trees and shrubs, as well as expansive vegetable gardens.

Concentrating in camellias, azaleas, flowers and palm trees, Raulerson made a business out of her gardening hobby. In fact according to Raulerson, several area foliage businesses, a few even as far away as Daytona and New Smyrna Beach, took root with plants from her backyard.

She later retired from her foliage business, due to restrictive zoning and business laws enforced more than a decade ago. Now gardening is again her hobby, and she has also undertaken the task of organizing hundreds of photos, that nearly fill one room of her home and some dating back as the late1800s, which chronicle the growth of Apopka. That seems only fitting for the individual who was a part of much of the city's history."

The Mahaffey Boys

Jim and Tom Mahaffey graduated from Apopka High School.

Let's take a little journey into the past and just imagine we were somewhere around First Street and Forest Avenue in the late 1920s or early 1930s. What was to be known as Edwards Field was being grubbed up by hand with shovels, axes, and grubbing hoes for a baseball field. The field was eventually finished and in the late afternoons, it was the hangout for the youngsters playing their favorite sport. In those days, that was either soccer or baseball.

Jim and Tom Mahaffey

A little to the west (Kit Land Park), was a large, producing citrus grove that covered the entire city block. The large, beautiful oaks you see today were only acorns at the time. Across First Street from where the tennis courts are today was the residence of the Mahaffey family who had moved to Apopka in the 1920s. Their two boys Tom and Jim were two of the many youngsters practicing their skills at baseball in the afternoons, when they were supposed to be working in the ferneries surrounding the area. They could hear their father's Model T Ford as he was returning home from work. It did not matter if they were pitching or playing third base, the rest of the boys knew when they heard that Model T, the Mahaffey boys were on their way home.

Baseball was good to the Mahaffey boys, especially Jim, who developed into one of the finest southpaws to ever pitch for the Apopka Packers of the Lake Orange League. The ferneries that they grew up working in were also good for these hard-working boys. Both of them went on to be very successful in the fern business.

In an interview with Jan Dunn of *The Apopka Chief* in 1986, Tom spoke of how different Apopka was in the 1930s. "My brother and I used to follow a pig trail (now roughly Park Avenue) up to and across Votaw Road, then go left at Thompson Road to Prevatt Lake [near today's Welch Road]. We would see 50-100 wild turkeys on the way," he recalled.

With a great deal of pride, Tom said the only man he ever worked for was Stewart Edwards. Other than that, he grew ferns for himself. Being the industrious young man that he was, Tom's first commercial venture was catching bullfrogs and selling them for ten cents. Catching bullfrogs is one thing, pulling ferns is another, but whatever the reason, Tom made a wise choice in choosing a career growing Boston ferns. He was very successful over the years.

Both boys went through the local school system, and graduated from Apopka High School. His senior year ended with a twist, Tom recalled. "The school board ran out of money, so they closed school a month early, to our delight," he remembered. But, there was no apparent harm, as he said his class had a near perfect grade average.

Tom also remembers when Apopka had two new automobile dealerships, in the 1920s. There was a Ford agency located where Stokes Hardware (Dunkin Donuts) is now, and a Chevrolet agency located on Central between Third and Fourth Streets.

During his school years, Tom was very active in sports. He was a member of the Apopka High School district championship soccer team of 1932, and played on the school's state championship baseball team that same year. His boyhood love of baseball that stemmed from his activities on the baseball field across from his house was later fueled by frequent visits to the area in the 1920s and 1930s by baseball greats such as Lefty Grove, Jimmy Foxx, and Mickey Cochran. Connie Mack, who was the owner/manager of the Philadelphia Athletics, spent his winters at the Mt. Plymouth Hotel and made up his missed Rotary meetings in Apopka. I am sure the other baseball greats followed Mr. Mack to Mt. Plymouth, where there was plenty of golf, fishing, and hunting.

One of my favorite Tom Mahaffey stories involves former Orange County Agricultural Agent Henry Swanson, who asked Tom how the old-time fern growers knew when a cold front was coming, since there were no weather stations to issue such reports. According to Tom, plant growers were generally "warned" of approaching cold weather by southbound trains. If the trains encountered cold weather further north, the engineers would give five long blasts on their whistles as they went through each farming community.

By the time I came along in the plant business in the early 1950s, we received our weather reports from W.T. Berry, agent for the Seaboard Railroad, who received his reports by telegraph and passed them along to interested growers. The Lakeland Frost Warnings Bureau came later; however, most growers agreed that Tom's old system of "five toots" had to be a better system.

Edgar King

Cowboy, U.S. Navy cook, sawmill man, grocer, butcher, and businessman, Edgar King was born in Portsmouth, Virginia, in 1909, the grandson of a wholesale grocer in Norfolk. In 1920, he moved with his father Thomas J., mother Christine, brother Thomas B., grandmother, and uncle to Florida. Christine told her grandchildren they lived at Diamond Springs in the Bay Ridge area. I would guess that she found that area all lively and sparkly.

When Edgar was very young, Morris Pike, Sr. gave him his first pony and that began his love for horses. His pony got loose one day and he tracked it all the way to Mt. Dora on the newly paved road. It is almost tempting to go looking down the road now to see if I can still see those tracks.

He attended Apopka schools, but since his mother taught music at Ocoee High School, he finished and graduated there. At that time, R.G. Pitman, Sr. was the principal.

Although he had a scholarship offer from Stetson University in basketball and baseball, his love for horses made him decide that he wanted to be a veterinarian. He attended the University of Florida, but left college to become a Florida cowboy.

Patsy, Edgar and Sarah King

He herded cattle, broke broncos, and worked for the state dipping cattle for tick fever at a lot of the big ranches in the Kissimmee and St. Cloud area. One of the largest was the McCrory ranch. This was a tract of land owned by the McCrory Chain Store magnate, consisting of some 100,000 acres of game preserve in Orange and Osceola Counties.

During open range time he would ride his horse sometimes through the Rosemont area, in water up to the horse's bridle, to gather up the cattle.

In 1939, Edgar B. King, a pioneer cattleman, claimed that he was "forced" out the cattle business by the trend of fencing in the land. He ran a herd of about 200 cattle in the area known today as Errol Estate, an exclusive housing development. During the spring months, he grazed these cattle on the Apopka marshland, but during the fall and winter months they "wintered" on the high ground where Errol is located now.

He married Rosa Caldwell in 1933, and they had five children, Patsy (Ryan), Sarah (Rich), Nancy (Thomas), Edgar, Jr., and Tina (Douglas). The family had moved closer in to Apopka and was living on a large piece of land.

Edgar and his father Thomas built a grocery store, King's Better Food Store, on Main Street between Park and Central. Unfortunately, the grocery business had to be closed because he was drafted into the Navy.

While he served two years in the Navy, stationed in the South Pacific, his wife Rosa was left without any transportation and five children to take care of.

After the war, he started a sawmill. His sawmill was portable and he moved it to different locations and worked the area until it was logged out. He covered the forests in the Apopka, Winter Garden, and Weewahootee areas. At the same time, he worked at a garage.

In 1949, when he decided to go into business for himself, he bought the Edwards property on the corner of Main Street and Central and started King's Service and Auto Parts. The building housed a restaurant, the White Kitchen, Dale Hall's barber shop, a pool hall, auto parts store, service station, garage, and a new home for his family.

Hwy. 441 was widened in 1957, and he bought the old Stauffer Chemical property on 441 and moved the business to that location. He sold that property and built a new building at 250 E. Third Street in 1973.

When he demolished the Stauffer Chemical building, he carefully salvaged the old beams, bricks, and many other useful items. The bricks were cleaned one by one to be used for his home that he built on Orange Avenue.

In addition to serving the needs of the muck farmers of the area, they started selling boats and motors. The business was expanded to include stores in Altamonte, Fairvilla, Haines City, and Kissimmee.

In 1974, the business was sold to his daughter and son-in-law, Sarah and Dan Rich. They retired in 2001, and their son Dan Rich, Jr. ran the business until it closed in 2009, sixty years after it began.

By far, the title of businessman will be remembered with the name Edgar King, for his contributions to the growth of our city with a business that carried through three generations.

Annie Belle Driggers Gilliam

Annie Belle Driggers Gilliam (known as "Belle") is a true Southern lady with all the spunk and grit of the antebellum era. She was the last of eight children born to Dixie and Mattie Ella Driggers on May 19, 1921, in Kingstree, South Carolina.

In 1923, Annie Belle, her mother, and four siblings departed Kingstree with her half-brother at the wheel of the family Model T Ford. At the same time, her two brothers and a cousin traveled in the coach section of a train while her father rode in one of the two chartered boxcars with their mules, Kit and Pet. They were all bound for a new life in Florida. After four days, the Driggers family arrived in Sorrento on Thanksgiving Day. This seemed appropriate, as her father's philosophy was that God came first, followed by his wife, then his children and afterward, his farm animals that helped provide their living, especially Kit and Pet.

Six years after their arrival in Sorrento, the Driggers family moved to Apopka, where Belle's father opened the Dixie Service Station on Hwy. 441, about a mile west of Apopka.

Belle's first job out of high school was with Mr. Bishop at the Economy Store, as his assistant and chauffeur for 25 cents an hour. Toward the end of her tenure, she worked her way up to $35 per week. During this period she also worked at her father's gas station, pumping gas and waiting on customers in general.

Her mother cooked and served food for the workers of the Pinaflora Packing House that was located next door to the Dixie Service Station. That old packing house building still stands on the corner of the Old Dixie Highway and Cabel Street. Belle later packed and bagged fruit for five cents a box and two cents per bag. She later worked at Plymouth Citrus, where her largest weekly check was $28.28. Belle's philosophy still remains: "It's not what you make; it's what you save."

Belle still remembers the Depression from her childhood days. While times were very difficult, she and her siblings never went to bed hungry. When there was no sugar, the family made syrup cookies, and her mother, an excellent seamstress, sewed for the entire family. In spite of all the hardships, Belle says, "I would not change any phase of my life."

May 16, 1946, was probably the happiest day of Belle's life. That was the day she married Garrett Gilliam. Blessed with two wonderful children, daughter Beverly and son Garrett, Jr., also known as "Boo," the family grew together with plenty of love and happiness.

Belle and Garrett bought his parents' grove service, changing its name from A.F. Gilliam and Son to Gilliam Grove Service, and at the same time worked their own groves. In 1956, the business was sold to Curt Haygood, so they could spend more time with their citrus holdings. After Garrett's death in 1975, Belle, with the help of her friend Calvin Williams, worked her groves until the freezes of 1983 and 1985. Then it was time for her to turn her attention in another direction.

Being more or less an Apopka native, she became interested in Apopka's history and involved herself with the Apopka Historical Society. Belle served the Society as president, vice-president, librarian, and curator and is presently on the board of directors. The greatest contribution she has given to the AHS is her memory. As the author of "Historical Tidbits," I can attest to that, as I have leaned on her memory many times to help me gather information for articles.

Belle is past-president of the Veterans of Foreign War Ladies Auxiliary #5335, and past-president of the United Daughters of the Confederacy-Florence Collier Chapter #1758. Belle received the UDC's Certificate of Recognition, the Judah P. Benjamin award.

The family homestead where I was raised stood approximately where the retention pond for SR 429 and Hwy. 441 is now located. The Dixie Service Station that the Driggers family ran for years was a little east of there, about where the Beverage Store stands today. Obviously, I have known Belle Gilliam all of my life, and because I previously mentioned the happiest days of her life, I can also attest to the fact that life has not been all roses for her.

Although her life has had its share of broken hearts and disappointments, she has always handled them steadfastly, with her beliefs and convictions. God has blessed this community with Belle. We should be thankful.

Grover Robinson

I can still remember Grover Robinson riding his bicycle down Highland Avenue wearing that classic paper sack hat. He would be singing praises to the Lord as he merrily peddled along. He always had a smile and kind words to anyone he met along the way. Mr. and Mrs. Robinson were faithful Baptists and lived only a block or so from the First Baptist Church on Highland. I can remember him well as a Sunday school teacher and member of his daughter Lucy Goolsby's choir in the church. He and his wife always enjoyed an early morning ride on their bicycles for exercise. They also enjoyed walking and reading, and he always liked to quote poetry. Cooking was one of Lena's favorite pastimes.

Lena and Grover Robinson enjoyed riding their bicycles on the streets of Apopka.

Young Grover Robinson watched a pretty, vivacious young lass growing up in his area, outside of Huntington, West Virginia, back in the early 1900s. There was something about her that caught his eye, and none of the other girls seemed to measure up. The only trouble was—Lena Wolfe was ten years younger than he!

But all good things come to he who waits, they say, and Grover waited a mighty long time before Lena "caught up," and he could ask to see her. The couple dated a year or more before they stood in her favorite cousin's home in Portsmouth, Ohio, and said, "I do."

In an interview with Shelby Macey of *The Apopka Chief,* Mrs. Robinson said, "While we were still dating, Grover made a trip here with friends, and kept sending me photos and souvenirs. I just fell in love with Florida, and wanted to live here. We had four children in the next few years, which held things up, but in 1923, three carloads of us, including Grover's uncle and two aunts, traveled here." Traveling with them was Mrs. Robinson's father; mother and brother in a 1914 Ford that Mrs. Robinson says "wouldn't pull the hat off your head."

They well remembered that first trip. It took them thirteen days in a 1912 red-wheeled Essex. Roads were not good in those days, and one day they traveled only twenty miles, having to hire a mule team to pull a certain 1914 Ford up the mountain. They came over the Midland Trail through West Virginia, and the only pavement was from Huntington to Charleston and a few other spots and places along the way.

The visitors spent their first winter at Lake Apopka, camping in tents. Wells Gap, then owned by "Uncle Lee" and Charles Wells, was a West Virginia settlement. Two other West Virginia families who came here at that time were the J. P. Harrises and the Edgells, who will be remembered by many older residents here.

The Robinsons were sold on Florida and kept coming back, making the other trips by train, but they had definitely decided to locate here. They liked the climate, the schools, and the First Baptist Church, where new friends made them feel so welcome, and in 1926 they purchased the property on Highland Avenue for their future home. It was an orange grove owned by Gillen McClure. In the fall of 1928, they came to live here in Apopka and Mr. Robinson went to work for T.J. King, who had a grocery and market in the Witherington building at the corner of Central Avenue and Fourth Street.

When the Robinsons first came to Florida, it never seemed cold to them. They went to the beach in the winter and never thought anything about it. On Christmas Day, they went to Rock Springs. Mr. Robinson says that after they got acclimated, they became "crackers" and began to feel the cold like everyone else.

In 1936, Grover Robinson left King's Better Food Store, purchased Allen's Store on Fourth and Central, and opened his own business. Although he dropped his grocery line after a few years, his meat market (when fish sold for three pounds for 25 cents) was prosperous for many years, until The Consumers and Veneer closed in 1945. The people that worked in the crate mill traded with them and would charge their groceries for a week or two at a time. When the mill closed, the people that worked there moved to Georgia or Alabama and left owing the Robinsons. It was during the Depression and times were hard. It took Mr. and Mrs. Robinson two years to get their wholesale bills paid.

Mr. Robinson retired a few years later and they began to spend considerable time at their home in New Smyrna Beach, resting and relaxing after a full and busy sixty years.

The four Robinson children, Lucy (Mrs. Ray) Goolsby, Mary (Mrs. Edwin) Fly, Alice (Mrs. J. L.) Goolsby, and Leon B. ("Bud") Robinson, all graduated from Apopka High School, and the family has had an active and important part in community life and affairs during all these years.

George McClure

The Apopka Chief used to run a series of articles called "Who's Apopka" by Jan Dunn. She would round up some of the old-timers in the area at the time and write some very interesting interviews. This interview was probably done in the 1980s. This week she chose an old friend of mine, George McClure. George was part of our "round table" group that had coffee every morning in the back of Robinson's Restaurant a few years back. As I have done so many times in the past, I want to quote Jan Dunn's interview in the time frame in which it was written.

"Apopka has had to vary its complexion during its century-plus history to best adapt to changing economies and environments. From its early beginning as a bustling lumber and mill town, to a thriving citrus community, Apopka now is gradually becoming more urbanized, and foliage nurseries have displaced citrus groves as the area's primary agricultural product.

But the core of Apopka, the very heart of the community, has remained rooted to the soil, and its long-time citizens have retained a down-to-earth nature.

Native Apopkan George McClure, as much as anyone, exemplifies the traditional personality of the community, yet he too, as a successful agribusiness man, has diversified his interests to adjust to and best meet changing times.

Born August 1, 1925, the grandson of a pioneer Apopka settler, McClure directs his foliage and citrus business from the same headquarters on South Hawthorne Street where he began his nursery business more than three decades ago. His office is adorned with photos and mementos of his family, and his two admittedly favorite past-times. "I love to fish and hunt" he said, "anytime, anyplace." In fact, in 1934 at the age of nine, McClure was the youngest charter member of the Apopka Sportsman Club.

Despite ravaging freezes in 1957, 1962, and three out of the last five years – that have virtually wiped out his citrus groves, McClure has repeatedly rebuilt his business, literally from the ground up. "In the last freeze I lost every acre of fruit and trees I had in Lake and Orange Counties," he said. "But it is the only thing I know," he said, in explaining his return to citrus farming.

McClure is one of an increasingly small, but deservedly proud group of Apopkans who can claim a two-to-three generation heritage in the Apopka area. His grandfather, H. H. McClure, came to Apopka from north Georgia after the War Between the States, homesteaded a site on Martin's Pond (on the S.E. corner of Main Street and McGee Avenue) and established a citrus farming business. In 1890, he gained a certain bit of notoriety when he displayed at the World's Fair a citrus tree he claimed to have 85 buds that represented 26 different citrus varieties. "It was the hit of the fair," McClure stated.

H.H. McClure was also very active within the growing town, serving as the police chief and mortician. He also ran the riverboat from Wekiwa to Jacksonville. "I still have a millstone from then in my front yard," McClure stated.

His father, George Gillen McClure, continued in the citrus business, began a fernery in the early days of the industry in Apopka, and was a commercial painter. He, too, served the city as a city councilman, mayor, and a county commissioner. McClure's mother was very active in the late 1930's in the PTA, and headed a committee to raise funds for a public health clinic.

George McClure led an idyllic country boy's childhood, hunting and fishing the abundant lakes and forests surrounding Apopka. He was one of 18 in the graduating class of Apopka High School in 1943. The highlight of his high school career, McClure said, was winning the district basketball championship as a senior. "It was the first time Apopka had won the district," he remarked.

Following a three-year stint in the Marine Corps, McClure attended the University of Florida, graduated in 1949 with a degree in agriculture, specializing in citrus. He married the former Nancy Brower of Philadelphia in 1948, and their family grew to include five children and five grandchildren. Nancy McClure is a professional interior designer, and has published a design column in *The Apopka Chief*.

McClure began working as the production manager for the Minute Maid Company in Orlando, but left in 1952 to become production and then general manager for Libby-McNeil-Libby. Under his direction, the company acquired 11,000 acres of prime Central Florida land.

In 1967, McClure left Libby to become a self-employed farmer. He has also become a large landowner, with 300 acres, and highly successful in foliage and citrus production. He has also been a well respected citrus industry leader, serving three terms as a governor-appointed member of the Florida Citrus Commission, from 1972 to 1982. The commission is charged with establishing the rules, regulations, and practices of the state's industry.

And like his father and grandfather before him, McClure served Apopka as a city councilman, in the early 1960s.

McClure still admits he will always remain a dedicated citrus farmer. He even maintains a mini-farm at his home in Apopka that produces grapes, peaches and pears. However, McClure said, he has not recently had a chance to savor his home-grown produce due to a localized competitor. "The squirrels beat me to it," he chuckled."

Dr. Tommy McBride

One of the most beautiful things in life is to be raised in a small town. I was lucky enough to be born and raised in Apopka. You remember so many little things that remain so dear to your heart. Simple things like Hwy. 441 being only two lanes or the Old Dixie Highway when it was all brick and nine feet wide.

You remember that little green schoolhouse where you attended elementary school or the friends you finished high school with. Along the way, there were certain individuals that were larger than life when you were growing up. In my case there were the local barber, Dale Hall, the Mahaffey brothers, Bob Pitman, Fred Odom, Perry Warren, and the local pharmacists, the Sheppard brothers; but most of all I remember the town doctor, Thomas E. McBride. So many people say that he reminded them of Milburn Stone's "Doc" Adams on "Gunsmoke." There probably were similarities. However, I saw Doc Tommy in a little different light. To me he was the perfect Southern gentleman. He truly was bigger than life.

Doc Tommy was born in 1896 in Paris, Missouri. He attended the University of Missouri and graduated from the Jefferson Medical College in Philadelphia, Pennsylvania and completed his medical internship in Erie, Pennsylvania. He moved to Apopka in 1926 and practiced here for the next fifty-two years.

As a young towhead growing up, I had all the aches and bruises that any kid has, including measles, mumps, tonsillitis, fevers, and earaches. In any case, it was always Mama first and Doc Tommy second. Every summer, we spent time at the local swimming hole, Dream Lake, and we would usually end up getting fungus in our ears. It was Doc Tommy to the rescue. The time I drove a rusty nail through my leg, it was on to the Doc's office and a tetanus shot. Lord, how that scared me.

Doc Tommy started out in 1926 in what was then the new Witherington Building on the corner of Main Street and Central. You may remember it as the Henry's Meat Market building. Dr. Cole

Carroll was the local doctor preceding Doc Tommy. After Dr. Carroll's death, Doc Tommy bought his office/apartment building on Park Avenue and Main Street. He moved his family upstairs and established his office downstairs.

He told of delivering four babies in one night, going from one home to the next. While he was at the first house where he was called, there were three other expectant fathers, each one pleading that Doc come immediately to his house. Doc said by morning all the babies had been delivered, and mother and child in each case were doing well. In those early days a lot more medical attention was given in the home. He said he had delivered many babies where the only light in the house was the blaze of crate mill chips burning in the fireplace. Doc Tommy delivered so many babies during his practicing days that he stopped counting at 3,000.

As my wife Joan and I were raising our children, I can remember taking our kids in when they stepped on nails, stuck marbles up their noses or smashed their fingers in the car door. They could be pretty ingenious. However, Doc Tommy had been there before, many times. On the smashed finger, I hysterically asked if he was going to have to cut the finger off. He very quietly looked up and said, "I don't think so, son."

Doc was married in 1927 to Helen Potts, whose parents lived on New Hampshire Street here in Apopka. They had five children: Paul Craig who died as an infant, Thomas Elliot Jr., Robin, Maria, and Mike. Mrs. McBride was a very active woman who strove to improve herself and the status of women in general. She was active in athletics, especially in tennis, but was mostly known as a cross-country pilot. She was the sole female pilot among more than 100 planes that flew to the New York World's Fair. I can also remember her participation in the Powder Puff Derby.

Dr. McBride was the dean of the medical profession in Apopka and Northwest Orange County. He was instrumental in establishing the West Orange Memorial Hospital in Winter Garden, and later on, was instrumental in starting the community hospital in Apopka.

He served as president of the Orange County Medical Society, was a life member of the Florida State Medical Association, and was also a member of the Southern Medical and American Medical Associations. His many professional awards are too many to list in this short article.

Probably the one civic accomplishment he was most proud of was fifty years of perfect attendance at the Apopka Rotary Club. Doc served as president of the Apopka Sportsman Club. He was elected a Harris Fellow of the Rotary International in 1977, and also received the Outstanding American Award from the Apopka Jaycees in 1972. Again, Dr. McBride received many other commendations for his services in local civic organizations.

Doc Tommy was the brother to a highly successful radio personality of the 1930s and the 1950s. She was Mary Margaret McBride, who broadcast five days a week in her folksy, warm Missouri voice. She always interviewed the people of the hour. That would include Bob Hope, Jimmy Durante, Frank Lloyd Wright, Carl Sandburg, Zora Neal Hurston, Elizabeth Taylor, and Admiral Byrd, to mention only a few. She talked to whoever had the spin of the day. Some have suggested that Mary Margaret was the Oprah Winfrey of her day.

You develop such wonderful relationships in a small town; however, the small town giveth but it also taketh away. Dr. Thomas E. McBride died just before Christmas in 1978. He was 82 years old. I know of no other individual who earned so much love and respect from his community as Doc Tommy.

W. R. McGuffin

W.R. "Mac" McGuffin moved to Apopka in 1964, and is best known for publishing Apopka's local newspapers and for his community service. After visiting with a friend in Orlando, Mac was encouraged to stay in the Orlando area, but being a small-town boy, he investigated Sanford, Kissimmee, St Cloud, Leesburg, and Apopka. After several visits to Apopka and attending local churches, Mac and his wife Delores and two children, Pat and Kathleen made Apopka their home.

Mac McGuffin was born into an Ohio River steamboat family. Educated in Ohio high schools, he was on his way to college when World War II began.

He enlisted in the Air Force and graduated from several military schools on his way to being assigned to an Inspector General's team. After a two-year assignment with the Strategic Air Command, he was promoted to the Pentagon, where he was assigned to the Information Collection Division of the Director of Intelligence.

While assigned at the Pentagon he met and later married Delores in February 1952. Shortly after he finished a CIA training activity, he was assigned to the Alameda Naval Air Station in California. Then he received additional training at a classified airfield in Nevada and spent the next two years working out of the Alameda NAS.

Following that assignment, he was reassigned to the Pentagon and after additional training was assigned to the field in England, Scotland, and France. It was when he was in northern England that he received the news that his son Patrick was born at Ft. Belvoir, Virginia, in January, 1956. Kathleen was born at the U.S. Army Hospital at Landstuhl, Germany. Later that same year, he was assigned to the headquarters of the United States Air Force in Europe at Wiesbaden, Germany.

From that assignment, he traveled quite often to the Middle East, and was in Iraq, Egypt, Iran, Saudi Arabia, Lebanon, and Jordan. Later trips took him throughout Africa, from the Union of South Africa to Cairo, and from Eritrea to what was Leopoldville, the capitol of the Belgian Congo, and to Alexandria, Egypt. Mac traveled and worked in forty-four countries during his military career, and held the highest security clearance possible at that time.

Following that four-year tour, he was transferred to San Antonio, Texas, to be the NCOIC of the Air Force Electronic Security Service intelligence data activities. He finally retired in 1964 and headed for Florida.

During his military career, Mac saw the first Air Force jet fly in 1943, six years before it was mass-produced. He has been in the White House, the Pentagon sub-basement, and the Situation Room (war room) on official business. He has seen the Egyptian Pyramids, the Sphinx, and Victoria Falls in Africa, and he has been forced down in an airplane by a sandstorm near Alexandria, Egypt. He was caught in a communist uprising in Tehran, Iran, along with a U.S. Army General and escaped to find the American Embassy.

Shortly after making Apopka home for himself and his family, Mac bought and sold several small businesses in Orlando and Apopka. Then he became interested in the newspaper business and started publishing a local weekly newspaper called *The Apopka Planter*. The name came from the people in the indoor foliage business, from which Apopka received its title of the Indoor Foliage Capitol of the World.

He had competition from *The Apopka Chief*, the city's newspaper which was established in 1923. After he received a lot of technical information from the publisher of the Leesburg daily newspaper, Mac stepped deeper into the newspaper business. He had not been prepared for the indifference Apopkans had for him and his newspaper. However, that slowly melted away and many of those indifferent acquaintances became close friends. They were not prepared for a newspaperman like Mac, who ignored some civic organizations in order to print what he felt was best for the community, not what was best for a few individuals. He later bought the *Apopka Chief* and made it into the top newspaper in Florida for its circulation category in 1974.

The *Apopka Chief* newspaper was well known under Mac's ownership for its strong investigative stories and hard-hitting editorials that helped to shape the Apopka community in the 1960s and 1970s. The papers were well respected in political circles, and presidential candidate Jimmy Carter stopped by the office. McGuffin also later met presidential candidate George H.W. Bush. Several Florida governors, senators, and representatives also stopped by in an attempt to get the endorsement of McGuffin's newspapers.

Mac sold the newspapers in December of 1979, and he and his wife traveled in their RV until she died in February 2000. He then turned his attention to writing fiction books, five of which have been published as of the date of this book. At age eighty-eight, he is still cranking out fiction books. His latest book, "High Heels," is in editorial review and will probably be published around Thanksgiving 2011.

Additionally, the McGuffins started Apopka Office Supply, Apopka Printing, and the *Florida Boater* magazine. They also built an apartment complex in Apopka and had other business ventures. Mac has also served Apopka as a city councilman.

Mac and Delores were active in raising money for the Florida Hospital Foundation for many years and chaired the Foundation when it was raising the money to expand the much-needed emergency room. He was also a founding member of the Foliage Sertoma Club, which has produced the Apopka Christmas Parade for decades. Raising money for worthy local charities became the McGuffins' primary focus after they sold the newspapers."

Warren "Ed" Lockeby

Kyle and Lorene Lockeby raised their family in Tifton, Georgia. Kyle had a chain of variety stores in South Georgia. In 1930, they traveled to Thomasville, Georgia, where Lorene's parents lived, for the birth of their son Warren E. "Ed" Lockeby in 1930.

The Lockeby family, including Ed's older brother Kyle, Jr. and Richard, lived in Tifton, Georgia, until Kyle, Sr. retired and the family moved to Daytona Beach in 1945. Ed, however, stayed in Georgia and attended the Darlington School in Rome Georgia, where he graduated in 1949.

Ed, Mary Ann, Warren and Greg Lockeby

After graduation, he attended the University of Florida from 1949 to 1950. He spent his summers between high school and his early college years working as a lifeguard on Daytona Beach. This is where he met Mary Ann Dykes from Montezuma, Georgia, who was in Daytona Beach visiting relatives. Their first date was a blind date, but Mary Ann would tell you, "That is another story."

In 1950, Ed joined the U.S. Air Force and spent most of his time at Reese Air Force Base in Lubbock, Texas. It was during this period that he and Mary Ann were married, and subsequently, their first son Warren, Jr. was born.

After Ed's discharge from the Air Force, he came back to Florida and re-entered the University of Florida. While in school, their second son W. Gregory was born, and the family moved back to Daytona Beach where Ed obtained his real estate license and worked as a broker until the late '50s.

When the real estate business slowed down, Ed began working with his brother in the construction business.

Ed and Mary Ann began traveling throughout Central Florida hoping to find a small town where they could invest in a growing community. They moved to Apopka in 1963 when they found property on Fifth Street and purchased it to build a shopping center where Ed opened Warren's 5&10. The 5&10 operated until 1979. You could find anything you needed in that store; it was a great addition to the business community.

Somewhere in the late '70s, a gang of thieves was terrorizing the local merchants, and Apopka Police Chief Johnny Holloway asked permission to sit on top of Ed's building as a lookout place to try to catch the thieves. Nothing happened that evening, so about midnight, they decided to give up and climb down. However, someone had stolen Holloway's ladder. He still does not remember how they all got down.

Ed was President of the Apopka Rotary from 1971 to 1972. He was a member of the Apopka Zoning Board and the Orange County Board of Zoning Adjustments. He also served as a volunteer fireman and EMT. At that time, Leroy Gilliam was the fire chief, and the Apopka Fire Department was all-volunteer. Ed was an honorary captain and always helped with the barbecue fundraisers which were held in the fire department's parking lot.

For years, Ed taught Sunday school at the First Baptist Church of Apopka and is currently enjoying retirement.

T. A. Shepherd

The time was the early 1930s. The place was West Orange County.

The kid knocking 'em over the fence of his hometown's Field of Dreams, not to mention scoring touchdowns and making baskets, was T.A. Shepherd.

Tom Allen Shepherd, a player on the first ever Ocoee football team later piled up the points for Lakeview High School in Winter Garden. Johnny Davis was his, "awfully good coach," whatever the game. "One coach did it all in those days."

The kid, who had come to Winter Garden as a toddler with his parents from Cuthbert, Georgia, a decade earlier, was good.

T.A. Shepherd's athletic talents had won him a ball-playing scholarship to Rollins College. He never got to use the scholarship. A sports injury during his senior year took him off the best high school team in Central Florida that season. It also ended his chances of playing for a college team.

On and off the playing fields and courts, T.A. Shepherd was a hard worker. When not in class or athletic competition, the teenager would be, "doing a little bit of everything" at his after-school job with Cappleman's Grocery.

Winter Garden was home for young T.A. Shepherd from 1920 to 1945. In 1945, he moved to Apopka where he has lived ever since. Apopka, however, was only one of several Florida towns in which he would spend his growing-up years.

"Daddy built roads for the Comb Company in Tampa, so we moved around," he said. Changing jobs took the family from one coast to the other, from Bradenton and Sarasota to West Palm Beach.

T.A. graduated from Bradenton High School; he then studied accounting and bookkeeping for two semesters at Walls Business School in Sarasota.

He then took a job with the old Florida Power, which was called Florida Public Service at that time. That brought him back to Winter Garden.

During World War II, T.A. was called up for service three times and was turned down three times. Unstable kneecaps kept him on the home front. His knee problems were, "Because when I was a kid, I played so much ball for high school."

In the early 1940s, T. A. Shepherd, not far into his 20s yet, he found his personal niche and calling in the business world. He started out in the dry cleaning and laundry business in Sebring, and made it his lifelong career.

On March 12, 1945, Shepherd became Apopka's dry cleaner. Fern City Cleaners had already been in business since around 1920 when Shepherd purchased it from Reuben Wells.

After forty-six years of owning and operating the dry cleaning company, Shepherd still shows up for work daily. He only takes time off for traveling, fishing, and hunting at a Georgia gun and boat club and camp, which he started with another Apopkan twenty-two years ago.

Travels have taken T.A. and his wife Jane to France, Portugal, Spain, Greece, Mexico, and other places. The International touring, however, "is more for Jane," he says. Jane, a retired Dream Lake Elementary School teacher and Mount Dora native was teaching at Tildenville and living next door to T.A.'s mother when she met her future husband.

The couple have been married fifty-two years. They have three grown children – Tom, Martha, and Anna – and four grandchildren.

"I'd rather be fishing or hunting," T.A. says. His interests over the years have also included community service work. He is a charter member of Apopka's Breakfast Sertoma Club, a former club president, and has been an Apopka Rotary member for twenty-three years.

He has been active in the Apopka Area Chamber of Commerce, "ever since there's been one," and is a member of First Baptist Church of Apopka.

At seventy-five, T.A. Shepherd does not ever consider retiring. "Why retire? You sit down and go crazy. I've seen too many people saying, 'I wish to hell I was back working.' So many tell me, 'I'd rather be working.'"

As long as the, "right good health," he now enjoys continues, and, "as long as I can hunt and fish when I want to, I'll stay on the job," he said.

Right now, the former ball player is eagerly contemplating some trips to Georgia, "two or three times a month, every chance I get, from the first of bow season through turkey season."

Walter Stokes

Walter Stokes stands by his display of trashcans as the traffic passes by on Hwy. 441.

Walter Stokes certainly could never say he was not a Florida cracker. His grandfather came to Florida in 1850 and homesteaded land in Marion and Citrus Counties, finally settling in the small community of Gaiter at the point where you cross the Withlacoochee River into Citrus County. He ran the ferry there for many years, and later Walter's father took over until they built a steel bridge somewhere between 1880 and 1890.

Walter's early schooling was at Gaiter, Dunnellon, and Ocala. Later, he lived in Jacksonville with his sister. During his days at Gaiter, he fell in love with his teacher. That was when he was twelve years old. He wrote her a letter telling her just exactly how he felt. Now, that might have been a mistake. The post office was in a local home, and the family opened his letter and showed it to Walter's father. His dad said, "If all you can think of is love, you can stay home the rest of the year and plow." That is exactly what Walter did.

During the Depression, Walter was in Jacksonville with his sister and finally secured employment with Florida Hardware, which was a wholesale hardware company. He worked there for fifteen years learning the hardware business. He felt that he had put in enough time in Jacksonville, so he moved to Gainesville and went to work for Folds Hardware Company.

Three years after getting married to his wife Pauline, they purchased a general merchandise business in Reddick, Florida, that they ran for about seven years. They did not care for the general merchandise business and were on the lookout for a hardware business.

They had friends at Florida Hardware, and they told him that Ryan & Company in Apopka wanted to sell their hardware store. He contacted Nat and Mark Ryan, and Walter and the Ryans came to an agreement. Walter and Pauline purchased the store at 212 E. Main Street, Apopka, to be known for the rest of its forty years as Stokes Hardware & Supply Company. This is where Dunkin' Donuts now stands.

Jeannine Loiacono, a *Sun* staff writer, said it well in 1990, when she wrote in an interview, "Walking into Stokes Hardware in the heart of Apopka is like walking through a door into the past. The air is thick with the smell of dust and iron. The scent invokes images of men who work hard for a living, who with just their hands and a few tools built houses or ran a farm. It is dark in the store, but where the sunlight filters through the front windows, a thin layer of dust can be seen covering the pots and the pans, the nails, and the ancient plow in the front window. Home Depot this isn't."

And that is the way Walter Stokes liked it. He bought that store in 1952 and ran it the same way until 1992. Of course, over the years, modern tools were added to his inventory. Power drills shared the shelves with their manual counterparts, but it was easy to get the impression that Stokes liked to do things the old-fashioned way.

Walter said," Stores like Home Depot and Scotty's have to pay rent, so their prices are higher. Well I haven't paid rent in forty-five years. I haven't borrowed money in twenty years, and I haven't had a sale in thirty."

Stokes never would give out his exact age; however, he would say he was well over eighty. "I've been married ninety-four years," he said with a laugh. Forty-nine to my wife and forty-five to this store. I've put more time into hardware than any other merchant in Florida."

Through the years, Stokes saw many changes in his business. "I've got a garden plow that used to run $4.95, now (1990) its $75.00. I've got locks in here that, if you asked for them at one of those chain stores, they wouldn't know what you were talking about. Competition from those chain stores doesn't bother me. I've got customers that have been coming here since I opened."

Stokes said, "I have seen plenty of changes in Apopka. The only thing that has not changed is that Apopka still has the same mayor as when I came to Apopka."

The growth of Apopka has not affected his business, Stokes said. "We get too much traffic out there," pointing his arm in the direction of Hwy. 441. "It doesn't bring people in, they are just bypassing town. They could close every chamber in Florida, and we would still be growing too fast," he said.

Stokes, who in the midst of talking about the store in his interview with Jeannine, pulled out some old photographs of bass he had caught over the years and said he had no immediate plans to retire. He loves the business, he said, but he could think of other things to do. "If I had time to golf, I'd go fishing," he said.

So you want to know his secret to running a successful business for all these years? "Have what they want, and do not overcharge them," he said. "That's all."

John Talton

Sheri Baker wrote an article about John Talton in *Florida Agriculture* back in 1979. I think it said a lot about who John was and something about the business he was in:

"People respond differently to opportunity, as the saying goes. There are those who wait for it to happen; those who watch it happen; and those who make it happen. John Talton has never been one to wait and watch.

Born in Apopka just a half a mile from his present home, Talton knew early in life he wanted to be a farmer. His father grew some citrus, but spent most of his time tending the small bank he started in 1911 – the only bank of Orange County to survive the Depression. One of six children, Talton worked in the groves while attending high school and it wasn't long before he decided to plant some of his own citrus and ferns.

'Apopka was known years ago as the Fern City,' Talton recalls. 'They grew millions of them. They raise a lot of them now, but they didn't raise anything but fern in the nursery business then.'

Time passed and Talton's business grew. So did his passion for farming. He expanded his operation by purchasing some cattle and chickens, and settled down to a rather hectic, but never dull, life on the farm.

To say that Talton is proud of his occupation would be an understatement. His family, however, brings him an even greater source of pride. He met his wife, Rudein, while both were working for a Florida power company and they were married during World War II. Their eldest daughter, Louise, is a pharmacist in Melbourne, and their other daughter, Ann, is pursuing the same career at the University of Florida. Although their son, John Jr., graduated from UF's college of agriculture with a masters degree in food crops, he has chosen not to farm for a living.

Said Talton, 'I remember the day John came to me and said, 'Daddy, I don't want to farm. You have to work too hard, there's no money in it, and it's too hot out there,' so he went to dental school and now works in his air-conditioned office in Georgia.

But Talton doesn't mind the perspiration and proved he could withstand a different kind of heat by spending 18 years on the Orange County Commission. 'I like politics,' said Talton, 'but being a public official is pretty abusive. I got clobbered more on the commission than I ever have in farming. You get calloused to it, though, and I guess that's why I don't get discouraged too much.'

Talton has actively participated in community-related agricultural endeavors, especially when the issues involved the land. He has been a director of Orange County Farm Bureau for about 30 years and also serves on Florida Farm Bureau's board as treasurer.

An average day with John Talton, if you could keep up with him that long, would take you winding through his farms by pickup truck, checking details and ironing out problems. He prefers to drive in silence, choosing not to have a radio or CB (says he has enough worries without people calling in with more).

'I often wonder just how young people are going to get into farming in the future. The first thing they must overcome is the economic problem of finances," said Talton. "If he doesn't have a father or a friend – someone that could help him – I don't know how he could make it.' Talton said he feels extremely fortunate to have made it and insists he would not be happy doing anything else.

I talked to this barber once who said to me that 60 percent of the people who sit in his chair hate to go to work in the morning. I love my work. I always have. I like horses and love cows. I like to round 'em up or just be around them. I like to ride through my groves, too. A citrus tree to me is one of the prettiest things I know of – the golden fruit, the white bloom, the green leaves. I love the fragrance, too, and of course if the price is right, it makes it all too much easier to smell the bloom.'

Talton readily agrees, though, that money cannot buy, nor does it guarantee, contentment. 'I've always told my kids the first thing in life they ought to look for is happiness. Money second,' said Talton. 'Money makes life a lot easier, but happiness in the mind is number one.'

Although he admits that one day he'd like to try farming in some of the muck out in his area, Talton said he's not shooting for too many goals in the future.

'I'm not trying to go to the moon or anywhere else,' he said. 'I've got good health, a lovely wife, and three super children. What more could you want?'

For John Talton, probably the only other thing he could want is more time. Time to spend doing more of the things he's already done. Appreciating the fact he'll never have more than 24 hours a day, he said he realizes the importance of making every minute count.

'I live by two sayings,' said Talton. 'If you don't have time to fish, you don't have time.' And his favorite, the one that describes his philosophy best, 'Take the time to smell the roses.'"

Bill Arrowsmith

Sometimes a little vacation can bring surprising results, especially when it happens here in beautiful Central Florida.

When Elizabeth and William Arrowsmith were living in Elmira, New York, their best friend was assigned to manage the Officer's Club in Orlando. At the friend's insistence, they came here for a two-week vacation and virtually never left. William fell in love with the area and said, "I'm not going back," so he sent his wife back to pack up and sell their home.

She flew down about a month later with Bill and his three-month-old twin brothers Pat and Mike. His sister Sandy remained behind to live with an aunt and uncle until she came to Florida and graduated from the University of Florida.

Bill was about eight years old, but he still remembers the magnificent smell of the orange blossoms when he stepped off the plane at Herndon Airport.

The family lived in the Winter Park area for a while, but Bill's mother wanted to live outside of the city. They found property off of Wekiwa Springs Road in Wekiwa Hills and built a home on Lake Alma in 1956. At that same time, they were blessed with beautiful little Tina. Bill can remember having to walk to Votow and Thompson Road to catch the school bus.

He started school at Apopka Elementary (now City Hall) in the 4th grade, and he recalls that his teacher was Mrs. John Anderson, and his 5th grade teacher was Virginia Walters. Bill went on to Apopka Memorial High School and graduated with the class of 1964.

During 1964 and 1965, Bill likes to say that he attended LSU (Lake Sumter Community College) while working part time at Winn-Dixie.

He was drafted into the U.S. Army in 1966, and after basic training, he returned home to Apopka and married Wanda Warren. He spent the next two years in Colorado Springs as a battalion supply sergeant. Bill and Wanda had three children – Natalie, Jon, and Robin. They now have five grandchildren – D.J., Anabelle, Luke, Cash, and Lily.

When Bill returned home from the Army, his friend Jay Gilliard got him a job with a department store distributor out of Atlanta selling men and boys clothing and textiles. He said that the job was good, and he was making $150 a week. He was proud that he was able to buy a new Camero and a new home. The problem with the job was that he was on the road constantly and was unhappy having to be gone most of the time.

He had met Stewart Green at the State Bank of Apopka many years before when he tried to talk his mother into letting him buy a 1965 Mustang when he was just nineteen. His mother had taken him to see Stewart, and Stewart wisely explained to Bill that he would probably be drafted soon, and it would be not fair to leave the burden of the car payments to his mother. This was the first time Stewart turned him down.

So, when he was tired of the department store business, he went to Stewart a second time and asked for a job at The State Bank of Apopka. Once more, Stewart said that he would not be a wise move for Bill at that time. However, Bill was persistent, and finally, Stewart hired him in the bookkeeping department in 1968. When he received his first check for his first two weeks of work, it was only $121, and he said, "What have I done?" In the long run, it was the best thing he could have done. He rose to vice president of marketing but left the job 1979.

The reason for leaving the bank was that his good friend Will Smathers owned a popular restaurant (The Lamp Post) in Mt. Dora. The two men met one night, and Bill said, "I want to go into the restaurant business." Will answered, "Would you believe it, I wanted to talk to you about going into the banking business." The discussion went like this: "Bill, you can come and work for me in the restaurant for a year, and after that, if you are still interested, I will help you every way I can to get established in the business." Well, Bill did go to work with him and did everything at the restaurant from washing dishes to tending bar, and he enjoyed it.

In 1979, Bill purchased property to build a restaurant in Apopka; unfortunately, that happened to coincide with a great recession at which time interest rates reached twenty-one percent. He found out quickly that this was not going to be a feasible venture.

The Bank of Central Florida hired Bill in 1981, and the bank flourished with his personal attention to customer service. The bank built a new bank building at the corner of Edgewood Dr. and Monroe where Bill was market president until 2002.

He began working at BankFirst at Wedgewood and Main in 2002 and continues to serve there as the market president.

Bill is presently married to Janine, and they will celebrate their seventeenth anniversary in February of 2012. They have worked at Dream Lake Elementary as mentors for the past twelve years. Bill said they found out that one of the children they were mentoring was not going to have anything for Christmas one year, so they gathered toys, etc. and took them to the child's house. Of course, that child was extremely happy. Bill said it is tremendously rewarding to see the faces of those children when he and his wife go to the school to read or play games with the children.

His dedication to the Apopka city government is amazing. He has served as a city commissioner for thirty-six years and is currently the vice mayor of Apopka.

He is a past president of the Apopka Jaycees and remembers that Arlen Mizell got him into the group, and that they all worked on the Foliage Festival that was held at the Bowling Alley (now Mosquito Creek). Robbie Roberson was a part of that group also, and Bill has fond memories of the many "road trips" in the motor home to football games in Kentucky, Auburn, Tallahassee, and Gainesville. Joan and I joined him on a couple of those trips ourselves.

Bill's legacy of community involvement is indeed impressive. He was a founding member of the Apopka Sertoma Club, past director and five-year coach of Apopka Little League, past trustee of North Orange Memorial Hospital and was instrumental in bringing emergency room services to Apopka for the past thirty years. As Chairman of the North Orange Memorial Hospital Scholarship Committee for the past thirty years, they have awarded over $550,000 to Apopka area students pursuing a career in medicine.

He has been president, trustee, or director of many more service organizations here in Orange County as well as Seminole and Osceola Counties. Bill received the "Rotarian of the Year" award and the Apopka Chamber's "Businessman of the Year" award. He is a lifetime member of the Apopka Historical Society and a member of Grace Pointe Church.

When I asked him what his plans for the future were, he said, "I plan to run for the City Council again next year in March. I feel that I represent the business side of the commission." I say, "Good Luck, Bill."

Catherine (Kit) Land Nelson

Kit wanted to make a difference in people's lives. She had so much influence on the people she came in contact with here in Apopka and far beyond.

Kit Land Nelson was a twin. She and her twin brother Jim, were born in Plant City, Florida in June of 1923 at the family home of her grandparents. Her mother, Josephine Land returned there to have her children while living on Alabama Avenue here in Apopka. She was raised with her six other sibling in a loving and active home. Her father, Bennett Land, owned and ran Consumers Lumber and Veneer, passed away in 1935. Josephine (Miss Jo, or "Nanny" to the grandchildren) raised the children on her own.

A graduate of Apopka High School, she and her best friend, Janet Connelly, attended Florida State College for Women in Tallahassee, Florida. She was active in her sorority, Alpha Gamma Delta and stayed active all her life. They both graduated in 1946. A little known activity was her interest in the Flying High Circus that Florida State was famous for. According to her brother, Mayor John Land, he believes that she and Janet were instrumental in bringing an exhibition to Apopka shortly after they graduated.

Following graduation, Kit worked as a social worker for Orange County for several years. At one time, she was a partner with Janet Connelly in the Fern Nook Gift Shop and worked as advertising manager of The Apopka Chief while Janet was the Editor.

In February of 1950, she married Brasher Parker (B.P) Nelson, from Orlando. They lived in Lakeland, Florida while B.P. worked for Hughes Supply and while there, adopted their first son, Mark. The family moved back to Apopka and shortly after that they added adoptees Stephen in 1957 and Kimberly in 1964, to complete their family.

Kit stayed busy raising her family, teaching at Lovell Elementary School and being involved in the community and many of the organizations. She was active in both the Girl Scouts and Boy Scouts. For years, her house was headquarters for the annual Girl Scouts of American cookie sale.

As a charter member of the Apopka Historical Society, she served as President. She was also a charter member of the Apopka Woman's Club, serving in many offices as well as president. She was instrumental in initiating the annual Folk festival sponsored by that group for many years, a key figure in the annual Apopka Art and Foliage Festival, and a charter of the Nasturtium Circle, which later became the Foliage Garden Club of Apopka.

Kit epitomized the "multi task" description of any person, as she was constantly into some kind of project. In 1977, she was recognized as the Apopka Citizen of the Year by the Chamber of Commerce. In presenting the award to Kit, Miss Burnie Roberts, executive director of the chamber, recited her many community activities. Miss Roberts was quoted as saying, "Kit Nelson was involved in 27 separate community projects, from start to finish".

Her brother, John related one of her Multi-task entertaining skills. Each year on New Year's Day, she would have Open House and invite everyone to drop by for hog jowls, black-eyed peas, rice, collard greens and some of her good corn bread. They would come by from 11:00 to 6:00 and she would make everyone feel welcome and happy.

While talking with her son, Stephen, he said, "I wish I had known her when she was in high school or college. I've heard stories from some very reliable sources (who shall remain nameless) that would surprise you. Who would have thought that my Mom, pillar of the community, would have done....well. Perhaps I should keep the secrets private. Let's just say that she had a great sense of humor and adventure. There are stories about spitting water from between her front teeth to wearing all of her skirts on a bus ride home from college (a luggage issue, I suppose). Perhaps the riddle of how she broke her finger while on a trip to Europe while traveling with her life-long buddy, Janet, is forever lost to us."

"One of the sweetest stories I will relate was Mom's love of the Thornwell Home for Children in Clinton, South Carolina. At our church each year, we took up a collection for the children living at Thornwell. The Presbyterian Women sponsored a child each year sending clothing and other items. I believe that this was a very special opportunity for Kit. Throughout her life and in a special memorial gift she supported Thornwell."

"She spread her love of family and community so often each year. For Valentine's Day each year, she baked valentine shaped cakes, iced them, and personalized them. Though we may have griped a bit about having to be the delivery service when we were old enough to "do duty", I think we all learned a valuable lesson of love and giving to others. Even after her death, I have tried three or four times to make those cakes. Not once did they match Mom's delicious cakes, but they were always delivered (and accepted) with many smiles and sweet remembrances."

Her dedication to the First Presbyterian Church kept her quite busy serving as a ruling elder, deacon, Sunday school teacher, Vacation Bible School leader, life member of Presbyterian Women where she served a circle leader and moderator. Her sister-in-law, Flo Nelson was quoted as saying, "When Kit asked for help on her multitude of civic and church projects, it was presented as an "opportunity" and rarely did anyone turn her down".

On the day of her death, two community members proposed to the city council that the City Park, the site of so many Foliage Festivals put on by the Apopka Woman's Club, be renamed in her honor. Her son, Stephen said, "She would not have wanted the honor, and she never knew of it as she passed away hours after the council approved the request. She now lives on not just in many folk's memories but in "her park" which is now Kit Land Nelson Park".

Earl Nelson

The Nelson family has always had strong ties to agriculture. In the early 1930s, Olin and Mabel Nelson moved to Palm Bay from Birmingham, Alabama, with their five-year-old son B.P. and baby Earl. There, Olin raised chickens for the eggs, and had two cows and a big garden.

When the family moved to Orlando in 1938, in keeping with his agricultural roots, Olin planted citrus trees in his yard. While still in high school, Earl built a greenhouse and a slat shed in the back yard. He started growing orchids, and as the business flourished, his mother Mabel became his partner. Together, they sold the orchids to neighbors and the Orchid Society.

One of his first jobs while he was in high school was at a grocery store where his main job was sweeping the floors for ten cents an hour. While working diligently to impress his boss, he accidentally broke a bottle of Roma wine. When Earl offered to pay for the wine, the owner made him pay full retail price, and that is when he quit that job and went to work for a another grocery store for fifteen cents an hour. That store eventually became Publix.

At his parent's home, enterprising Earl had forty-three rabbits which he kept well fed and sold them to the store where he worked. One day, he called his mother and asked her to skin two rabbits because he had a sale that day. She never skipped a beat and had them ready for Earl to deliver to the store immediately. I get the impression that there was a special bond between Earl and his mother.

Both B.P. and Earl graduated from Orlando High School and attended the University of Florida.

After several tries to pass a hated humanities course at the University of Florida, B.P. decided to leave and seek his fortune with Hughes Supply in Orlando. B.P. married Catherine "Kit" Land, an Apopka native, and they settled in Apopka. They had three children – Mark, Stephen, and Kim.

Like so many families at that time, they started a small greenhouse in their backyard, which led B. P. to visualize going into the nursery business on a larger scale.

In 1950, B.P. talked his father into getting into the foliage business. That was the beginning of O.F. Nelson and Sons Nursery. They bought twenty acres on Sheeler Road where they started growing indoor foliage plants under a slat shed. Olin ran the nursery until B.P. left Hughes Supply and came to join him in the nursery.

Back then, there was no plastic to cover the slat sheds, and the nursery was heated with grove heaters. One of the hardships of keeping the plants from freezing was that either the heaters burned up the plants or the plants froze because they were out of range of the sporadic heat. In a heavy freeze in 1957, they lost a great deal of their plants.

Earl graduated from the University of Florida in 1957, and in the same week married Flo Johnson. They had met at Memorial Jr. High School in Orlando, and they both attended the same church. Earl's dad asked him where she came from. When he told him that she was from Georgia, his dad smiled and said, "She's okay, Son."

After graduation, Earl had been working as the assistant county agriculture agent in Manatee County. He left that job in 1958, and he and a very pregnant Flo moved, and Earl joined his dad and brother to become the grower at the nursery. Earl and Flo's son Bryan was born that September, and their son Scott was born two years later during Hurricane Donna.

They built the nursery up to where it covered thirty-four acres. In the beginning, they grew mainly pertussum and philodendrons. Earl recalls one of the biggest deals in the early days of the business was when they were finally able to fill one-half of a semi-truck with boxes of plants for shipment. They went on to fill many semi-trucks throughout the years they were in business.

When they found a need to diversify from indoor foliage plants, Earl, who loved flowers, went to see a small rose grower in Bradenton. He was out of roses but had some rootstock for sale. Earl purchased the plants and planted them by Flo's clothesline in the yard at his house. Sheets and diapers got tangled in the roses, but there they grew. Earl experimented with cutting and grafting the Fortuniana rootstock onto various roses. He developed a rose that was to be strictly grown here in Florida. The company decided that raising roses offered the diversification that the nursery needed, so they started propagating them.

They grew about 500 roses on the first trial, but they didn't sell. They were dejected and almost gave up until orders started coming, and they sold all of them. That inspired them to start growing in a big way. They named them "Nelson's Florida Roses."

In the 1960s, the Nelsons revolutionized the growing of roses when they developed an assembly line method of producing container-grown plants on a hardy rootstock which could thrive in a variety of conditions here in Florida. According to Henry Swanson, "The success of Nelson's...mass-producing almost a hundred different varieties of roses on this new root stock made the name Nelson's Florida Roses almost a variety name rather than a trade name."

Over the years, in one way or another, the entire Nelson clan has participated in the nursery. Kit and Flo worked in the office for many years. All of the children – Mark, Bryan, Kim, Bryan, and Scott – pulled weeds and did other chores at the nursery. As adults, Mark, Bryan, and Scott had a significant part in running the business. Now Mark, B.P.'s son, is the owner of Nelson's Florida Roses and is continuing the family tradition of raising the best blooming plants in the industry.

Bryan, Earl's son, left the nursery to start his own insurance agency and then added a political career as state representative for District 38. Bryan and his wife Debbie have two children – Reed and Linda. Reed is with the credit department of Old Florida National Bank, and Linda, now Mrs. Doug Knudsen, works with her dad at the insurance agency.

Scott, Earl's youngest son, worked both at the nursery and then had his own nursery. He then left to pursue his other love, hunting, and to work in sales at Gander Mountain. In 2009, he had a tragic accident which has rendered him a quadriplegic. He and Sandi have two girls – Sarah and Amanda. Sarah is a budding craftsman, and Amanda is in pre-nursing at Seminole State College.

Earl is readily recognized for his vast assortment of suspenders. A belt was never enough to keep his trousers up, especially when he was carrying trays of plants at the nursery. One Christmas, B.P. gave him a pair of L.L. Bean red suspenders. B.P. swore Earl's productivity increased a hundred fold, as he no longer had to hold up his pants with one hand while carrying trays of plants with the other.

After retiring, Earl volunteered with the International Executive Service Corps., traveling to Ghana, Egypt, Macedonia, and Ukraine. To keep his fifty-two year perfect attendance in Rotary, he made a special effort to make up meetings in all the foreign countries he visited. Flo and Earl now live their quiet life surrounded by what else, beautiful "Nelson's Florida Roses."

Fred Brummer

When Fred and Cathi Brummer arrived in Apopka in 1981, it was clear that this town was very different from their South Florida Hollywood home. They could feel the sense of community in that, in Apopka, people knew their neighbors and cared for them. Fred and Cathi were aware that Apopka had a long, rich history, and they knew they wanted to be a part of that history.

Fred attended Newberry College in Newberry, South Carolina, for two years and graduated from Florida Atlantic University in 1968. FAU was only upper division college at that time. He was awarded an MBA from FAU in 1974.

A certified public accountant, Fred Brummer succeeded Charles Wicks, C.P.A., in serving family businesses in the indoor foliage industry. In the early 1950s, Mr. Wicks had succeeded C.E. Baker who had served families in Northwest Orange County since the early 1920s.

Fred's relocation to Apopka made practice development his first priority. At that time, as is true today, business development in Apopka means being active in the Apopka Area Chamber of Commerce. In 1981, General John Raaen was the executive director of the Apopka Chamber.

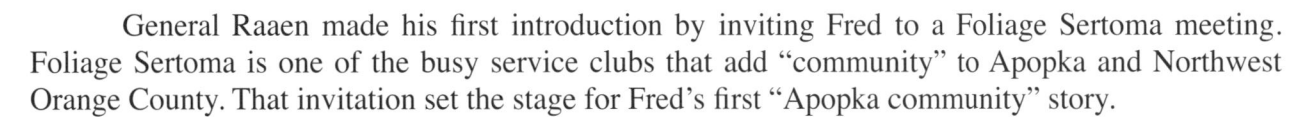

General Raaen made his first introduction by inviting Fred to a Foliage Sertoma meeting. Foliage Sertoma is one of the busy service clubs that add "community" to Apopka and Northwest Orange County. That invitation set the stage for Fred's first "Apopka community" story.

A few weeks after joining Sertoma, Fred was in line at the local supermarket checkout behind Apopka Mayor John Land. Fred reached for his wallet but realized he had left it in his truck outside. Fred lamented out loud to no one in particular, "Wow, left my wallet in my truck."

Mayor Land had recently met Fred at Sertoma, but Fred doubted Mayor Land knew Fred's name. No matter. Much to Fred's surprise, Mayor Land asked, "Do you need me to loan you some money?" That was the first example Fred saw of Apopka's sense of community.

Fred arrived in Apopka experienced in the commission manager form of government. To tell the truth, he was in disdain of the "old-fashioned" strong mayor government even after the supermarket checkout line event; however, that was not for much longer.

For some reason, Fred had to call Apopka City Hall. The phone rang four times, five times, six. Then a male voice answered, "City of Apopka." Taken aback by the voice recognition, Fred said the only thing he could think of: "Is that you, Mayor?"

That call changed Fred's opinion of Apopka's form of government and led to a campaign contribution to Mayor Land's 1982 re-election campaign.

As any good campaigner, Mayor Land acknowledged the campaign contribution with a thank you letter. Fred's respect for the Mayor's fiscal conservatism grew when he saw that the thank you letter was on letterhead from Mayor Land's 1949 campaign!

In 1983, Cathi and Fred moved the accounting practice into the two-story building on south Park Avenue adjacent to City Hall. The building is a community landmark that had served for more than fifty years as the medical office of Dr. Thomas "Doc Tommy" McBride.

The reception for the opening of the accounting office was "old home week" as most of the attendees recounted the bumps, bruises, broken bones, colds, fevers, and illnesses they had treated in the same office years before. All that reminiscing was overshadowed by the arrival of the mayor's wife (Doc Tommy's nurse) Mrs. Betty Land.

In 1985, while leaving the weekly Rotary Club meeting, Fred was approached by Apopka's longtime chiropractor Dr. Harry Ansley. Doc Ansley asked, "With the way your practice is growing, would you be interested in buying my building?"

Talk about your full-fledged jaw dropper! Fred had admired Doc and Glena Ansley's building on the corner of Park Avenue and Third Street. In 1981, while searching for an office for the firm, Fred had driven past the fine new building and wondered whether the chiropractor would lease some of the space the huge building must have. Of course, Fred did not have the courage to stop and ask. Cold calls are for sales people, not accountants.

The euphoria was short-lived, however, as the realization set in that such a fine building would not be in the budget of the growing accounting practice. What happened next was another "only in Apopka" moment.

Fred dutifully called Dr. Ansley with the report that as much as Cathi and Fred would like to buy, the numbers for the purchase just would not work. The "only in Apopka" moment occurred two weeks later when Doc Ansley called Fred and asked whether a lowered purchase price would work.

What makes a person reduce the price of an asset to help a fellow businessperson buy it? Fred believes it is the sense of cooperation that permeates the business and residential communities. He had also seen the same thing happen in the indoor foliage industry. Industry members helped to advance another's project or business without apparent self-interest.

In 1988, Fred learned two important things. First, all politics are local, and second, Apopka was yet a small community.

In that year, Roger Williams, Northwest Orange County education icon and retired longtime principal of Apopka High School, visited Fred's office and asked for a moment of his time. Roger's son, Roger F. Williams or "Little Rog" (a full-grown man, of course) had decided to run for the Florida House of Representatives against the incumbent who had represented the area of east Orange County and Winter Park.

Roger Williams was to be his son's campaign treasurer and was seeking Fred's assistance with treasurer compliance and reporting requirements. Fred explained his limited experience in the matter but offered to help as he could.

Shortly thereafter, the political landscape changed abruptly. Representative Fran Carlton, Florida House member for Apopka and Northwest Orange, announced her intention not to seek re-election to the Florida House but rather to run for Orange County Clerk of Courts.

Roger F. Williams immediately moved home to Apopka and declared his candidacy for the Apopka seat.

Soon thereafter, likely the very next Saturday, Fred was working in his office when he heard his name called from outside his window. The caller was Apopka veterinarian Bob Sindler. Bob had decided to run for the Florida House in the seat being given up by Representative Carlton and wanted Fred to act as his campaign treasurer.

Fred explained he was willing but there were two problems. The first was that Bob and Fred were not of the same party affiliation. Bob stated the party difference was of no concern.

Fred then explained he had committed to help Roger Williams with the campaign reporting in the same race. Bob recognized this as substantially important. Bob and Fred agreed they would both speak with Roger Williams to request Fred's release from his commitment. Of course, Roger Williams agreed to release Fred.

Well, Roger agreed at first. Over the weekend, he must have had second thoughts. Roger came to see Fred early Monday and insisted he needed Fred's help.

Fred pointed out he was going to help Bob Sindler. He made it clear he would also help Roger only under the condition that no questions would be asked of Fred that might breach the confidentiality of the opponent's campaign information. Roger readily agreed. The matter was then broached to Dr. Sindler, who also agreed.

Bob Sindler had a primary opponent he easily defeated. Roger F. Williams had a three-way race that resulted in a second primary or run-off. Roger won in a close, very heated run off.

Fred was pleased there were no questions that would have compromised his confidentiality. There were no regrets or recriminations expressed by either campaign that the arrangement had not worked. Fred believed that was another reflection of a closely-knit community.

Interestingly enough, Mayor Land asked Fred to be his campaign treasurer in his upcoming 1988 re-election effort. The mayor had handled his own campaign treasurer duties in all his previous campaigns; however, with the changing dynamics of an Apopka municipal election, Mayor Land believed it was time to seek help. Of course, Fred agreed and served as treasurer for several of the mayor's successful re-election efforts.

Service club membership added to the fun things of being an accountant. Fred realized that "fun things of being an accountant" is not an expected phrase.

Some of the fun things of being an accountant were that Fred and his staff have served as tabulators for the Christmas parade judges' score sheets. They also handled the judges' scores for the wildly popular Little Miss Apopka and Little Miss Cutie Pie contests.

But one of the most rewarding and memorable assignment was when W.R. "Mac" McGuffin asked Fred to be Santa Claus in the Christmas parade. Fred said, "You have not known honor until you see the look in children's eyes seeing you as Santa Claus."

Cathi Brummer sewed the Santa Claus suit and arranged the other costume accoutrements: beard, wig, eyebrows, and glasses. Santa was accompanied in his sleigh by elves – the grandchildren of Carole and John Fredricks. Later, Santa got to climb to the top of the Apopka Fire Department's ladder truck.

This perspective gave Fred the view of children who believed in Santa Claus. The responsibility of being a good Santa Claus requires an appropriate performance and appearance. It was a responsibility Cathi and Fred both took seriously.

The challenges of the weather and wearing the heavy Santa gear are small compared to the looks on those children's faces. Fred would love to be Santa Claus again.

Fred was continually blessed to be able to serve the community. He was recognized by the Apopka Area Chamber of Commerce as Businessman of the Year in 1991. In 1995, the Chamber gave Fred its Community Service Award.

Cathi Brummer was acknowledged for her service to the Apopka Rotary Club in 1993 with a Paul Harris Fellowship. Fred served as president of Apopka Rotary for the 1991-1992 club year.

In 1997, when Representative Bob Sindler announced his intention to leave the Florida Legislature to run for Orange County Commission, It was decision time for Fred and Cathi. Fred had always been interested in government and politics, and for the previous nine years was actively involved in local campaigns.

With Cathi's blessing and help, Fred jumped into the Florida House race. He had learned a huge amount about campaigning while being a treasurer, but realized he knew little about a campaign once it was his own. Fred was willing to learn and to work.

After a grassroots campaign based on door-to-door voter contact, Fred won a three-way race, taking more than fifty percent of the vote in the primary.

Fred has said that entering the Florida House chamber for the first time and seeing your name on the vote board might be an even greater honor than playing Santa Claus.

The eight-year term limit for Florida House members sounds like a long time, but it passes in the blink of an eye.

During the eye blink, and with a substantial amount of good fortune, Fred was successful in passing the legislation necessary for the completion of the beltway around Central Florida. The Wekiva Parkway was and is a foundation issue for Fred's campaign for public office. The completion of the beltway will change the economy of Northwest Orange County. Residents will be able to work where they live.

After the limit of his term in the Florida House, Fred was elected to the Orange County Commission. The 2006 campaign was a four-way race where Fred won fifty-four percent of the vote in the primary, making a run-off unnecessary. Fred was re-elected in 2010, gathering seventy-five percent of the vote in the general election.

Chapter VII - Sportsmen's Club and Old Hotels

Mt. Plymouth Hotel

Wouldn't it be neat if somewhere frozen in time there was a "hotel heaven" where all good hotels, boarding houses, and inns go after their illustrious careers are over? The chosen ones from the Apopka area would be The William Edwards Hotel (Kings Inn-Palms Hotel), The Tinsley House, The Biltmore, Oaks Hotel, Plymouth Dell, Lake Standish Hotel, San Carlos, Wayside Inn (The Apopka House), Zellwood Inn, and Holly Arms. However, the queen of them all was about seven miles to the north of Apopka in Lake County, simply known as the Mount Plymouth Hotel.

In 1926, the Mt. Plymouth Corporation was formed by William Edwards, J. Stewart Edwards, W.D. Rogers, and Carl Dann of Dubsdread fame. They purchased the Over the Top Ranch and several other parcels totaling over 5,000 acres to develop a playground city. There were plans to build business and residential areas, a large resort hotel, four golf courses, and an airport. In 1927, a highway was built from Apopka to the property.

The hotel originally consisted of 150 rooms and was constructed for $350,000. Old-timers say that a lot of the material used in the grand lobby and ballroom (the largest in Florida at the time) was sent over from Europe by ship, down the St. Johns River to Sanford, and delivered to Mt. Plymouth via oxen. These same old-timers say there was a stagecoach running between the Sanford Port and the hotel. We have no pictures to verify that. Having personally seen the lobby and dining rooms, I can vouch for the fact that the hotel was very elegant. The initial success of the resort was so encouraging that forty rooms were added in 1929.

Four 18-hole golf courses patterned after the St. Andrews courses in Scotland were originally planned for the resort. However, the real estate crash of 1929 prevented completion of three of the four courses. The course they did build is now called Mt. Plymouth Golf Club and remains operational today. Although the Florida real estate crash kept the other three courses from being completed, the hotel became the center of activity in the area and was a winter golf retreat for the famous and the infamous.

The Apopka Rotary Club received a windfall when Connie Mack, the legendary manager of the Philadelphia Athletics, began to winter at the hotel in 1929. Tom Mahaffey said, "Rotary always looked forward to Mr. Mack making up his meetings at the Apopka club, where he gave his yearly progress report on the Athletics." Belle Gilliam says her brother Marvin Driggers (my brother-in-law) caddied for Connie Mack. A couple more of the famous who wintered there were the "Bambino" himself, Babe Ruth, and Kate Smith, a popular singer of the times who made "God Bless America" famous during World War II. Some of the more infamous visitors were Al Capone and some of his mobster friends from Chicago and New York. Big Al insisted on a bulletproof door to his room and a private line to his bodyguards at all times.

The airfield accommodated flights from all over the state. There were a lot of twin-engine planes bringing in groups of fifteen to twenty passengers daily. The airport stayed pretty busy, and, at times, they put on air shows for the guests. When the stock market crash in 1929 sent the nation into its worst depression, tourism in Florida suffered, and the Mt. Plymouth Hotel was no exception. I think it is fair to say it never really recovered.

Florida Central Academy purchased the hotel and surrounding grounds (not the golf course) in 1959 and operated a boy's school, with grades 7-12. The school closed in 1983.

On January 6, 1986, the hotel burned to the ground. The following day, two teenagers confessed to setting the fire. I am sure that the Mt. Plymouth Hotel made it into that hotel heaven in the sky, for it served its guests in the finest manner that it possibly could. There are a lot of us who have fond memories of this majestic hotel.

The Palms Hotel

The building changed hands many times before it became the Palms Hotel.

With the completion of the 1925 paving projects, real estate excitement accelerated in Apopka. The paving had opened up more property to be developed, and twenty lots were sold within a week. By 1925, about forty new homes were completed or under construction. The growth of Apopka was accompanied by even more extravagant expansion elsewhere in the state, which caused some difficulties. Congested railroad lines made it difficult to get supplies. Lovell and Harris stopped construction on Phoebe Towers' new home because of a lack of materials. Ryan and Company explained that it had several carloads of lumber on the way, but they were caught in the railroad jams. Highways were also becoming crowded. A traffic count showed 2,019 cars passed Fourth Street and Central Avenue in a twelve-hour period in September 1925.

The increased automobile traffic was creating a demand for new kinds of accommodations. By 1920, people were stopping at Apopka and pitching tents for brief periods. These "tin can tourists" were numerous enough that the city provided a campground in 1922. But the board of trade recognized the need for commercial tourist camps. The Mynatt Camp west of town and the Apopka City Camp on the Ocoee Road, both established in 1925, were intended to meet this new demand. The city contracted with Mrs. Gertrude Gould to build cabins at the Ocoee Road Camp in 1926.

At the urging of John Jackson, C. Ellwood Kalbach, and A.M. Hall, the Chamber of Commerce named Mayor Morrey, J.G. Grossenbacher, J.S. Henderson, Sam Sadler, A.M. Hall, and Wilber L. Tilden as a committee to plan a suitable hotel. Capitalized at $150,000, the Hotel Corporation offered shares to the public at $100 each. Each week, a goat was given to the sales person who topped his quota by the largest margin. A final sales drive in April 1926 sent total subscriptions to $163,000, and the hotel was assured.

The old Apopka City Hall on the corner of Central Avenue and Fourth Street was razed to make room for a forty-room structure, which was built by O.P. Woodcock of Jacksonville. After a spirited contest sponsored by *The Apopka Chief*, the new hotel was named the William Edwards. It was formally opened under the management of A.A. Roby, formally of the Manavista Hotel at Bradenton, in June 1927. With justifiable pride, *The Apopka Chief* applauded the ceremony as the "most notable event in the history of the Fern City." The event brought predictions of future growth and prosperity for the city.

In 1933, the William Edwards Hotel was leased to R.R. King of North Carolina, who reopened it as the King's Inn. When the Apopka hotel was unable to settle an outstanding mortgage in 1936, the King's Inn was sold at auction to A.D. Rainville of New York who managed it until 1938. He then sold to A.H. Albee of New Hampshire. Albee planned to keep it open year-round as the Palms Hotel.

In 1941, he sold to Glover Burney. In early 1944, C.L.C. Bruner purchased the Palms Hotel and rented rooms with kitchen privileges to the military personal stationed in Apopka at the time. With business on the slow side, the practice of renting rooms continued after World War II.

On June 2, 1962, the First Federal Savings and Loan Association moved into Apopka. They reached downstate to the Palm Beach Federal to bring in Willis Warren as their branch manager.

In 1964, First Federal bought the old Palms Hotel on Fourth and Central and built the very modern building you see today. Willis said, "The old hotel had the only elevator in town." Willis also stated, "We had to take up seventeen septic tanks when we were demolishing the old hotel."

At the grand opening, many of the guests were complaining about the bank using artificial plants instead of live plants for decorations. After all, Apopka was "The Indoor Foliage Capital of the World." General Manager Joe Croson did not take long in having Willis Warren remove all artificial plants and replace them with live plants.

Life Before Air Conditioning

We are rapidly approaching that time of year when the hot days of summer will keep a lot of us indoors with our glorious air conditioners. I am sure there are a lot of you who do not remember what life was like or how homes were built before the air conditioner was invented. Willis Carrier patented the first apparatus for treating air in 1902, but it wasn't until 1925 that it really hit the big time with the installation of Carrier units in the Rivoli Movie Theater in New York City. It was probably after World War II before the window units were mass-produced to the point they would become economically available to rural Orange County.

The first attempt at building an air conditioner was made by Dr. John Gorrie, an American physician, in Apalachicola. During his practice in the 1830s, Dr. Gorrie created an ice-making machine that essentially blew air over a bucket of ice for cooling hospital rooms for patients suffering from malaria and yellow fever.

In 1881, when President James Garfield was dying, naval engineers constructed a box-like structure containing cloths that were saturated with ice water, where a fan blew hot air overhead. This contraption was able to lower a room temperature twenty degrees Fahrenheit, but consumed half a million pounds of ice in two months.

With all of this emphasis on lowering the temperature, houses throughout the state of Florida may have been laid out a little differently than homes in other parts of the south, as there was a special emphasis on protection from the heat, mosquitoes or hurricane winds.

The first thing I remember about the house that I was raised in were the porches. A lot of the homes in Apopka had wrap-around porches. However, we did not. Since our house was located on Hwy. 441, the front porch faced the road with a swing on one end and an assortment of wicker at the other. The porch had no screen and seemed to be used mostly by the kids in the family, especially while entertaining their guests.

The back porch, however, was something else. It seemed to address some of the problems we had with hot nights and mosquitoes. It was completely screened and nestled under the old oak tree, and in the evenings, it was about as cool an area as we had. My mother would sit out on that porch in the evenings shelling her black-eyed peas for the evening meal, and my dad spent his evenings in the rocking chair smoking his pipe. The icebox was also on that porch so the iceman could service it without going inside the house. My brother and I were usually out playing Fox and the Hounds with the neighborhood boys, while wearing shorts and no shirts.

Everyone was either outside or on that porch until it cooled down enough to go to bed. By the time I came along in the family, we had that screened porch and screened windows. Before that, if you opened the windows to cool the room, you would be eaten alive by mosquitoes. Since you dared not take on the mosquitoes, you could count on having a hot, sweaty night.

I mentioned the icebox on our back porch a little earlier. Well, I think we can say that the icebox was the predecessor to the refrigerator. The term "refrigerator" was actually coined by a Maryland engineer back in the 1800s. Today, his so-called refrigerator would be called an icebox – a cedar tub, insulated with rabbit fur, filled with ice, surrounding a sheet metal container for transporting butter from rural Maryland to Washington, D.C. The only point being made is that he called his icebox a refrigerator. The refrigerators as we know them today did not come into mass production until the '50s.

The icebox was not too much different from the refrigerator. It opened at the top to put in the blocks of ice. This area was the so-called freezer. Below were the shelves for the food, just like the "fridges" of today. You had to have an ice pick to chip the ice into small pieces for your water, tea, etc.

Every town had its icehouse. Apopka's icehouse is still standing on South Central Avenue. You could either pick up your ice or have it delivered. If you were having it delivered, you had a dial with the numbers 25-50-100 on it. If you wanted the iceman to put twenty-five pounds of ice in your icebox, you dialed that number. If you picked up your own ice at the icehouse, you had to have ice tongs that griped the ice block so you could carry it a little easier. It was always interesting to watch the men at the icehouse handle large shipments of ice with their tongs.

Some cars in those days had ice racks on the running boards for a twenty-five-pound block. I guess that was pretty clever, since I could not imagine what would keep the ice still while the car was moving.

Henry Land's Essay

Henry Land was always a leader and a visionary in whatever endeavor he participated. This trait began to show at an early age as it did in the first edition of the *Apopka Acorn*, the official publication of the Apopka schools many years ago. Since Henry graduated from high school in 1929, we can only assume he wrote this essay mid or early 1920s.

Young Henry wrote an essay of what the future had in store for us as far as air travel by the year of 1957. Some of these prophecies were amazing and others have yet to be realized. He called his essay "The Future of Aviation." Here is Henry's essay as it was written those many years ago:

"In 1957, someone will look up in the skies and see something that looks like a huge bird traveling along at an almost impossible rate of 500 miles per hour, so fast that it can be barely seen as it goes by.

The airplane of that time will be as far advanced upon the airplane of today, as the old-time horseless carriage was compared with the modern automobile.

There will be many and varied improvements so that the airplane will be safer than the car is today and accidents in the airplane will be practically unheard of. The automobile, express and passenger trains will gradually phase out and be supplanted by huge airplanes that will carry many tons of freight and as many as twenty passengers.

Among the new inventions will be an airplane that will rise vertically in the air and will not require runways as the planes of today do. These planes will be propelled by propellers at the top of the plane and driven by powerful motors.

The plane will be equipped with an enlarged type of parachute attached to the top of the plane.

If there is any engine trouble that necessitates an immediate landing, the plane will glide safely to the ground without injury to the plane or its occupants.

The plane will be equipped with small balloons at each side. If it is wished by the pilot to stay in the air when the engine was not working and there is not suitable place to land, these balloons will be inflated immediately by some special machinery on the plane for that purpose and the plane will remain in the air until a suitable landing place is reached, then the air will be released by a special valve and the plane will taxi slowly to the earth.

There will be a new kind of gas found that will be much lighter that the gas of the present and will go many more miles to the gallon. By the use of this gas, many long trips can be made without overloading the plane.

The new planes will be very small and built of much lighter materials than those of the present. The nose of the plane will be pointed as the sharp edge of an ax to lesson air resistance.

The planes will be built on the principle of the stabilized glider and if there is any engine trouble, the plane will glide gracefully to earth.

All planes will be equipped with a rudder and propeller such as is used on ships and the bottom shall be the shape of a boat so that if forced down on water, it will not sink and the plane will also be able to navigate as ships.

All planes will have radio transmitters and receiving apparatus, parachutes, rubber boats and unsinkable suits for the protection of the passengers. The plane shall be equipped with an earth inductor compass, barometer, speedometer, altimeter, and many other things for recording the speed, etc., of the plane. There shall be air charts for sale just as there are road maps today.

High altitude planes shall consist of a plane with an air-tight chamber for the pilot and the plane will be outfitted with an oxygen-condensing machine which shall keep air at all times pure, removing the carbon dioxide also. By the use of this plane, flights may be made as high as twenty miles above the surface of the earth.

In short, flying will be a very safe means of transportation as well as a quick one. Everyone will own a plane and they will be as cheap as the automobiles of today. Any New York businessman will be able to go to Paris to spend the weekend if he so desires."

After graduating from the University of Florida, Henry Land began his public service life by being elected to the Orange County Commission in 1940 as the youngest man ever elected to that position at twenty-six. He was forced to resign eighteen months later to go to war, where he was awarded the Bronze Star for Valor.

After he returned from the war, he served in the Florida House of Representatives for twelve years and chairman of the powerful Appropriations Committee. He was selected by the Florida Press as one of the "Ten Outstanding House Members" in 1955, 1957, 1963, 1965, and 1967.

Henry's crystal ball served him well throughout his business and public careers

Ryan Field

Finding an airfield in the Apopka area in the early 1930s wasn't exactly an easy thing to do, but at least there was a grass strip on the corner of Welch and Thompson roads that ran north to south, parallel to Thompson Road. Pilots would come in over the weekends and offer rides to the more daring residents. It was a thrill to take off over beautiful Lake Prevatt.

In 1935, under the auspices of the Federal Emergency Relief Administration, construction was started on a community airport located north of Apopka on Rock Springs Road where Dream Lake Elementary is located today. There were 150 acres involved. About twenty-five men went to work in August of 1935, and the field was dedicated in October 1936. At the dedication, the field was named Ryan Municipal Airport after Mayor E.J. Ryan, who had recently passed away. It was also proclaimed an emergency landing field to be maintained by the state.

Immediately after the grand opening, the Apopka Aviation Club was formed by R.A. Lassiter, Dr. C.H. Damsel, Dan Colbert, and Park McCall. By this time, flying was a popular avocation for several Apopkans, and E.C. Kerlin was busy as a flight instructor.

The hanger, which faced north, was located about where Maters & Taters is located now. There was the 2,800-foot, north-to-south runway that ran from the hanger north, parallel to the Rock Springs Road. The east-west runway started at the north-south runway and ran somewhere along Ryan Street toward the high school. These runways were grass strips.

In 1938, a U.S. mail plane landed at Ryan Field in observation of Airmail Week and brought Postmistress Minnie Vick and her assistant, Park McCall, their first 261 pieces of airmail.

Proponents of the airfield continued to lobby for another hanger, gas tanks, and additional improvements. After the unexpected recession of 1937, additional funds were appropriated for Works Progress Administration projects, and a second airport project was undertaken. With only a small outlay by the city, the federal government spent about $20,000 providing work for about thirty-five men for nearly a year. In 1940, the municipal airport was leased to R A. Lassiter and E.G. Kerlin, who envisioned a civilian flight training school there.

Mrs. T.E. McBride and Mrs. Alice Hamrick were two of the first women to take up aviation. They received their pilot's licenses in the mid-1930s. By 1939, Mrs. McBride had become a competitive cross-country flier. In January, she flew to Miami and Havana in a national air meet, and in June, she participated in a gigantic aircade to the New York World Fair. Out of more than 100 planes sponsored by the Florida Branch of the National Aeronautical Association, she was the only female pilot.

Between 1946 and 1951, she entered and placed well in numerous air races from Miami to Cleveland, Ohio, and Windsor, Ontario. In the latter year, she was general chairman of the All-Women's International Air Race from Orlando to Windsor, an event that attracted extensive notice to Central Florida.

Helen McBride leased the airport from 1942 to 1952. She purchased four planes out of Miami and had four locals that included John Jackson, Robert "Boo" Burgust, and a fellow from Orlando, name unknown. Mrs. McBride was a cross-country racer and was in the process of being a World War II flying instructor. She had a contract with the military to train pilots to fly her planes.

I can imagine seeing our good friend Boo Burgust breaking in some of Carol Hamrick's wild broncos; however, it seems a little difficult seeing him in the cockpit of some of those early planes at Ryan Field. But that was the case. The four planes flew back up the coast and stopped in Ft. Pierce to refuel, and then continued to the grass strip at Richardson's Clarcona Airport. I have no idea why they did not fly into Ryan Field.

Mrs. McBride did not renew her lease in 1953, and the city sought ways of disposing of the airfield. After considering its sale to developers for much-needed housing, the city sold a portion in 1954 to the Orange County School Board as a site for Dream Lake Elementary School. A few years later, the balance of the land was sold to developers.

Sportsmen's Club

Over the years, things have not changed a lot in the world of hunting and fishing. In the weeks preceding the opening of hunting season, hunters are busy fixing up their camps and stands for that traditional opening day. In the early days, things might have been a little different, because there was no hunting season.

In the early 1920s, hunting and fishing was so popular that it became a concern that the game and fish might be eliminated unless conservation measures were implemented. Florida first required fishing licenses with limits on what was caught, and soon instituted a hunting season from August 1st to December 1st. After this, I am sure the excitement of opening day grew by the year. It was not long before the Orange County sheriff appointed a special deputy to, "Look out for the out-of-season predators of game in and around Apopka and Sanford." Our local hunters and fishermen said, "Young turkeys were being killed when frying size, the young deer were dying from no protection, the fish were being dynamited, seined, trapped, and caught by the thousands."

Apopkans took these new game laws very seriously. Civic leaders such as Mark Ryan, John Steinmetz, Walter Schopke, and Jim Oliver formed the Wildlife League and supported the statewide movement for better wildlife management. They later renamed the League "The Apopka Game and Fish Association" and were instrumental in having Chip Buchan

This monument contains the names of the club's first members.

Front: George McClure, T.O. Mahaffey, William Hamrick
Standing: Mayor John Land, Raymond Hogshead

appointed as county game and fish warden in 1926. Chip was already serving part-time as a state warden.

The Apopka Sportsmen's Club was formed in the early 1930s to promote sports in Apopka. They sponsored a baseball club that played in the Lake Orange League, as well as a gun club and a tennis club. Bennett Land, Sr. (John Land's father) was the first president and V.W. Haygood was the secretary. The seventy-five members were conservationists at heart, so they leased land to form The Mill Creek Game Preserve in order to practice the game management they believed in. By 1934, they had leased 7,000 additional acres between Rock Springs and Wekiwa Springs.

Dues at that time were a $50 initiation fee and $15 per year. Clyde Love was appointed as the patrol rider against poachers, and Mallory Welch was the game warden for the Rock Springs Preserve. With this excellent game protection in place, the club was provided with an abundance of wildlife, and by 1938, they cut their membership back to fifty members.

In 1941, the Apopka Sportsmen's Club purchased the 3,500 acres they had been leasing from the Wilson Cypress Company. Through the years, as more property was purchased, each member paid their share of the cost. During World War II, those who were in the service had the choice of paying their share at that time or after the war. For twenty years after the war, the Apopka Sportsmen's Club managed their land very well.

When the announcement came in 1969 that Walt Disney World was moving to Orlando, most of the Sportsmen's Club members did not want to see the beautiful land that they had been managing caught up in the changes that were about to happen in Central Florida. After four years of negotiating, the club finally came to an agreement with the State of Florida to sell the club land and some additional properties for $2,700,000. This was well below the market price of land in Central Florida. This sale was totally contingent upon the fact that the land would be a state park and open to all of our citizens for their enjoyment.

In terms of size, the Sportsmen's Club was to make a very large park for the state, as it covered almost ten square miles of land that was rich in natural beauty. There was eight miles of riverfront property, seven on the Rock Springs River and one on the Wekiwa. It had one spring, Witherington Springs, located within its boundaries, as well as two lakes.

In September of 1991, the surviving members held a reunion at the Wekiwa Springs State Park to dedicate a monument in honor of those who participated in the club and managed the land so well.

An inscription on the marker reads, "MONUMENT DEDICATED TO…The animals and birds of the forest and streams and to the past human users of this land. First were the Indians, and then came early explorers searching for gold or the fountain of youth. Early pioneers farmed this land and part was a pre-civil war cotton plantation, sawmill, gristmill and turpentine stills used the forest and streams. Their signs still seen, the Apopka Sportsmen's Club were the next owners practicing conservation to protect wildlife and preserve the natural beauty. Members' names appear on this monument now to be used as a spot of natural beauty and healthful recreation for the people of Florida. It is hoped that future generations will use it well."

All of Central Florida owes a tribute to these members who contributed so much to the conservation of this land for the future use of our citizens.

Dr. Cole Carroll

Sometimes known as "the most beautiful building in Orange County," the quaint two-story building on the corner of Main Street and Park Avenue was built by Dr. Cole Carroll in 1932. W.G. "Bucky" Harris was the contractor. As I was growing up, it was always known as the Carroll Building. Sometimes I hear it referred to as the "McBride Building," and that is understandable.

Dr. Carroll was a handsome young bachelor who never married. He came to Apopka in 1913, after graduating from the Atlanta School of Medicine (Emory University). He was the doctor preceding Dr. Tommy McBride. Actually, their tenures overlapped during Dr. Tommy's first eight years. In Dr. Tommy's unpublished writings on "The History of the Practice of Medicine in Apopka," he stated that, "Dr. Carroll was not only a good doctor but a good businessman."

Dr. Cole Carroll was a doctor and businessman.

Carroll bought the old Converse Drug Store (now torn down) that stood directly on the corner of Main and Park. He lived and practiced medicine in Apopka for more than twenty years. He later sold this building to his friend from Lamont, Florida, W.B. Sheppard, a pharmacist. After the death of Dr. Sheppard, his widow, Lillian Sheppard and their three sons, Leon, Laurie, and Walter, known as "Buster," ran the pharmacy for many years. I never had a pharmacist other than the Sheppards, even up until Buster's retirement from the Winn-Dixie Pharmacy in recent years.

Dr. Carroll was also a successful citrus grower and a director and vice-president of the State Bank of Apopka, one of the few banks in Florida that was not forced to close during the Depression. Many people had confidence in Dr. Carroll's integrity and business ability, and this was a factor in the stability of the bank.

In an interview with Laurie Sheppard, son of W.B. Sheppard, Janet Connelly wrote in *The Apopka Chief* in 1991 that Laurie recalled that Dr. Carroll was extremely well liked and a very popular, eligible bachelor. Sheppard also remembers being very impressed with Dr. Carroll's new office building which cost $6,000, a great deal of money during the Depression years of 1932.

Dr. Carroll kept birddogs and was said to have done a lot of hunting.

But along with all his business and other activities, there are reports he answered medical calls day and night, sat for hours at the bedside of diphtheria or even migraine headache patients. There were eyewitnesses to his weeping over the death of a patient he could not save.

Dr. Carroll would generally take his meals at the Wayside Inn (approximately where CVS stands today), and he had an intense liking for lemon pie and baked sweet potatoes. He sometimes dined with Mrs. Lillian Nolle.

Dr. Carroll lived to enjoy his new building for about one year, and then he suddenly died. The cause of Dr. Carroll's death is somewhat of a mystery. It was presumed to be a heart attack.

His niece, Mrs. Maudie Carr said he did not eat right. She said, "If he had fed himself as well as he fed his dogs, he might have lived longer." One of Mrs. Carr's sons was named Cole after Dr. Carroll.

Prominent Apopkans were pallbearers. A delegation followed the body the 200 miles to Lamont, north of Perry, for the burial.

It was not long afterwards that Dr. McBride, who started his practice here in 1926, bought the building and continued his practice until his retirement about fifty years later.

Dr. Carroll's building is now owned by the City of Apopka.

State Bank of Apopka Bank Robbery

Pictured: W.G. Talton, D.E. McGuire and Frank Burgust

At four feet, eight inches, Grace Van Sicklen was a small lady who enjoyed her job working the ledgers at the State Bank of Apopka on Main Street. She may have been small in stature, but she was about to experience one of the biggest episodes of her life. It happened close to noon on a beautiful fall day in 1934, as Grace's boss Frank L. Burgust, cashier at the bank, was working with the combination of the walk-in vault at the rear of the bank.

They were especially proud to be associated with the only bank that did not have to close its doors during the Great Depression. Actually, the economy was slowly rebounding, and the bank's deposits had increased $125,000 in the last year. A few years back, when the banks in Orange County were having to close because the customers were withdrawing their funds, the State Bank of Apopka held on because the people of Apopka had a great deal of faith in the bank's management at the time. William Edwards, W.G. Talton, Frank Burgust, and Richard Whitney were some pretty influential names in those days.

As Mr. Burgust had finished his business in the vault that morning, he turned to close the door when a voice behind him said, "Do *not* close that door." As he turned, he could see Lonnie Parrish and his men, a notorious local gang, at the front and side windows. They instructed Mr. Burgust to open the safe inside the walk-in vault; however, it was on a timer, and Lonnie Parrish had to settle for the cash at the cashier's window. When they left the bank, they had $4,000 in cash. They took Mrs. Van Sicklen and Mr. Burgust as hostages.

Grace was moving too slowly for the robbers, so they left her on the street. As the car pulled away, she ran into the Argonne Thrift Shop and told everyone that the bandits had robbed the bank and escaped in a Cadillac. She drew this conclusion because one of the bandits said, "Get in the Cadillac." Mr. Burgust was seen riding on the running board. As they passed local merchants, Bob Willis and his brother, who were busy with their daily work, saw Mr. Burgust waving desperately for help, but the unsuspecting merchants just smiled and waved back.

He was eventually dropped off on the east side of town, and immediately ran behind one of the big oaks on the street. As the gang disappeared over the hill, Mr. Burgust went into the Gillen McClure House and called authorities.

Orange County Sheriff Harry Hand did not have radios at the time, and he had to dispatch deputies to various points in the area. One was in Seminole County at the Five Points in Longwood on the way to 17-92. The deputy was parked along the road waiting to apprehend the robbers in a Cadillac. Actually, the Parrish gang was in a 1934 Ford, and went through the blockade.

Within two weeks, authorities captured the gang somewhere in Texas. It has never been recorded if the money was recovered or not, but justice prevailed, and this gang spent quite a few year behind bars.

The facts in this article came from tapes in the Museum of Apopkans and a personal interview with Robert Burgust, son of Frank Burgust. History is not to be forgotten, but treasured forever.

Richard Whitney

In researching some of these articles for "Historical Tidbits," I cannot help but notice the extraordinary leadership the Apopka area had in the '20s and '30s. Citizens like William Edwards, John G. Grossenbacher, Henry Witherington, and John J. Anderson kept popping up whenever something had to be accomplished. Others like John T. Pirie and Richard Whitney showed a lot of faith in the area and invested accordingly. The old saying that if you have never been in the valley, you can never appreciate the mountaintop might be especially true of Richard Whitney.

Richard was a banker and investment counselor born in Beverly, Massachusetts. He descended from immigrants who arrived in Massachusetts in 1630. His father, George Whitney, was a leading Boston banker. Richard graduated from Groton and from Harvard, where he was elected to the prestigious Porcelland Club. He moved to New York in 1910 and became a member of the New York Stock Exchange in 1912, at the age of twenty-three.

Whitney served on virtually every significant committee of the Exchange, including the Business Conduct Committee. In 1929, he was vice-president and acting president of the Exchange. He then served five consecutive years as president. During this time, he was the spokesperson for "the Old Guard," which came increasingly under attack from the newly created Securities and Exchange Commission, a part of the New Deal of Franklin Roosevelt. He appeared as a witness at congressional hearings throughout the period from 1931 through 1935.

Whitney chose not to run again for the presidency of the Exchange in 1935; instead, he became more heavily involved in his speculative investments he had made in firms manufacturing apple brandy, peat humus, and marine colloids. It was the peat humus that had brought him to the Zellwood area a few years earlier.

In 1920, he had purchased the bankrupt Zellwood Farms Company, which included several thousand acres of muckland, with the idea of mining the peat. By 1922, he changed the name of the company to the Alpha Peat Company and hired Lindley Wood as its first manager. By 1925, he once again changed the name of the company, this time to the Florida Humus Company. The firm was mining, drying, and shipping its product in both bulk and small containers suitable for sale to nurseries and gardeners. After lengthy experiments costing over $1,000,000, the company finally developed a satisfactory system of processing muck by 1933. By 1935, Whitney was operating in the black.

In 1931, Whitney purchased John G. Grossenbacher's Florida Insecticide Company and hired

William B. Goding as general manager. In 1933 and again in 1935, they expanded the plant substantially, and in 1936, they merged with Stauffer Chemical out of Texas. A year or so later, Whitney sold Stauffer two-thirds of his interest in the company. Stauffer Chemical was located on Hwy. 441 where McDonalds is today.

Apopkans were very proud of their association with Richard Whitney. He was a stockholder and vice president of the State Bank of Apopka. On his annual dove hunting trips to his 30,000-acre preserve, he was always very liberal with his invitations to old friends in the area.

In order for Whitney to keep all of his business interests afloat, he was borrowing heavily from friends and acquaintances, using his ties with J.P. Morgan as a type of "influence collateral." In March of 1938, his world collapsed. New and tighter reporting regulations on personal finance revealed that Whitney had been a terrible manager of his own and other people's money. Investigation of his affairs demonstrated that he had been borrowing against funds in his trust since at least 1926. During this period, Whitney quietly disposed of his State Bank of Apopka stock and resigned as vice president before the scandal was made public.

Within days, events snowballed, and Whitney and his company would both declare bankruptcy. An astonished public learned of his misdeeds when, on March 10, he was officially charged with embezzlement by New York County District Attorney Thomas E. Dewey. Following his indictment by a Grand Jury, Richard Whitney was arrested and eventually pleaded guilty. He was sentenced to a term of five to ten years in Sing Sing Prison in upper New York

As a model prisoner, Richard Whitney was released on parole in August of 1941, after serving three years and three months in Sing Sing. He was permanently banned from dealing with securities and planned to retire to his home in Far Hills, New Jersey; however, Richard could not give up his dream in the Zellwood investment. In 1946, Whitney decided to plant Ramie, a fibrous plant which seemed suited to the production of rope, twine, and bagging. He decided to grow it on a large scale and build a plant which could turn it into shoe thread – 10,000 pounds in a week. After about three years, the project was abandoned, and Richard really retired this time. He still spent his winters at the Mt. Plymouth Hotel. The Zellwood muck had extracted too much from him, and he was willing to let others try to tame it. Richard Whitney died in 1974.

Edward's Field

For many decades, Edwards Field was a spot where members of the Apopka community gathered for baseball games.

If the kids were not on their hands and knees weeding the ferns in the many ferneries in the area, they were pounding the baseball around in the vacant lots north of First Street and Forrest. Every evening before the sun went down, you could hear the baseball chatter, the old wooden bats cracking one into the nearby woods, and possibly a dinner bell ringing for the boys to come home. They certainly did not have a baseball field in the true since of the word; however, the roots were planted for Apopka's everlasting love for baseball.

At some point in time (maybe the early 1900s), the good citizens of Apopka formed the Apopka Baseball Club in order to purchase land to build a baseball field for the kids on First and Forest. This was a private venture where stock was sold to raise the funds for the purchase. They chose approximately a city block adjacent and east of what is known today as Kit Land Nelson Park. William Edwards spearheaded this drive and purchased a considerable amount of stock to insure its success. To this day, the field is known as Edwards Field, in honor of his perseverance. The Baseball Club was incorporated in 1924 so they could borrow the funds to install the field and some wooden bleachers for the fans.

In 1922, Apopka and several other towns formed the Lake-Orange League, which maintained an excellent caliber of baseball for the next three decades. The Apopka Club dominated the league during the first four years and fielded winning teams for years.

Both the Apopka Club and the Lake-Orange League had difficulties during the 1930s, when the Depression was at its worst. The Apopka Club had not paid taxes on Edwards Field since 1929, and the community was pushing for a lighted field so baseball could be played at night. The merchants were unable to close their stores in the afternoons for baseball games as they had in the past. The community also wanted shuffleboard and tennis courts to make the town more attractive to winter tourists.

The recreational committee, composed of W.G. Talton, Charles Sickles, George Kerr, and J.C. Robinson, noticed that the WPA was favorable to such improvements in other towns in the area. Realizing the WPA could only work with municipalities, they proposed that the city acquire Edwards Field and apply for a WPA project. After some negotiations, the Apopka Baseball Club deeded the field to the city and the WPA agreed to spend about $14,000 improving it. Work on Edwards Field and Ryan Airfield provided a payroll of about $1,000 per week in 1938-1939.

Despite the popularity of their baseball team, Apopkans consented to the leasing of Edwards Field for use as an army base during the war. In conjunction with the Fighter Command School at Orlando, the 351st Coast Artillery Search Light Battalion, with about 250 men, converted the ballpark into an army post.

The Lake-Orange baseball league was restored after the war and the Apopka Baseball Club continued to win more than its share of games. When the army ended its lease of Edwards Field, the city purchased the improvements which were left there. They were then sold for more than enough money to restore the field, and $200 of the surplus was used to purchase uniforms and equipment for the team. In 1949, the Apopka Athletic Association – John Talton, John A. Jackson, James F. Parrott, R.G. Pittman, Jr., and John H. Land – leased the city owned field for ten years, installed new lights, and agreed to maintain it.

From 1947 until the late 1950s, crowds numbering in the thousands turned out to watch the Apopka teams win many victories in the Lake-Orange league. With the advent of television and the increasing recreational use of the automobiles, attendance at the games dwindled. The Lake-Orange League was discontinued in the late 1950s, a victim of modern technology and changing use of leisure time.

You can't help but wonder, as the Apopka Little League team was receiving its 2001 National Championship trophy, if they could hear the echoes of the boys of the early 1920s on First and Forest. It was from this humble beginning that produced the Zack Greinke's, Rodney Brewers, and others who took their love for baseball to the highest level.

Hall's Feed Store

I was wondering the other day, what is the oldest family-owned business in downtown Apopka? Without checking with the real Apopka historians, Belle Gilliam and John Land, I would have to say Hall's Feed Store on Fifth Street is the oldest. I say this because it has been a continuous business in downtown Apopka since 1929.

Back in 1921, Albert Curtis Hall was working for the U.S. Department of Agriculture in Baltimore, Maryland. That same year, Mr. Hall decided to move to Florida to open his own insecticide company. This effort was successful until the fruit fly nearly ruined the local citrus industry. It did ruin Mr. Hall's chemical business. He picked himself up and got a job as an accountant with an insecticide company in Apopka. It would be my guess that this insecticide company was Florida Insecticide, owned by John Grossenbacher of Plymouth.

By 1929, Hall decided he wanted to be in business for himself. Because of his agricultural background, he chose to open a feed and grain store on Central Avenue, and called it Hall's Tuxedo Feed Store. The business prospered.

Hall married Juanita Womble, who was also an Apopka resident, and they had a son named Les. Like most fathers in that day, he brought his son up in the family business to be his eventual successor, which he did in 1942.

Those years were difficult ones for the feed and grain store. There was a feed shortage because of World War II, and the Halls had trouble getting enough goods to supply their customers. Les Hall notes that he often had to ration feed to the area farmers, and sometimes they would wait at the store for hours to have first chance at a new shipment. People would buy anything; cattle feed to give their pigs and chickens or chicken feed to give their cattle. Les said that they bought whatever they could, and used it wherever they could.

While Les was trying to locate feed for his customers, Juanita would often have to manage the store, and load and deliver the feed by herself.

A crisis arose in Apopka when the draft board was considering drafting Les. They planned to close the store and allocate its feed ration to other stores. The farmers in the Apopka area were upset. They formed a committee and had a petition signed by most of the people in the area to have Hall given a deferral because he ran a necessary business, and the draft board finally agreed.

The business has changed over the years. In 1962, it moved from its location on Central to the new building on Fifth Street.

Les was semi-retired, and he handed over operation of the company to his wife, though he still took an active role in the management of the business.

Aside from the business, the Halls have been active in the life of the community. "Ducky" Hall was a volunteer fireman with the Apopka Fire Department for forty years, and Juanita Hall served as a pink lady at the Orange Memorial Hospital in Orlando for thirteen years and was active in the PTA and other school organizations. The Halls are members of the First United Methodist Church of Apopka.

Les also followed the tradition of his father and brought his son, Leslie "Butch" Hall into the business. Butch took over the operation of the store in 1980. One of the first things he did was to add bait and tackle to the product line.

In 2007, Butch retired and, true to family tradition, his son Chris assumed ownership. Chris has added new technology to the business with the addition of computerized sales and inventory controls. He has remodeled the store and continues with new product expansion. However, they still offer some of the same products they did when his great-grandfather started the business.

They sell a full line of seeds, feeds, garden supplies, pet supplies, seedling plants, flowers, fertilizers, rabbits, chickens, and quite a bit more, including the famed "Silver Queen" variety of sweet corn. Above and beyond all else, customer service has been and will continue to be a very important aspect of their business.

Chapter VIII - World War II & Heros

World War II

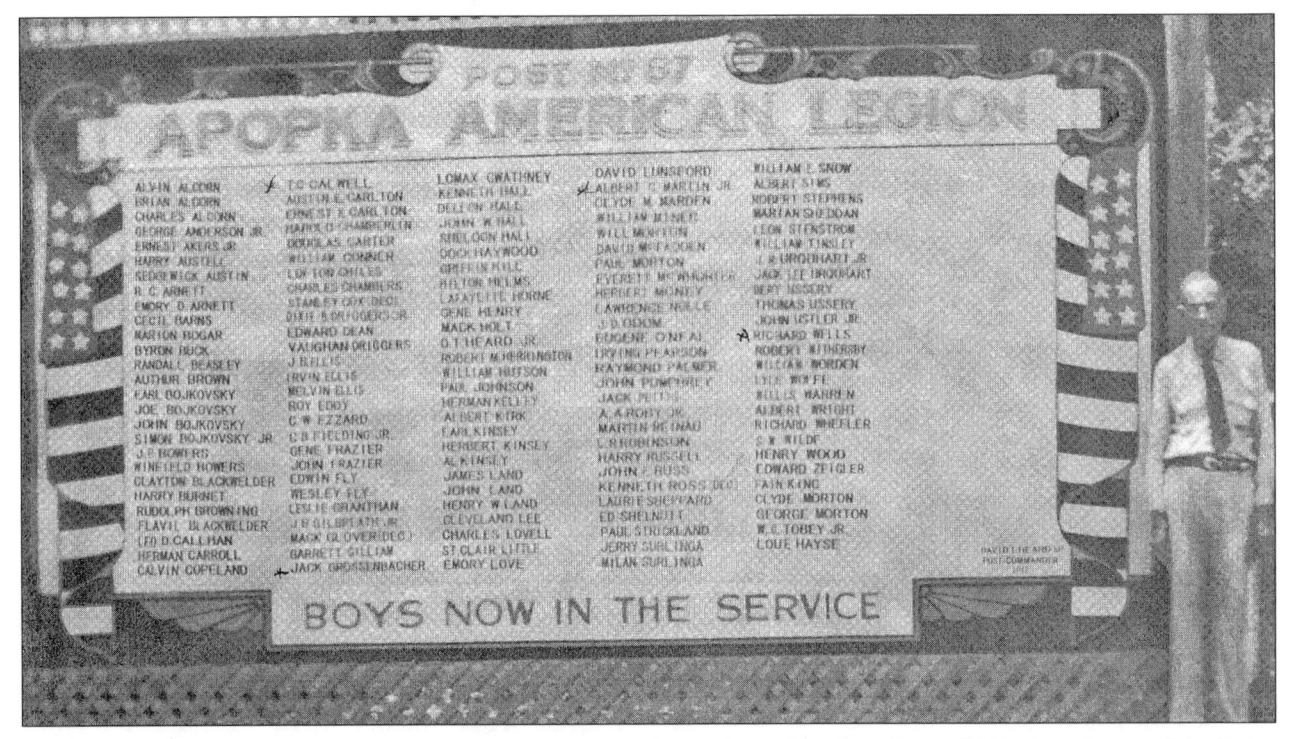

Davis Thomas Heard, Sr., Post Commander, American Legion Post #67 stands next to list of Apopkans serving in WWII, which was located in front of City Hall on Main St. in 1944.

The bombing of Pearl Harbor by the Japanese on December 7, 1941 surprised and shocked the people of Apopka as well as the nation. At the same time, it removed doubts about the economy, as well as the dispute over America's role in the expanding world war. The isolationists immediately joined President Roosevelt and the internationalists in a sustained, determined effort to defeat the Axis powers – Germany, Italy, and Japan and save the free world democracies. The dilemma of Communist Russia being on the side of the allies was deferred for the duration.

The sudden unity of the nation against a common enemy also restored the confidence of Americans in themselves and their system. Men enthusiastically flocked to the colors, ready to fight for their nation. Men and women alike demonstrated their readiness to make the sacrifices necessary to support the armed effort. In doing so they replaced their doubts of the past decade with an enthusiasm and self-confidence that buoyed the nation for another generation. During the ensuing four years, seventeen-million American men and women served in the armed forces all over the world and the industrial system – about which there had been such doubt in the 1930's – became the "arsenal for democracy." Exceeding the most optimistic patriots, American industry supplied the munitions and logistic support for the allied forces on all fronts. A confident nation was prepared for a leading role in international affairs after the war.

The Pearl Harbor disaster should not have been such a complete surprise. Much had already happened to suggest that the United States was being drawn into the war. The irreconcilable dispute with Japan may not have been clear to Americans on the street, but the sinking of the Reuben James by a German submarine half-way across the Atlantic Ocean should have emphasized the gravity of our lend-lease shipments to the allied nations. Infinitely more recognizable than either of these matters was the first peace-time draft of American youths for military training in 1940. By the narrowest possible margin, Congress authorized the conscription of young men for one year of military training. Men between the ages of twenty-one to thirty-five were registered for selection. On October 22, 1940, 600 men from Apopka registered for the draft. To the popular strains of "I'll be Back in a Year Little Darling," several of them reported to Camp Blanding during the following months. It would be much longer than a year before most of them returned. Most would have their term extended to "the duration and six months."

Some local youths had not waited for the draft. Jack L. and John R. Urquhart, Randall Beasley, George Anderson, Jr., Alvin Alcorn, and Woodrow Foxworth were among the area residents who enlisted as early as June 1940. After Pearl Harbor, there were more enlistments and the draft was extended to include all between the ages of twenty to forty-four. Registration for the expanded age group occurred on February 2. This added 317 residents of Northwest Orange County to the list. By May 1942, there were 122 of them already in the service, and numerous others would be added during the next three years. In October, the American Red Cross honored Simon Bojkovsky, who then had five sons in the military service. The D.F. Halls and Josephine Land were among those who had four sons in uniform.

The war soon reached Apopka in many other ways. Mobilization for war created enormous demands for goods of all kinds, and military needs had priority. Many items of food and equipment were rationed. Non-military construction was sometimes restricted.

Rubber supplies had been cut off by the Japanese invasion of Southeast Asia, and at the same time, military needs for it increased demand. Tires were rationed in early 1942. Gasoline was rigidly rationed for passenger cars, but allowances were made for farm machinery and trucks. Sugar and other commodities soon followed suit.

Children assisted the war effort through drives to collect paper and scrap iron for recycling. Everyone bought war savings bonds and stamps. In the schools, children bought stamps on a weekly schedule. Some firms offered payroll deductions for war bonds. Everyone was willing to sacrifice for the war effort. Most felt, that whatever was done on the home front was the least they could do, "for the boys over there."

After Germany capitulated in the spring of 1945 and the Japanese surrendered in August, Northwest Orange County's soldiers began returning home. They were received enthusiastically by families, friends, and entire communities.

Despite the sacrifices, it had been a satisfying experience. The enemy was clearly identified, issues were clear and popular, and there were good feelings from having pulled together on the home front and overseas in accomplishing victory over the dictators.

With the Depression far behind them, and continued full-time employment appearing likely, the people easily made the transition from war to peace.

Albert Martin

World War II claimed the lives of four of Apopka's finest young men. It seems as though those lost in battle were always the very best we had to offer. In Apopka's case, Albert Martin, Jr., Dick Wells, Harold Caldwell, and Jack Grossenbacher fit that description perfectly.

First, we highlight and honor the memory of Albert Martin, Jr., a native Apopkan, born on December 6, 1919. He attended Apopka schools and Orlando High School and was attending Stetson University before entering the U.S. Army Air Force.

Albert was raised on Alabama Street across the street from our Mayor John Land. Although Albert was a year older than John, they were close friends and playmates growing up. John says that Albert always wanted to be a pilot, and as a teenager, he learned to fly at the old Apopka airport at the corner of Welch and Thompson Roads and got his private license prior to entering the Air Force.

Died over Anzio Beach.

A lot of his socializing was done at the Orlando Country Club or at various sporting events around town. He was said to be an excellent dancer and figure skater. At an early age, he built his own boat and enjoyed the beauty of the Rock Springs and Wekiva Springs runs.

Albert Martin, Sr., whose brother was the governor of Florida, owned a dairy on the land where first Townsend's, and later, Captain and the Cowboy restaurants were located.

When World War II broke out, Albert enlisted in the U.S. Air Force and received his wings in March of 1943, at Marianna. He was later attached to the 514th Bomber Squadron, 376 Bomber Group in the European theatre.

First Lieutenant Martin commanded a Liberator named *The Confederate Clipper*, and his last mission was over Anzio Beach, Italy, on February 12, 1944. The plane was heavily damaged in an air battle and went down over the Mediterranean Sea less than 100 miles from an American base. Life rafts from the plane were found. However, there were no survivors.

Part of a letter President Harry Truman wrote the family is as follows: "He stands in the line of patriots who have dared to die that freedom might live, and grow, and increase its blessings."

Lieutenant Martin was awarded the Air Medal with Oak Leaf Cluster and the Purple Heart posthumously.

Dick Wells

Another one of Apopka's finest was Dick Wells. His family lived in Apopka on Central Avenue near Dream Lake during the cooler months of the year. In the summers, they went north. He graduated from a northern high school, but when he was here, he went to school in Apopka with the class of 1937.

"Dick was a grade ahead of me, a very nice fellow," remembers J.C. Hethcox, who was in John Land's and Jack Grossenbacher's class. He was a pilot in the Air Corps. and flew a P-38 or P-52. It is believed Dick was killed over the English Channel.

Dick's father, a local school board trustee, was instrumental in renaming Apopka High School as Apopka Memorial High School in honor of all the Apopka boys lost in World War II.

Harold Caldwell

Pfc. Harold Caldwell was the son of Mr. and Mrs. J. D. Caldwell of Apopka. He graduated from Apopka High School with the class of 1942. After graduation, he was employed by Skipworth's Service Station (now Walgreens) on the corner of Hwy. 441 and Park Avenue.

Harold enlisted in the U.S. Army in July of 1943, at the age of twenty. He was sent overseas in October of that same year, serving with the 75th Division, 289th Infantry.

The family received letters from him as late as January 26th, stating that he was just back from the front but only for a short time and would be returning to the front soon and that he "had seen plenty of action."

Pfc. Harold Caldwell was killed in action during the Colmar Offensive on February 2, 1945, in the small town of Wickerschwihr, France. He was buried with full military honors at the American military cemetery in Epinal, France. His body was brought home after the war and interred at Edgewood Cemetery in Apopka.

Harvey Caldwell of Zellwood remembers his big brother as being, "hardworking and super, super nice. I remember he loved to fish, but mostly he was always working, giving whatever he earned to our mom."

Jack Grossenbacher

We honor the memory of another young Apopkan lost in World War II. He was Captain Jack Grossenbacher, son of the late John G. Grossenbacher of Plymouth.

Jack graduated from Apopka High School, where he was elected president of the class of 1938. He is also well remembered for his activities in basketball and football. Jack had completed two years at the University of Florida as a roommate of John Land when the war broke out.

When he enlisted as a flying cadet at MacDill Field in Tampa on September 26, 1941, he was assigned to the Bonham Aviation School at Bonham, Texas. He completed his training at Randolph Field, Texas, and was assigned to the 434th Fighter Squadron, 470th Fighter Group, and 8th Air Force at Santa Maria Field, California. Before sailing overseas, he was temporarily assigned to the School of Applied Tactics at the air base in Orlando.

His group was based in Wattisham, Suffolk, England. On May 15, 1944, his group flew their first mission. On his 104th mission, he flew his P-38 Lightning fighter plane as an escort for a group of bombers whose mission was to attack the enemy's ball bearing and airplane parts factories at Schweinfurt, Germany.

The enemy flak was intense and accurate, scoring slight damage to the engine of a B-17, which was forced to slow down. With his wingman Lt. Simpson, Captain Grossenbacher remained behind to protect the bomber and crew from enemy aircraft. His supply of oxygen ran out, and he was forced to fly at a lower altitude. His plane was struck by flak and caught fire. The last report was that he had parachuted from the burning plane, and it was believed that his chute got tangled on the tail of his falling plane. He was reported missing in action, and later, when the victorious allied army liberated the territory where he was last seen, they recovered his body, which had been buried by the enemy in a rural area around Frankfurt.

On January 13, 1945, Major Edwin House, at a special ceremony at the Orlando Air Base, presented Jack's father with the Air Metal, one Oak Leaf Cluster, and the Purple Heart for his son.

Jack Grossenbacher's former roommate Mayor John Land issued a proclamation to name the streets in the developing Apopka Terrace area to honor these boys who gave their lives for our country. They are Grossenbacher Drive, Caldwell Street, Wells Street, and Martin Street.

In a 1992 interview with *The Apopka Chief*, Mayor Land said he was reminiscing about the old days with his old high school pals concerning four of his fallen classmates from high school and college. "We think, every now and then, about how life might have turned out if the war had not stolen from our midst four of Apopka's most promising youths during the era," John Land said. "Sometimes something draws the memory back to those days, and you can't help wondering how they would have matured and about things we would have done together. All of them would have made good citizens and made good contributions to the community."

Observation Tower

It was not long after the bombing of Pearl Harbor that the United States government started setting up procedures to protect the shores of the United States. German submarines were stalking the U.S. Eastern Coastline, and there was some concern about a Japanese air attack on the West Coast and a German attack on the East Coast.

A Civil Defense program was established in every county and community in the country in order to defend civilian society from military attack. Apopka's own Carl Jackson served as chairman of Orange County's Civil Protection Committee. There was an enthusiastic response to Apopka Mayor Ted Waite's proclamation of Volunteer Defense Registration Day, and after Pearl Harbor, an air raid blackout plan was completed. Fred Risener was chief warden, and F.L. Burgust was his assistant. The first test was announced on January 1942, and the response was very good. Then, in late May, an unannounced test interrupted the city council meeting while important business was being discussed. The city did its part, and the meeting was resumed only after the "all clear" sounded.

Frequent reports of oil tankers being sunk off Cape Canaveral by German submarines, and the revelation of a submarine landing three spies on Ponte Vedra Beach in 1942 aroused concern. When officials of the Aircraft Warning Service asked that communities erect and man observation towers against possible air attacks, the people again responded. Towers were erected in both Apopka and Zellwood. There would be 15,200 observation towers throughout the country, with 480 on the East Coast alone. The Apopka tower was located behind the old Apopka City Hall (behind the Bank of America today). Don Kenney was named chief observer for Apopka and S.M. Coen for Zellwood. Volunteers readily signed up for the shifts. These volunteers monitored the skies for air traffic and reported any flights to a central station in Jacksonville, where the information was cross-checked with authorized flight plans.

But the duty soon became drudgery, and it was difficult to find enough volunteers. Mayor Waite called a meeting at which Aircraft Warning Service officials emphasized the importance of a twenty-four hour watch. Kenney resigned as chief observer, and Oscar Vick succeeded him. For a while, the volunteers resumed their duties. The midnight shift was most difficult to staff.

At a February 1943 meeting in the UDC chapter house, Mrs. Howard Anderson declared that if the men would not man the observation post during the night shift, then the women must, "do their bit." Nineteen women signed up. Enthusiasm again waned after a few weeks. In May of 1943, A.E. Dymond, who had replaced Oscar Vick, called for volunteers for the midnight shift to, "prevent another Pearl Harbor."

I recall there was a gentleman named Pop Doan serving as chief observer during the later days of the observation tower. As a final effort, he enlisted high school students for the midnight shift. I was one of those thirteen- and fourteen-year-old volunteers who could not tell a Japanese Zero from a German Messerschmitt. As you might suspect, this project eventually proved unsatisfactory. By early 1944, people became convinced that it was a long way from Tokyo to Apopka, and the observation posts were discontinued.

Harvey Caldwell

Sometime in the early 1920s, John D. and Katie Mae Caldwell came to Florida from Nettleton, Mississippi, with their three children – Harold, Harvey, and Jean. John went to work with Wallace Champney, growing azaleas, and remained there until he passed away in 1952.

Harold graduated from high school in 1942 and worked at Skipworth's Service Station (where Walgreens stands today) before enlisting in the U.S. Army in 1943. He was sent overseas, serving with the 75th Division, 289th Infantry and was immediately sent into the heat of battle. The family received letters from him stating that he was just back from the front, but only for a short time and would be returning to the front and that he "had seen plenty of action."

One Sunday morning in February of 1945, young Harvey accepted the telegram with the gold stars notifying the family that Harold was killed in action during the Colmar Offensive in France. It was a terrible blow to the entire family.

During World War II, the City of Apopka consented to the leasing of Edwards Field for use as an Army base for the duration of the war. In conjunction with the Fighter Command School at Orlando, the 351st Coast Artillery Search Light Battalion, with about 250 men, converted the ballpark into an army post.

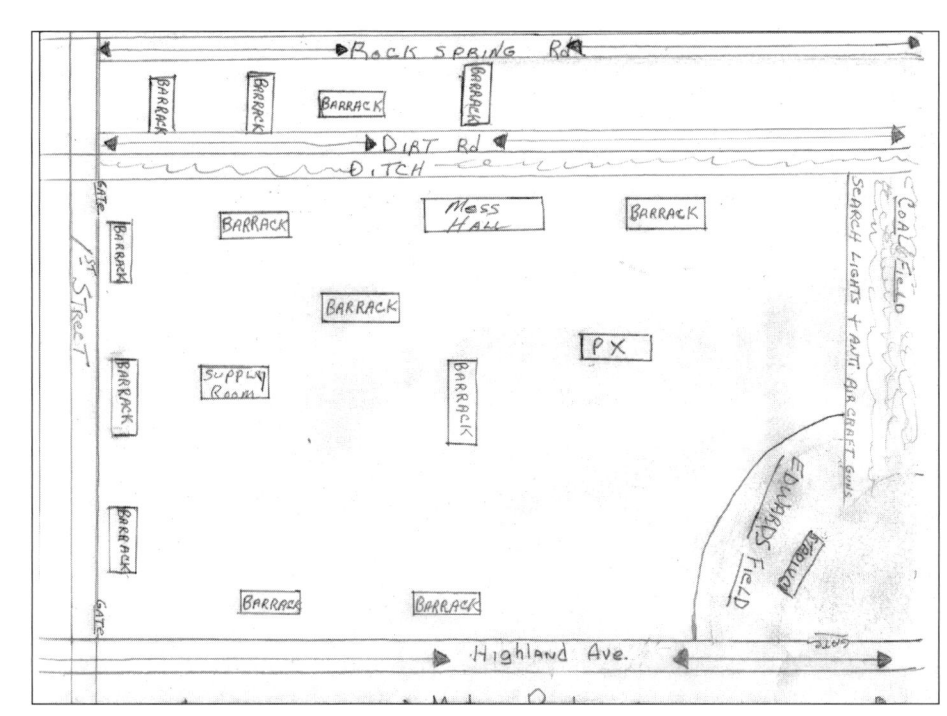

Maybe it was fate that the Caldwells lived across the street from the new army post and young Harvey sort of grew up in the midst of the many men stationed there. He would quite often invite some young men over for a home cooked meal, and pretty soon, Mrs. Caldwell found herself cooking for ten to fifteen young men with heavy appetites. It all worked out well as they all pitched in for food costs. Strong bonds were developed between the boys and the Caldwells. I am sure Mrs. Caldwell had a place in her heart for all of these boys, who were possibly away from home for the first time.

Harvey knew the layout of that base (as seen in a sketch at the museum), and he remembers the old potbelly stoves heating the barracks and the coal piles used for heating the entire base. He recalls an obstacle course they had laid out from the McBride property to Thompson Road.

He would ride along the path beside the course on his bicycle as they put out canisters of tear gas for the boys to go through.

The sergeant in charge gave Harvey a gas mask in case of emergency. When the troops came through, Harvey would circle back and go through the course with the boys. When they saw Harvey put on his gas mask, they knew trouble was right behind.

Every so often, the men would be shipped overseas, and Harvey would lose a lot of his old friends. There was the case of Francis Sturgis, who as he was leaving, handed Harvey his Bible to keep, as he felt he would not return. Recently, Harvey tried to contact Mr. Sturgis and found he had survived the war but passed away since. Harvey offered to return the Bible to the family.

It was at the base that Harvey developed his love for softball. Being a ten-year-old boy, he developed his skills at pitching, using the old windmill windup. As he grew older, he developed a mean fastball, as well as a good curveball and slider. Harvey's softball future was looking good.

Harvey found out, however, that Vienna sausage cans, firecrackers, and little boys just do not go together. One Fourth of July, he was piddling around in his back yard with firecrackers, when one failed to ignite under the sausage can. When he was checking it out, the firecracker went off, and the can hit Harvey in the left eye.

He lost the sight in that eye. After spending some time in the hospital, he was released with a patch over it. Later, he was standing with Glenn "Fireball" Roberts while the boys were throwing palm seeds at each other. When one of those palm seed missiles was thrown toward Glenn, he ducked, but Harvey didn't, and the palm seed hit Harvey directly on the patch over his bad eye. That sent him back to the hospital.

Losing the sight in one eye did not hold Harvey back from his love of softball. He learned to cock his head in such a way that he had full vision of the batter with his right eye. Now, this did not exactly help the batter, as his fastball was doing around 100 mph. I used to help Harvey warm up, but it did not take me long to find something else to do. Boy! That fastball hurt!

By the time Harvey was sixteen, Walter Hudson had him pitching for Denmark's Sporting Goods in Orlando. It was there that he got to pitch with Ollie Barker, a pretty good fastballer himself. Little Harvey must have felt intimidated by a guy like Ollie who was a huge specimen of a man. Harvey later pitched against Herb Dudley of the world champion Clearwater Bombers and beat the King and His Court at Edwards Field here in Apopka. He continued pitching for about twenty years, and then turned his interest into teaching kids the game of softball. He taught in most of the high schools in Central Florida before spending his last four years at Lake-Sumter in Leesburg.

Harvey, who just turned eighty, is retired, and he and his lovely wife Honey live in Eustis at the present time.

Ted Waite

When Leslie P. "Ted" Waite passed away in 1974, *The Apopka Chief's* editor at the time wrote in his editorial, a brief history of the man so beloved by his fellow Apopkans. It is presented to you in the time frame as it was written:

"It was a privilege to know L.P. "Ted" Waite, because he was ahead of his time in thinking of the future and assessing the present. He was our friend, and had words of encouragement for us during difficult times. His death on Tuesday was clearly a loss to the entire community and to those who knew him.

Most Apopkans of these modern times will remember Ted as they last saw him. We decided to go back in history and tell our readers about the young, vigorous Ted Waite when he was about 30 years old and in the prime of his life. But, before we tell you about him at that age, let us tell you about another marvel seldom heard of in the present mobile society of America.

He was born, raised and lived all of his adult life in the same house located on the southeast corner of Central Avenue and Orange Street. Thus, for 81 years, Ted Waite was able to command a view of Apopka and its growth and activities of its citizens. We are fortunate to have sat on his porch and talked with him about the past history of Apopka; and on one occasion, Ted's life-long friend, the late J.B. "Doc" Standard, joined us on the shaded coolness of Ted's porch. By chance, we had a tape recorder and we let it "run open" as Doc and Ted sorted through personal memories of events and Apopka personalities for well over an hour. We doubt that they missed discussing a single event or personality – all of which adds luster to the history of Apopka.

Ted Waite was proud of Apopka; it was his hometown. He was born here, educated here, was in business here, served his community in civic and political affairs, retired here – and died here.

We reviewed the pages of the old *Apopka Chief* and started with the earliest records on file. We found that, in 1924, Ted renewed his subscription to the *Chief*. He was elected to the city council in an unusual election in 1924. He received every vote that was cast in that election, including the votes for Ted Waite instead of L.P. Waite.

He was a conservationist at least 50 years before it was fashionable to protect the environment and was elected secretary of the Orange County Fish and Game Protective Association. The pages of *The Apopka Chief* contain many references to his love of the outdoors and his hunting and fishing activities. Only a few weeks prior to his death, Ted Waite continued to be a familiar figure seated in his lawn chair on the bank of Dream Lake, wearing his long billed cap and fishing beside a youngster of 10 or 12 years of age.

In 1924, he was a member of the Apopka Baseball Club, and despite a weak stick, he was really tough on the field. He was recorded as handling 91 put outs at first base before being credited with an error. Ted retained his interest in baseball throughout his life and always held the Apopka Baseball

Club in the Lake-Orange League, in high esteem.

Ted was no stranger to the free enterprise system, because the records show that he was a part of the local agricultural scene as a fertilizer dealer, until he moved into real estate just prior to the great Florida land boom in the mid-20s. It was in the mid-20s when he became interested in politics, and while serving on the city council, he led the way in pushing for a Clean-up Week in Apopka.

In 1924, Apopka boasted a population of 1,003 people, a first class postage stamp cost one cent for one ounce, and the council instructed the mayor to enforce a town ordinance, which called for keeping the chickens in a pen since 300 vehicles a day were recorded passing through the town. Ted served on the committee, which resulted in a three-story hotel being built in Apopka (the Palms Hotel).

Although 50 years passed from his activities in 1924-1974, Ted Waite remained aggressive and civic-minded. He was always there whenever a call for assistance was made and continued to serve city government in an advisory capacity. He was a member of the city-appointed study group on restructuring and streamlining the administrative functions of the city. Ted was mayor of Apopka for two consecutive terms during the tough and lean years of World War II and was fully aware of the tenacity needed to operate on a slender budget."

The community of Apopka will miss Ted Waite.

Sneed

When I was a young boy growing up in Apopka in the 1940s, my brother, Gene and I were very close with the Cox family that lived on the west end of Fourth Street. Their father had a meat market on South Park Avenue across from Consumers Veneer and Lumber. There were three boys and one girl in the family – Billy, Bobby, James, and a sister named Carolyn. Both Bobby and James were roughly the age of my brother, so where my brother went, I tagged along just enough to be a pain.

Drawn by Mary Jane Cox, James Cox's wife.

A lot of years have flowed through the dam since those early times. Billy has a bison ranch in Tennessee, Bobby and my brother have passed on, and James and I have resumed contact when I accidentally picked up a book in the Museum of Apopkans he had written entitled, *"Dustballs – The Adventures of My Lifetime."*

After James retired as a member of the national board of directors for TG&Y, a variety store chain, he began teaching the art of writing autobiographies for seniors at Louisiana State University. *Dustballs* included a story that I was very familiar with that he called, "Sneed." I think you will enjoy it:

"When I think of Tom Sneed, known to most people only as 'Sneed,' I fondly remember the city dump in my central Florida home town of Apopka.

It was the city dump that Sneed called home, existing there in his loosely fashioned shack of tarpaper, cardboard, and pieces of metal, burlap bags and old license plates. His residence flowed in perfect harmony with its environmental setting.

I came to know Sneed from his sometimes visits to my father's grocery store, which was an old house my dad had gutted and converted, and where I acquired my education in the grocery and meat cutting business during my high school years.

The dump was in the woods several miles from the store, so Sneed had quite a walk when he made the pilgrimage to town. But I suppose he picked up plenty of old shoes at the Refuse Supermarket where he lived.

I'm not sure how he got money; he never had much. All he ever bought was canned dog food. He said it tasted good. At ten cents a can, it was somewhat of a bargain even in those days. He must have picked the dump for other food.

We lived in the country, had a barn, and kept two horses in the stables. Many times, I'd throw the 40-pound saddle on Lady, my chestnut mare, and ride through the woods to the city dump. There my nostrils would be greeted with three acres of smoldering trash plume of acrid smoke and fumes.

Amidst all this foul smell and smoke was Sneed's rumble-tumble shack at the edge of it all, near trees that provide shade and protection from the wind.

On the occasion of my first visit to Sneed Manor, I called out this name while still astride my horse, being unsure what his reaction to a visit would be. At age 15, one could imagine strange happenings here. 'Hey there…anybody home?' I shouted. I heard movement inside.

He emerged from the cocoon of his handiwork looking as if he had been buried by the Mexican earthquake, and had just been pulled out. Filthy, dirty skin, matted hair that probably had not been washed or combed for years, worn out sandals (or old shoes cut in strips), no socks, and emaciated feet. He squinted through the cracked scum on his face, raising his hand in a gesture of salutation. 'Ho,' he said.

After the first trip, it became a lark to periodically ride out to visit Sneed, sometimes with buddies who had horses, sometimes alone; it began as a joke, a fun thing, see the freak.

My fascination with this man was inspired by my youthful curiosity to learn why any human being would choose to live like this. But a few trips later, squatting around a fire roasting hot dogs, which I provided, on a sharpened palmetto stem, Sneed recounted the stories of his life that brought him to this point. The stories came only in small snatches of conversation.

I watched, curiously, as he meticulously put two more hot dogs on the sharpened stick, squatting in the flow of the fire like an Australian Aborigine. As he talked in his squeaky voice, I began to realize this man was not a freak to ridicule, but a man, no matter how far he had fallen.

Still a living, breathing person just likes me, who had many failures and tragedies visited upon him over the years, and was not strong enough to handle it all, and so, dropped out of life. I had never before pitied anyone so. But I can only guess how he came to be there. It was evident he wanted no part of people or the establishment any longer. He must have wandered, dejected, and beaten, a bruised and battered man with nowhere to go. He probably had no money, and lived by scavenging for some time, and finally, through trial and error, arrived at the Apopka City Dump, where he was left alone, and nobody cared if he stayed or went, lived or died. He was the original dropout. The first hippie, He was home.

I had my own feelings for situations back then, and have reflected on those feelings each time I see the 'Sneeds' of this world

I experienced many things growing up in Apopka, but I'll always remember the city dump and the human lessons I learned from Sneed that he never knew he taught."

Zellwood Drainage District

VEGETABLE FARM AREA — In the foreground is a portion of Lake Apopka which is two feet higher than the farm area. In background is the pump house located in the #2 Unit of the District. A system of canals, ditches and mole drains enables each farm to maintain its own water control levels.

This article was taken from Henry F. Swanson's book, Countdown for Agriculture in Orange County, Florida. Henry's book was first published in 1975, and most of the information contained was prior to the State's buyout of the Zellwood Farms:

"The clouds of World War II began to appear on the horizon in late 1940 and interest in national food production began to accelerate. This "rekindled" interest in the marshland area near Zellwood that was abandoned some 23 years before.

As who did what, where, and when, in this second attempt to re-develop this area, several versions exist. However, nearly everyone agrees that the late Judge Charles O. Andrews, Jr. was really the "father" of the Zellwood farm area in that he created the legal vehicle which brought the Zellwood Drainage and Water Control District into existence. When Judge Andrews was a member of the Florida Legislature (House of Representatives), he drafted the necessary legislation to create the Zellwood Drainage and Water Control District Act. It was this Act that secured the necessary financing and engineering to bring this development into being.

In 1941 the Zellwood Drainage and Water Control District was organized as a municipal corporation under a special Act of the State Legislature (Chapter 20715). Those familiar with the legal aspects of this Act credit Judge Andrews with creating a landmark piece of legislation. If this Act had not been properly drawn up so as to withstand all kinds of legal attacks and maneuvers, the District would probably have failed during the trying years of the area's early development. It should be pointed out also that Judge Andrews served as President and legal advisor to the Board of Supervisors of the District from its inception until his death in September of 1969. Thus, Judge Andrews guided the District through its financial problems and its struggles with various groups as well as controversies relating to Lake Apopka.

Mr. George B. Hills prepared the original engineering design for the District. Following that, a local citizens committee was required to establish the value of the land proposed for development. According to E.S. Marsell of Zellwood, he, Harlow Barnett and Leroy Smith, both of Tangerine, set the value at $150.00 an acre. With the value of the land to be developed established and a plan for development drawn up, an application was made to the Reconstruction Finance Corporation for creation of the Zellwood Drainage and Water Control District. A Reconstruction Finance Corporation loan was granted in the amount of $142,500 for Unit #1 (approximately 2,589 taxable acres) and $257,500 for Unit #2 (approximately 6000 taxable acres). In the course of construction, addition funds became necessary and the R.F.C. granted a supplemental loan in the amount of $87,500.

During these early years, Mr. Richard Whitney, of New York, was a principal owner because his properties were pledged for loans from a New York bank. When Mr. Whitney encountered financial difficulties in the repayment of these loans, the bank sent their troubleshooter, John F. White, to assist in liquidating these properties. In 1945, Mr. White bought the New York bank's interest and obtained a loan for $200,000 from Connecticut Mutual Company to create the Florida Humus Company, of which he became president.

Proper management of the water was the primary requirement of the Drainage District and a network of major canals was built so that the water level on each farming tract could be maintained individually and without regard to the other tracts. Gus Wenzeloof, the first Superintendent of the Zellwood Drainage and Water Control District, was replaced by Arch Hodges on March 1, 1946. According to Hodges, a section of land (640 acres) was normally ditched as follows; one ditch 660 feet from the line, followed by a second ditch 1,320 feet from this one and two more ditches 1,320 feet apart followed. A final ditch 660 feet from the proceeding squared off the section giving it a uniform grid system of water control.

Units 1 and 2 each had its own pump house, with three diesel pumps handling 42,000 gallons per minute. Lake Apopka was two feet higher than the nearby farmland so water from the lake could flow into the District canals by gravity flow. Pumps moved the water throughout the network of canals. From the main canals, each individual farm tract can regulate its own water levels.

Moving water from the District back into Lake Apopka required extensive pumping because of the two-foot difference in elevation.

This elaborate water system was supervised full time by the superintendent who was answerable to the Board of 5 Supervisors. This Board was set up to provide the overall management of the District. It also sets the annual tax per acre that provides funds to maintain the 11 miles of levees separating the lake from the farmland, together with all the bridges, roads, canals of this 9,000-acre private tax Drainage and Water Control District.

This system of managing its affairs under a municipal corporation responsible to the taxpayers within the District has withstood the test of time. The sound thinking of the late Judge Charlie O. Andrews, Jr., made the landowner responsible for his own destiny. This vital principle was not employed when the area was first opened to farming at the turn of the century and at that time it was impossible for each farmer to control the water level adequately within his farm area.

Of the farms that began back in the trial and error period when the District first opened, Hooper Farm was one of the most successful. In 1948 the father, M.M. Hooper, a station manager in North Birmingham, Alabama, retired from the Southern Railroad at the age of 62. The family operation consisted originally of Mr. M.M. Hooper and sons Foley and Eric. Later the younger brother Frank joined the operation as did Foley's son, Robert and Eric's brother-in-law, Pat Green.

They farmed 1,700 acres of muck soils in Orange and Lake Counties. In July of 1948, Mr. Hooper and his son Eric, (then in the service) toured Florida looking for a suitable site to start raising cattle. On this trip they happened to visit the newly developed Zellwood Drainage and Water Control District. Both were impressed with the possibilities of the area for vegetable production rather than for cattle operations. Their enthusiasm was such they purchased 265 acres in Unit #2 of the Zellwood District from J.W. Piowady. In October, 1948, Foley, the oldest son, left the American Cast Iron Pipe Company in Birmingham and brought his family, father, mother and younger brother, Frank, a fifth grader to Zellwood.

The second son, Eric, an Annapolis graduate, class of 1946, still had a year of military service to complete but after completing his military service in 1949, he too joined the family in the Zellwood farm venture. As the family farming operation expanded over the years, the roles of the various members changed. Brother Frank completed college, and joined the family operation. Eric's brother-in-law, Pat Green, and Foley's son, Robert did likewise. M.M. Hooper, now in his late 80's, assumed an advisory and bookkeeping role, which left the other members free to concentrate on production and marketing of the various crops. What began originally as a cattle safari to Florida grew into one of the areas most successful vegetable farms."

CHAPTER IX - THE JOHNNYS COME MARCHING HOME

Johnie McLeod

Prakash Gandhi of the *Orlando Sentinel* staff wrote an article back in 1990 titled "Lawyer not afraid of a tough fight." With this headline, there was no doubt he was referring to our good friend Johnie McLeod of Apopka. Johnie never backed away from a battle he considered just. Although Johnie has passed away, his firm is still representing the same causes under the leadership of his two sons, Raymond and Bill. Let's take a look at just how this attorney became such an advocate of "justice for all."

Keep in mind this is quoted in the time frame that it was written:

"Johnie McLeod learned about battling against the odds at a very early age.

McLeod was three when his family moved to Sanford in 1924 from Portland, Oregon. One year later, the family moved to Lockhart, where McLeod went to elementary school.

He started working when he was six. Later, he swept classrooms each afternoon at Apopka High School. 'It made me a very independent person and made me respect people's rights to earn a living,' he said.

McLeod completed his under-graduate work before the war and entered law school after he was discharged from the Marines. He borrowed money from the Apopka Rotary Club and worked in an Orlando grocery store to pay for his studies. He started at the University of Florida's law school, but transferred to Stetson University in Deland, where he graduated.

McLeod opened a practice three doors from his current office at 48 E. Main Street. The city had a population then of less than 2,500 and the workload was light, he said. While running his private practice, McLeod spent 16 years as a Justice of the Peace. He figures he handled more than 100,000 cases, holding trials in his office, issuing warrants and for eight years, signing death certificates.

In 1972, he launched another chapter in his long legal career when he became Apopka's city attorney, a part-time position he held for 13 years. McLeod resigned his position as city attorney after clashing with high school classmate and long time Mayor John Land over a proposal to annex a large area of land.

Over the years, McLeod has gotten himself involved in many zoning issues, representing citizens he believes have been wronged with dogged determination. Often he represents clients for free.

Land, who has known McLeod for more than 50 years, said that his fierce drive is one of his strongest features. 'When he gets to doing something, he will hold on with bulldog tenacity and carry the job through to the end,' Land said. 'I think that is one of the things that has gotten him as far as he has.'

McLeod's office has the usual symbols of his profession – the scales of justice, the bundles of legal papers on his desk and on the floor. Leaning back in his chair with a foot propped on the large desk, he speaks philosophically about himself and the law, citing legal opinions to add ammunition to his arguments. His thick gray hair sweeps across part of his forehead; his bushy eyebrows move up and down and he gestures a lot with his hands.

McLeod feels passionately about the importance of the U.S. Constitution and about the role of elected officials. A person who goes to an elected official with a problem should get it addressed by the official and should not be referred to staff, McLeod believes. 'I do not know why public officials become adversaries once they become elected,' he says in a voice that constantly alternates between softness and great strength. 'They are fine people until they become public officials and then they lose their goodness.'

Last year, he argued before the Florida Supreme Court that Orange County's charter, which voters passed in 1986, should be scrapped. McLeod thinks charters give too much power to non-elected bureaucrats and too little power to the average citizen.

In the 1960s, he fought an ordinance that required dog owners to license their dogs before they were vaccinated against rabies. McLeod considered it 'taxation without representation.' He won and the judge dismissed the law as too vague."

Mayor John Land

In 1920, Bennett Land, Sr., with his wife Josephine, her uncle Albert Schneider, and others, purchased Consumers Lumber and Veneer Company (CL&V) from the Starbird family.

Bennett was at a CL&V company board meeting on November 5, 1920, the evening John Land was born in Plant City. John is the middle child of nine. His older siblings were Henry, Bennett, Lydia, and Josephine, and the younger ones were the twins Catherine, known as "Kit," and Jim, Sara Jane, and Mary. Bennett Land moved the family to Apopka when John was one year old. Mrs. Land returned to Plant City for the birth of Kit, Jim, and Sara Jane at the home of her parents, Mr. and Mrs. William Schneider. Mrs. Schneider died in 1926, and John's sister, Mary was born in Apopka on November 29, 1928, at the family home on Alabama Avenue.

Bennett Land, Sr. died March 4, 1935, in the middle of the Great Depression when John was fourteen years of age. At twenty-one, Henry became the president of CL&V, and he and Mrs. Land kept the family and the business together.

John enjoyed growing up with all the activities available to a young boy of that time: hunting, fishing, athletics, school plays, HiY, FFA, and observing national, state, and local political campaigns.

Before the age of ten, along with his buddies, he would fish in the small lakes two or three blocks away from home. Later, they would drive to Lake Apopka and more distant lakes such as Lake Harris, Lake Eustis, and Lake Jessup.

John and his childhood friend, Albert Martin, Jr. had their own playgrounds with the rolling hills of Alabama Avenue and the Martin Dairy pastures. They built their own boats and paddled on the Wekiwa River and Rock Springs Run, as well as the small lakes of Central Florida.

When John was fifteen years old, his mother gave him an L.C. Smith double-barrel shotgun. He and his friends and a bird dog named Mary walked about a half-mile from his home, where Mary found a covey of quail, and in the excitement of his first shot, he pulled both triggers and managed to bag a quail. From that time on, John was hooked on quail hunting.

There were outside chores for the boys of the family. They cared for the chickens, ducks, rabbits, pigeons, turkeys, goats, horses, and dogs. There was also a garden, along with citrus trees, a yard, and a cow. John also had two pigs to raise for an FFA project. Henry had honeybees and family pets. The girls had inside chores.

To John, living on the Land three-acre homestead was like living in Norman Rockwell America. This all changed when the whole world was drawn into the flames of war in the 1930s.

John attended Apopka High School, graduating with the Class of 1938. He entered the University of Florida in the fall of 1938, pursuing his education in agriculture and forestry. He participated in the activities of the Lambda Chi Alpha Fraternity and received Army ROTC training in Field Artillery.

Reporting for active duty in the U.S. Army on June 25, 1942, John was assigned to the First Battalion Field Artillery Replacement Training Center at Ft. Bragg, North Carolina. He saw action in WWII at the end of the Battle of the Bulge, with General Patton's Third Army with Corp Artillery in V Corp. The war in Europe ended May 8, 1945, while John was in Czechoslovakia, having crossed Germany from Belgium.

Captain John H. Land returned home June 3, 1946, and returned to work in the family business. He had met Betty Ross Hall at a school dance while he was home on military leave. John and Betty dated when she was home from Georgetown University, where she was earning a nursing degree. She graduated in 1948, and they were married in 1949.

John and Betty have three children – Suzanne Larkin, Catherine Waters, and John, Jr. They also have five grandchildren – Catherine, Jordan, India, Samantha, and Caroline.

The year John and Betty were married, John was elected mayor of Apopka and became the youngest mayor in the history of the city. His three-year term started January 1, 1950. In 1950, Apopka's population was 2,254, and the city government still operated much the same as it had during the Depression of the 1930s. Officials had worked hard and were successful in keeping the city together and did not default on bond payments, as did some cities. Mayor Land, as a businessman with four years leadership in the Army, wanted to move the city into the future more quickly.

With the exception of one three-year term out of office in the 1960s, Land has been the mayor of Apopka. He holds the state record for longevity in the office of mayor in Florida, and could very well be the longest-serving, full-time mayor in the United States.

But I must digress from talking about John Land the person and talk to you about John Land the true historian and molder of Apopka, the city that he has done so much for and that he loves so very much.

The following are a few of the early accomplishments of his multiple terms of office, starting in 1950:

> The city purchased a modern garbage truck for $12,000; and by saving trips to the dump, the truck was paid for in three years.

> The land that is now Kit Land Nelson Park was purchased for just under $6,300.

> Construction began on a much-needed Sewer Plant (a campaign promise).

Property was annexed for the first time since 1882.

Sand rut roads were converted to twenty-four-foot clay roads, with large road improvements, the first since the 1920s. Revenue Certificate Bonds were used.

The city changed the charter to increase the number of council members from three to five.

Mayor Land went to New York to sign bonds worth $3,900,000 to build the Lake Apopka Natural Gas District.

In 1965, he was invited to attend a meeting with Governor Hayden Burns and Walt Disney.

He supported the need to preserve land needed for parks, such as Wekiwa State Park, which was purchased in 1969.

The city purchased the former high school, which was remodeled for the New City Block Campus, which included a new fire station, police department, Emergency Operating Center, and forty-person jail. It also included a location set aside on the northeast corner for the Apopka Chamber of Commerce.

Land met with Richard Mark, who planned to develop Errol Estate, formerly owned by the Pirie Family. At the meeting, Mr. Mark requested that Errol Estate be annexed into the City.

He instituted the first full-time, paid fire department.

He served on committees in an effort to improve Lake Apopka and save the muck farms area.

Mayor Land worked with the governor and legislature as they moved to pass legislation to buy farms.

The City adopted a new charter. This was needed for a larger city and change in the state.

Oh, yes, these things were accomplished in his first thirty or forty years. While under his leadership, the City of Apopka has grown from a small town of 1.25 square miles with a yearly budget of $31,000 to a city of over 33 square miles with a population of 41,000, and it still on the rise. His innovative ideas continue to keep Apopka growing, year after year.

Take Mayor Land any place in the thirty-three square miles of town, and he will tell you the history of that area. He can explain how the area came to be within the city limits, as well as all of the details involved.

Mayor John Land has received so many awards, honors, and accolades that it would be impossible to list them all here. However, over the almost sixty years that he has represented Apopka, everything has been done with the good of our town as his foremost thought.

Recently, he said, "Looking back in 2011, one can see that since 1950, Apopka has changed from a Mayberry-type farming community to the second largest city in Orange County." While reminiscing about the past, Land commented, "We did have lots of fun in those good ol' days gone by; however, we are now living in the best of times!" He has a saying, "Don't let the past be an enemy to the future."

Dr. Charles Henry Damsel

A Naturopathic physician, Dr. Charles Henry Damsel was known and honored throughout the state for his ability and professional integrity. He headed professional organizations and was a member of the Florida State Board of Examiners of Naturopathic Physicians.

Dr. Damsel also served his fellow citizens in numerous public capacities, including as the mayor of his home community, Apopka, from 1947-49. His record as mayor was one of business acumen and administrative ability, which was of benefit in establishing permanent policies of government and many civic improvements. A good example of that was his purchase of a fire truck from the city of Orlando for $1. He was succeeded by a twenty-nine-year-old veteran by the name of John H. Land. Damsel was an active member of the First Presbyterian Church of Apopka and was one of Florida's renowned Masons.

Dr. Charles Henry Damsel was born in Columbus, Ohio, on February 15, 1900, the son of Fred P. and Mary Murphy Damsel. His father, an accountant, was the son of Charles Henry and Lillian Damsel of Columbus.

Dr. Damsel began his education in Columbus grade schools. He graduated from Indianola High School and obtained his degree of Doctor of Chiropractics at Ross College in Ft. Wayne and his degree in osteopathy from Metropolitan College in Cleveland. He took post-graduate courses in proctology and was licensed to practice in Ohio, South Carolina, and Florida. In 1936, after taking his exams, he was granted a license to practice medicine.

His attraction to this beautiful state and to the climate of Florida compelled him to leave an established and lucrative practice in the city of his birth and start anew in the small but beautiful city of Apopka. In 1938, he built a small hospital and residence on Central Avenue.

During the World War I period, though too young for military duty, Dr. Damsel was the youngest superintendent of shipping for the United States Food Administration, servicing at Columbus, Ohio. The executive ability he displayed then proved to be of extraordinary benefit to the people of Florida and to his professional colleagues. He has served as president of the Florida State Naturopathic Physicians Association, and for three years was on the State Board of Examiners by appointment of Governor Spessard Holland. He also served a long term on the Board of Governors of the Naturopathic Physicians Association.

Dr. Damsel was a member and past master of Orange Lodge No. 36, Free and Accepted Masons, and past district deputy grand master of the fifteenth district. He was an officer in the Ancient and Accepted Scottish Rite; a member of the Ancient Arabic Order of Nobles of the Mystic Shrine; a member and past chancellor of the Knights of Pythias; a past monarch of Grotto; a past worthy patron of the Orange Chapter No. 137, order of the Eastern Star, and a member of the Woodmen of the World.

By 1936, flying was a popular avocation in Apopka. At that time, the Apopka Aviation Club was formed by Dr. Damsel, R.A. Lassiter, Dan Colbert, and Park McCall. The doctor was a real flying enthusiast, and he logged many hours in the air. He was a charter member of the Civil Air Patrol of Florida, serving as a wing medical officer.

Dr. Charles H. Damsel married Dorothy M. Carter of Columbus, Ohio, and they had a daughter – Dorothy Jeanne and a son Charles "Chubby" Henry, Jr. Their daughter was born in Columbus on July 19, 1920. She received her elementary and junior high schooling in Columbus, but graduated from Apopka High School and attended Southern College at Lakeland. Chubby was born in Columbus, Ohio, on April 30, 1929. He received his early education in the grade and high schools of Apopka, graduating in 1946. He attended the University of Florida and received his law degree in 1956. He now has a very successful law business in West Palm Beach, Florida.

Coach Howard Beckert

It seems almost impossible that it has been more than a year since our good friend Howard Beckert left us for his heavenly home. And it seems like only yesterday when he showed up as the new, twenty-six-year-old football coach at Apopka High School. I wasn't sure whether he was our new starting guard or our new coach. He seemed to be pretty young to me.

And young he was. Born January 1, 1920, in Pittsburgh, Pennsylvania, Howard was the second son of Walter and Rose Beckert. He was actually raised in West View, a little north of downtown Pittsburg, and graduated from Perry High School in 1938. His love for sports was nurtured there as he lettered in football, basketball, and baseball.

After high school, he attended Slippery Rock University in Slippery Rock, Pennsylvania, and graduated with a bachelor of science in education, specializing in math and physical education. While at "The Rock," he played varsity football and lettered for three years. Upon graduation, he was recruited by the Philadelphia Eagles, but he did not pursue their offer. I suppose he felt that he would be drafted one way or the other, so he joined the U.S. Navy during his senior year (1942) and received his ensign's commission at Officers Candidate School at Columbia University. After receiving his commission and while he was home on leave, he dated Margaret "Peg" McQuistion, who two and one-half years later would become his bride.

On reporting back to active duty, he was assigned to LST 375 (Landing Ship Tank) with the amphibious forces in the European theatre. He saw action in the landings in Sicily in July 1943, the Salerno landings in September 1943, and the Invasion of Normandy in June 1944. During this period of time, he was serving as a communications officer. At Salerno, his ship received a 1000-pound shell, a 250-pound shell, and eight 88s from German coastal artillery batteries. Upon being declared unseaworthy, LST 375 put in at Bigerti for repairs.

Ensign Howard Beckert

After repairs were made, they left the Mediterranean and proceeded to England to participate in the granddaddy of them all, the D-Day landings at Normandy on June 6, 1944. Howard missed a couple of trips across the channel due to the fact that he had to have his appendix removed. Well, having your appendix removed is one thing, but where you have it removed is something else. The operating room was in the bar of the Weymouth Hotel in Weymouth, England. Ensign Beckert recovered and returned to the trips across the English Channel for the duration of the invasion. After the war in 1945, he returned home to marry the girl he dated two and a half years earlier. While still in the service, he enrolled at the University of Pittsburg to pursue his master's degree.

After graduation, he and Peg moved to Florida to be closer to Peg's parents. He and Peg had two children – Howard Jr. of Winter Haven and Dorothy Rhodes of Apopka. While still in uniform, Howard was hired by Bob Pittman, Sr. to coach at Ocoee High School.

Howard was officially discharged from the U.S. Navy in January of 1946. He applied for and got the coaching position at Apopka High School that same year. The high school was located in the buildings that City Hall occupies today. Actually, he coached football and basketball, and he coached them well. In his eight years as a coach, he won many conference championships in football and basketball and coached the first undefeated football team in Apopka's history.

I felt as though he had the attention of the majority of the boys with the possible exception of Curt Haygood. One evening, coach was giving us a little "talking to," when he stopped in the middle of his lecture and asked, "Curt, are you listening?" Curt replied that he wasn't. Coach Beckert replied, "If you do not pay attention to me, I will rub your nose in the dirt." Curt replied that the coach was too slow for that. Well, the next thing I knew, they were both at the left field fence, and Coach Beckert was rubbing Curt's nose in the dirt. From that day forward, Coach Beckert had the attention of all the boys.

In 1954, Howard left coaching to enter the administrative side of his profession. After serving as assistant principal at Apopka High School and principal of Apopka Elementary, he took over the new Dream Lake Elementary, where he remained until his retirement in 1977.

Before his retirement, he lost his beloved wife Peg to cancer in 1973. Two years later, he lost his brother Bob in Pittsburgh to a stroke. Life was getting very lonely for Howard until his good friend Bob Pittman, Jr. stepped in to help fill that emptiness with weekend fishing trips out of Cape Canaveral. He continued his weekend fishing until he had a heart attack in 1986.

After his retirement from education, he married Marjorie Chambers, who had served as media specialist at Dream Lake for seventeen years. Marjorie passed away recently.

Howard was active as an elder and deacon in the First Presbyterian Church in Apopka. He was a former member of the Apopka Rotary Club, a Paul Harris Fellow, and a fifty-year member of the Masonic Lodge of Apopka. Howard belonged to the Orange County Retired Educators Association and Slippery Rock Alumni Association. He was highly respected as a leader in Apopka and a man with great presence.

Charles H. Damsel, Jr.

Charles H. "Chubby" Damsel, Jr. was born in Columbus, Ohio, but his family moved to Apopka, Florida, when he was six years old, where his daddy was a small town medical practitioner and the mayor. Attending such a small school in Apopka gave Chubby an opportunity to be involved in extra-curricular activities, including football and basketball. Of his 1946 graduating class of thirty-six students, it is believed that thirteen of them are still living.

In the fall of 1946, he entered the University of Florida, continued to be interested in extracurricular activities more than scholarships, and was a member of Kappa Sigma social fraternity. He was active in the Florida Players, the Florida Radio Guild, and many other productions, particularly Gator Growl. He was the president of the Florida Players, Alpha Phi Omega, and Alpha Kappa Psi. In 1950, Chubby was chosen to the Florida Blue Key, the highest leadership fraternity, and to the University of Florida Hall of Fame. He received his bachelor of science in business Administration in 1950.

In February 1951, he enlisted in the U.S. Army and served for two years as a special agent in the Army Counter Intelligence Corps, and in August of that year, he married Margaret W. Damsel, who had been the dietician and his boss when he was working for his meals in the University of Florida cafeteria. Just before they returned to Gainesville to attend law school in September 1953, they were blessed with the birth of their son Charles H. Damsel, III.

During his time in law school from 1953 to February 1956, he managed 144 Florida-Vet apartments for the University. He once again got involved in extra-curricular activities. He was executive director of the 1953 and 1954 Gator Growls, and was a member of Phi Delta Phi Legal Fraternity. He and Peggy were blessed with the birth of their daughter Cherie in August of 1955. Chubby graduated with his LLD in January of 1956.

After law school, Damsel went to work with Gurney, McDonald, and Handley in Orlando, working predominantly on insurance defense cases. Thereafter, he moved to West Palm Beach where he became a partner with Jones and Foster and continued on the defense side of litigation for over twenty-eight years.

During that time, Chubby has conducted over 250 jury trials, including the usual automobile cases, those including catastrophic injuries, medical malpractice cases, hospital negligence, product liability, and other liability matters.

He has been admitted to the Florida Bar, the Federal District Court, the Trial Bar of Federal District Court, the Fifth Circuit Court of Appeals, the Eleventh Circuit Court of Appeals, and the United States Supreme Court.

In addition, Chubby has been a member and past president of the Palm Beach County Bar Association, a member and past president of the Florida Defense Lawyers Association, a member and past local president of the Federal Bar Association, a member and past vice-chairman of the Florida Bar Board of Legal Specialization & Education, a member and past vice-president of the Federation of Insurance and Corporate Counsel, a diplomat of the Florida Academy of Professional Mediators, and a member of the Florida Academy of Certified Mediators.

He was recently awarded the Federal Defense Lawyers Association's Douglas P. Lawless Award for his contribution to the alternative dispute resolution areas of the association.

Tommy Staley

Life was very pleasant during the 1930's, as James and Edna Staley were raising their two boys Merritt and Tommy in Macon, Georgia. If there was a problem, it was that James was a coffee distributor in the Southeast and had very little time to spend with his family as he was on the road five days a week.

Mr. Staley had a brother-in-law who was a celery farmer in Oviedo and who often encouraged Staley to join him in Florida. Finally, in 1937, the Staleys made up their minds to move to Florida. Mr. Staley bought a Gulf Oil Station in downtown Oviedo and immediately started getting up at 4:00 a.m. to service the farm equipment in the area with gasoline at twelve cents a gallon and distillate (similar to kerosene) at five cents a gallon.

Tommy was in the seventh grade and immediately pursued the two sports that the schools offered, which were baseball and basketball. He graduated from Oviedo High School in 1943 and two weeks later joined the U.S. Navy, and left for the Great Lakes for eight weeks of training. After basic training, he was sent to Key West for twelve weeks of training as a sonar operator and came out as a 3rd class petty officer. He moved on to Norfolk, Virginia, where he joined his crew of 321 for destroyer school. After schooling at Norfolk, the entire crew boarded their new ship, the U.S.S. Stern DE 187, at the Brooklyn Navy Yard. Tommy would spend the next two years and four months aboard the ship. The Stern escorted five convoys to different ports in Europe, including Casablanca, Bizet, Tunisia, Normandy, Plymouth, Liverpool, Belfast, and Londonderry.

The Navy later moved the U.S.S. Stern through the Panama Canal to Pearl Harbor and westward to the Leyte Gulf. Next came Iwo Jima, where the U.S.S. Stern escorted the landing barges to the beach.

It was somewhere around the middle of the morning of February 23, 1945, that Tommy heard bells ringing, sirens and foghorns blowing, and troops cheering. Tommy glanced to the top of Mt. Suribachi and saw Old Glory waving in the gentle South Pacific breeze. This, of course, signified the advancement of U.S. Marines on the Japanese fortress on Suribachi. The troop commander did not feel that the flag was large enough for all the troops on the beach to see, so the infamous seven men were sent up the mountain for the second time where one of the most famous pictures of World War II was taken, the raising of Old Glory on the top of Mt. Suribachi on Iwo Jima. Tommy Staley was fortunate enough to have witnessed this memorable part of history.

The U.S.S. Stern moved on to Luzon to form a group for the invasion of Okinawa. It was during this campaign that they shot down five kamikaze planes. It was an honor to receive a message from Admiral Kincaid, commander of the Seventh Fleet. The message was, "Your continued good shooting is taking its toll on the enemy. Well Done." It was also their last campaign in the Pacific, and they headed back to San Pedro, California, where they began converting the U.S.S. Stern into an attack personal destroyer for the invasion of Japan. The crew was given a thirty-eight day leave. While they were on leave, the A-Bomb was dropped on Japan, and the Japanese surrendered. The ship was delivered to Green Cove Springs for mothballing, and Tommy received his discharge in Jacksonville on March 4, 1946.

While Tommy was in the Navy, his father had sold his gas station and was farming a small celery farm in Oviedo. Tommy worked with him for about two years and then married his high school sweetheart Martha Carraway on June 4, 1946. The celery business started going through an overproduction period, so Tommy went to work for the Clonts Farm in Zellwood and stayed there about two years. He then moved down to Delray Beach, Florida, to run a 200-acre farm for the Hoopers.

Wanting to be back in Central Florida, Tommy went to work for George Long, an uncle to Billy Long. In 1954, Tommy made his final move to Zellwin Farms as a field foreman. Over the years, he worked his way up to production manager.

In 1979, Martha passed away. Tommy later married Lou Laughton Norton. Each of them has three children.

In 1983, Zellwin Farms was having a bus tour of Germans. They had stopped at the carrot fields when Tommy noticed one of the Germans was off to the side and crying. Being curious, Tommy asked the German's wife what the problem was. It seems the gentleman had been a German prisoner of war in World War II and had been held in a prison camp in Leesburg. They were brought in to work the Zellwood muck farms during the day. This was the first time the German had seen the farms since, and he was touched.

As it turned out, the couple was Fritz and Marriane Fitting of Mauchenheim, Germany. Tommy exchanged addresses with the German couple, and he and Lou regularly corresponded with them over the years. In 1992, Tommy and Lou went to Germany on vacation and visited the Fittings, who owned a winery in Mauchenheim and lived in a home that had been in the family for 400 years.

In 1995, the Fittings visited Tommy and Lou here in Apopka. They have exchanged visits a couple of times since.

Tommy retired from Zellwin Farms in 1988, after thirty-four years. At that time, the farm had 10,000 acres and 700 employees. He went into politics in 1989, and was an Orange County Commissioner for the next eight years.

Roger A. Williams

Attention! – At ease – Thank God It's Friday! If you went to school in Apopka after 1946, you would know from those words the subject of my tidbit is none other than Roger Williams.

Mr. Williams, as we all would forever call him, came to Apopka through the urging of school board members Clem Womble and Charlie Wells.

Mr. Williams grew up on a farm in Antrevill, South Carolina, near Abbeville. He attended school there and developed a deep and abiding faith in God, a burning love for America, and a character distinguished by pride, determination, and humility. His brothers and sisters gave him the nickname "Babe."

He graduated from Erskine College in 1931, with a double major in social studies and religion. Mr. Williams chose Chipley, Florida, as the place to begin his career in education. His first assignment included teaching and coaching. From Chipley, he moved to Bonifay, where he spent seven years as supervising principal.

After teaching in Bonifay, he felt the need to enlist in the U.S. Air Force. During his four-year tour of duty, he was honored by the 20th Air Corps with a Commendation for Distinguished Service for developing a Guam education program.

When he first came to Central Florida, he had every intention of attending school for three months in Orlando. However, a good friend loaned him a car, and he drove out to Apopka and met with Charlie Wells, Hermit Smith, and Clem Womble. They convinced him that they could make a call to the county supervisor of education, Judson Walker, and get him a job at an Apopka school. They drove him around Apopka, and his first impression was that he liked the people and the town.

In 1946, he had three job offers. Mr. Williams said, "I did a lot of praying before I accepted the position as principal of the Apopka twelfth-grade school," where he remained for thirty-four years.

I was privileged to be one of the first students to learn and feel the strong hand of discipline that he brought to our school. It was late in the afternoon in a study hall class. I was minding my own business, and all of a sudden, I was whacked on the back of the head with an eraser wielded by J.C. Hicks. I immediately picked it up and was in full back swing when Mr. Williams walked into the room. Wouldn't you know it? I was the one who was called to the office, and I was the one who was given the choice of going home or taking a couple of whacks from his famous paddle. Well, I was smart and said I would just go home. That was a mistake. When I got there, my dad asked why I was not at school, and when I told him, he said, "Fine, now you can get on top of the slat sheds and put moss in for shade." I did that for a while, but it was so hot, I decided to go back to school and take my whipping from Mr. Williams. I was careful from then on.

Mr. Williams master's degree in school administration was received from Duke University in 1950, and in 1952, he earned a doctorate degree equivalency from the University of Florida. At some time, he went to school with the Presbyterian minister, Arthur Ranson, and later became a member of his church.

His keen interest in high school athletics led him to join with other Central Florida principals in forming the Orange Belt Athletic Conference. He was honored by his colleagues who appointed him as the conference's charter president.

Over the years, AMHS has received many honors for its high scholastic standing and can boast of many outstanding athletic teams. Mr. Williams was always the most enthusiastic supporter of the teams and always tried to instill a winning spirit in his students.

In 1954, a young science teacher Elizabeth Smith was hired at AMHS. Roger and Elizabeth were married June 14, 1956, and were blessed with three children – Roger, Jr., Lisa, and Rose. Roger and Elizabeth have four grandchildren.

In reflecting on his fifty-six years in Apopka, he enthusiastically acknowledged that Apopka afforded him and his family a wonderful, happy life that he would not exchange for living anywhere else.

Also important to him was that he was considered to have been the catalyst that helped racial desegregation in our schools. He felt that Apopka took the fall for integration. People were on pins and needles as to what might happen when integration started. As it turned out, their fears about problems at Apopka High School were unfounded, because Mr. Williams had been so proactive in addressing the situation.

When listening to the comments from his former teachers, you hear accolades like the one from Janet Connelly, "I admire him as a man of conviction. He is willing to listen to other people, but he not afraid to state what he believes in."

Bill Arrowsmith, class of 1964, said, "He ran a real tight ship. He kept everyone in line. It's too bad they can't run schools like that now. He was a wonderful administrator. He was a great inspiration to the community."

Roger Williams and Howard Becker were being interviewed for *Tater Tales*, an Apopka Historical Society oral history project, and Howard said, "Mr. Williams did more for education than anyone ever had in Apopka."

For the recording of *Tater Tales*, Mr. William said, "I had a knack for hiring the right people. I know how to size people up. The Lord gave me that gift." He further said, "The problem with the school system now is that Washington is setting the curriculum instead of the local school board."

In that same interview, Mrs. Connelly asked about any incident that stood out in both men's memory, and they both remembered that while Coach Beckert was getting the football team ready for a game with Eustis, he said to Mr. Williams, "If anyone gets hurt tonight, it will be Jack Christmas." Well, sure enough, on one of the first plays of the game, I ran into a Mack truck and ended up on the ground with a broken collarbone. The bad part was that Mr. Williams had to go and tell my parents that I was hurt and in the hospital. When Mr. Williams woke my dad up and told him what had happened, my dad blew his top (and said some unsavory things), because he had no idea that I was playing football, and he had never given me permission to play. Finally, my mother intervened, and by the next day, my father went and apologized to Mr. Williams.

Williams is recognized as one of the outstanding educators in the state. He constantly took stands against concepts of education that would lower the quality of the education our young people receive.

Although he has received many awards and honors, he feels his proudest achievements were his fifty-year tenure teaching what is now known as the Roger Williams Sunday Class at First Presbyterian Church, and his induction into the Florida High School Activities Association Hall of Fame.

Mr. Williams was admired by the teachers and students over the years, and he made Apopka a better place for us to live. Thank you, Mr. Williams, for your dedicated service.

CHAPTER X - APOPKA'S FINEST

Jack Hall

With the war ending in both the Atlantic and Pacific, you would have to consider 1945 a vintage year. Boys were returning home from the war and in a lot of cases, they continued their education in high school and college. This was made much easier with the G.I. Bill.

The G.I. Bill made it pretty tough on the high school kids entering college in pursuit of an athletic career, while competing against the much older and mature veterans returning from the war.

This was the case with Jack Hall, a 1946 graduate of Apopka High School, where he was all-conference in football. Along with five other local high school graduates and veterans, Perry Warren, Julian Roberts, "Red" Rickerson, Jack Urquhart, and his brother Bob, Jack enrolled at Norman Park Junior College, a Baptist school in Norman Park, Georgia, where he played fullback and linebacker. He received his AA degree in 1948.

In those days, a few extra bucks were hard to come by, and hitchhiking was more acceptable than it might be today. On one of

Jack Hall coached several sports.

Jack's regular trips home over the holidays, he often stopped off in Gainesville on his way back to school, to visit a couple of his old friends from Apopka, T.L. Rogers and Glenn "Fireball" Roberts, who were enrolled at the University of Florida at the time. On one such trip, Fireball suggested to Jack that he would be glad to drive him out to the town of Alachua because getting a ride from downtown Gainesville might be difficult.

The three of them loaded into Glenn's souped-up race car. T.L. was crammed into the back and Jack sat on an orange crate up front with Glenn, who was safely strapped in under his roll bars. Well, it did not take long for Glenn to hit 100 mph in second gear. By this time, T.L. was screaming for mercy. He wanted out and swore never to ride with Glenn again. He did hitchhike back to campus. Jack got out in Alachua with shaky knees, and he immediately stuck his thumb up for a more tranquil ride on into Georgia. Jack probably did not stop off in Gainesville too many times after that trip.

After two years in Norman Park, Jack received a scholarship to Newberry College, a Lutheran

~ 233 ~

liberal arts college in Newberry, South Carolina. There, he excelled not only as a running back, but also as a kicker. He lettered in football, baseball, and track. He graduated in 1950 with a bachelor of science degree in history and political science. He obtained master's degree in school administration and history from the University of Georgia in 1956.

Jack's military service began while he was still in college in 1948, with his enlistment in the National Guard. He was called to active duty as an Infantry SFC in 1953, during the Korean War. He also served short recall sessions during the Cuba, Grenada, and Panama problems. Jack retired as a colonel from the ready reserve after thirty-seven years of service.

While serving at Ft. Jackson in South Carolina, Jack coached the football team to an All-Service Championship in football and an All-Army Track Championship.

When Jack took his first high school coaching position in Aynor, South Carolina, he was the head coach of the baseball, basketball, football, and track teams. This school had never won a state championship in any sport. During Jack's first year as coach, they were runners-up for the state championship in football, and by the second year, they had won it all.

Coach Hall spent the next few years coaching Boone High School in Orlando, where he was eventually voted into the Hall of Fame.

Jack's first college coaching job was at the Citadel in Charleston, South Carolina, from 1960-65. He was an assistant football coach for the Citadel freshmen for three years and served as defensive backfield coach for the Bulldogs. His 1964 defensive backs were ranked number ten nationally in pass defense. Jack was also the Southern Conference track and field coach of the year in 1961-62. His 1961 team finished first in seven of sixteen events, and six members of the 1961 team are in The Citadel's Athletic Hall of Fame. In October of 2007, Jack Hall was inducted into the Citadel Athletic Hall of Fame.

Due to his outstanding accomplishments in track and field and also as a defensive backfield coach, Jack moved up to Duke, where he spent the next five years as co-coach of Duke's track and field team.

In 1970, Coach Doug Dickey recruited Jack to Tennessee where he was the head freshman football coach and head recruiter.

When Doug Dickey went to the University of Florida, Jack went along as one of his assistants and head recruiter. Jack spent eight years at the University of Florida and then moved on to a recruiting job with the New York Jets. When Jets coach Walt Michaels was fired, his entire staff went with him.

Coach Hall only needed a few years in order to retire from teaching. He took a position as the track and field coach for Santa Fe Community College in Gainesville. When he got there, he was informed that he was also the women's tennis coach. As for coaching tennis, Jack had never played a game of tennis, but he accepted the challenge with the tenacity that had carried him all the years of his life. "The girls," as he loves to call them, came in fourth nationally in the junior college ranks.

Jack is now retired with his lovely wife Trudy. They live in the suburbs of Gainesville. I think that when his mind drifts back to all of his accomplishments during his coaching career, it is still "the girls" that have that special place in his heart.

This area is very proud of the accomplishments of Apopkans such as Jack Hall. The thing that we treasure the most is that he is still proud to call Apopka his hometown.

"Fireball" Roberts

BEACH RACE 1948

"Fireball"

Glenn "Fireball" Roberts has been dead for forty-four years, but he is still remembered and loved by his old hometown of Apopka and Northwest Orange County. Many of the racing elite still believe to this day that he was the greatest stock car driver of all time.

Glenn grew up in Apopka, where his father worked for Consumers Lumber and Veneer Company and was in the grove business. The word on the street is that Glenn got his name "Fireball" as a baseball pitcher in the sandlots of Apopka. He played high school football; however, he never played any organized baseball.

His family moved to Daytona Beach following his sophomore year at Apopka High School. He joined the U.S. Air Force and after six months, he received a medical discharge because he had asthma. The problem with asthma is that it never goes away. Throughout his racing career, Roberts would have to have oxygen after every race. The asthma eventually contributed to his death. He could not wear the fireproof clothing available at the time because of his asthma.

Dr. T.E. McBride, his physician in Apopka, said, "Well, he had a bad case of asthma. Many nights I didn't think he would last until morning. We had to move everything out of his room except a porcelain table. We were trying to keep everything dust free."

After his discharge from the Air Force, Glenn returned to Florida and got his GED, making the highest score ever attained in the state, and graduated with his class of 1947 at Apopka High School. He attended the University of Florida for three years before he left to pursue a racing career.

Like any race driver, Roberts did not start at the highest level. He worked his way up by racing at such bullrings as Seminole Speedway, Jacksonville, Greenwood, Hendersonville, Newberry, and countless other tracks across the South. In Greenwood, many veterans of stock car racing love to tell about that skinny kid from Florida they had never heard of who came to town and blew out all the locals.

Roberts had several great years in racing, but 1962 was special because he took racing to a new dimension. That year, he was named the Hickok Professional Athlete of the Year for all sports. No race car driver had ever come close to such a prestigious award. Fireball was actually the first superstar of NASCAR. In March of 1963, *Motor Trend* magazine said Roberts was the most aimed-at driver in racing history and the man with whom most comparisons are drawn.

"Fear-boll, Fear-boll, Fear-boll," the French chanted as Fireball Roberts roared down the front stretch at Le Mans in 1962. It marked the first time in auto racing history that a Southern stock car driver had truly gained international racing acclaim.

Sadly, only a short time after his trip to Le Mans, Glenn Roberts would die in a tragic racing accident at Charlotte Motor Speedway.

As he strapped into his race car that fateful day, a friend dropped by and handed him two dollars that he had borrowed. Glenn stuck the crumpled bills in his shirt pocket and finished the strapping-in process. Less than four hours later, Junior Johnson would plow into the rear of Ned Jarrett's Ford, which in turn would put Fireball into the wall. As his car burst into flames and rolled to a stop, he struggled to unstrap his belts. While being assisted by the heroic Ned Jarrett, Glenn called out, "My God, Ned, I'm on fire! Help me!"

Glenn suffered burns over seventy-five percent of his body and was rushed to Charlotte Memorial Hospital where he lay in agonizing pain for six weeks. Glenn Roberts passed away on July 2, 1964, at the age of thirty-four in what had become known simply as "the wreck."

There is irony in Roberts' death. He was planning to drive two more races and then retire. "He had already signed his retirement papers," according to his fiancée, Judy Judge. "He was going to work for Falstaff to do color commentary for the races. He was going to drive in the Firecracker 400, which he had won in 1963, and the Southern 500, which he had also won in 1963, and then he was going to announce his retirement. That was signed, sealed, and delivered. He said he was happy for the first time in his life."

John Land, mayor of Apopka, said the people of his town continued to think of Roberts as their own, even though he had moved to Daytona Beach. Land said Roberts made race fans out of the local people but after "the wreck," they lost interest.

The fact that Roberts became one of the most popular drivers of all time was no surprise to Roger Williams, Apopka High School's principal. "Glenn had a very outgoing personality," Williams said. "He was friendly, well liked, and popular with students, teachers, and the people in the town."

Those of us in Apopka and Northwest Orange County have always had a place in our heart for those who were raised in our midst and went on to pursue their dream in whatever field they may have chosen. Edward Glenn "Fireball" Roberts pursued his.

Bob Pitman

Back in 1982, Jim Carfield of the *Orlando Little Sentinel* wrote an article about Bob Pittman II titled "Baseball's First Free Agent." Again, I will use the time frame in which it was written:

"When you toil in baseball's minors, it's one long bus ride after another, playing for next to nothing and dreaming of someday becoming a wealthy free-agent like Dave Winfield of the New York Yankees. That's sort of the way things are done today.

Most of the game's historians regard free agency as a modern phenomenon, which simply didn't exist in the 'good old days.' But, like everything else in this world, there's always an exception. Free agency really isn't a recent development or a new road to athletic riches. It is as old as the game itself.

Half a century ago, becoming a free agent was possible too. Few players were interested, though. In those days, when Babe Ruth, Lou Gehrig, and the New York Yankees were dominant, obtaining your release from a contract was a one-way ticket to the minors. Free agents rapidly turned into paupers.

Except for infielder Bob Pitman, Jr., signed off the University of Florida campus by the old Boston Braves in the early 1930s.

Pitman, born in Blountstown and a resident of Apopka since 1917, was baseball's first successful free agent. He asked for his release from the Boston club after the 1933 season in order to become the highest-paid part-time player of his era. Not as a major leaguer, but as a minor league star.

Actually, Pitman never made it to the big leagues. After signing with the Braves, he was assigned to their Harrisburg, Pa., farm club. In his first game there, he broke his left ankle sliding into second base. While recuperating, Pitman was offered the head-coaching job at Bartow High School and took it.

For him, free agency was a way to stay in the game, negotiate for himself, and command the largest possible salary.

Basically, Pitman's formula was the same as the strategy used by today's stars with a few exceptions. It didn't make the Gators first baseball All-American a millionaire overnight. He didn't hire a business agent to do his wheeling and dealing, and negotiated only with the minor league teams in the old Florida State and Carolina Leagues. Pitman's fielding and batting skills were all the marketing tools he needed.

'I did just the opposite of what most ball players do,' says Pitman, who turns 71 next month, but remains active in the family citrus and foliage business. 'That injury taught me a baseball career was risky stuff. Besides, it was during the middle of the big Depression and you just couldn't afford to pass up a steady job.'

'All I wanted to do was supplement my income by playing summer ball. Back then, the minors attracted lots of interest and drew pretty big crowds (5,000-6,000 fans). A top player could make $250 to $300 per month plus room and board. By becoming a free agent, I could dicker with anyone in any league and I'd usually wind up getting offers from all over.'

'Nobody else was content to stay in the minors – all the other players were aiming for the majors.'

Pitman even spent one summer playing in two different leagues. He led Gastonia, N.C. to the first half title of the Carolina League in 1938, and then finished out the season playing for the Sanford club of the Florida State League. At Gastonia, he earned $300 per month and hit .420. In previous summers, he starred for Gainesville, which won the FSL title in 1936 and 1937. Everywhere he went; his salary was three or four times more than what his younger, starry-eyed teammates were paid.

'We played a shorter season, of course, but my compensation was fairly comparable to the average major league salary of the day,' said Pitman. 'Back then, $10,000 was big money. For four months of baseball, I pretty much matched my salary as a teacher-coach at Bartow High. Those were hard times and you could buy a full course dinner for a quarter. Today, that's not even a good tip.'

Pitman, also an avid angler, spent 13 summers in the minors and also organized and coached the Bartow entry in the old Orange Belt League. He also was one of the most respected prep coaches of his era, winning football titles at Bartow and then moving to Bradenton, where he coached the first unbeaten, championship football team in that school's history in 1941. He later served as the Gators' wartime baseball coach and football backfield coach before retiring from active coaching in 1946.

Now only five pounds heavier than his playing weight of 185, Pitman doesn't consider himself a pioneer.

'There's a different emphasis nowadays,' he said. "Anybody who averages .250 and hits 20 home runs is considered a good player. Not in my time. Back then, you were ashamed when you struck out. And you weren't considered much good unless you could hit .300.'

'Today's free agents are talking big figures, and it looks like they could kill the game.'"

Rodney Brewer

Rodney Brewer was one of the top all around athletes ever to come out of Apopka High School. He was a six-foot, three-inch, 210-pound, left-handed quarterback who ended his high school football career by being the most sought-after quarterback in the state of Florida. He was also an outstanding baseball player who struck out 161 batters in 109 innings his junior year. He was drafted by the Toronto Blue Jays in the twenty-fifth round of the 1984 amateur draft, but he chose to attend college so he could play both sports.

In choosing a college, he had finally boiled it down to the University of Florida, Alabama or Florida State. All three schools wanted him to play football only. However, Rodney's mind was made up that he wanted to play both baseball and football, and he made this perfectly clear to all three schools. He finally accepted a full ride with the University of Florida to play both sports. In an interview with Glenn Miller of the St. Petersburg newspaper, he stated, "If I couldn't play baseball, I wouldn't have come here."

Well, Rodney ended up joining the Great Summer Quarterback Derby of 1984. This included Dale Dorminey, Roger Sibbald, Brian Massingill, Clifton Reynolds, Donnie Whiting, Darryl Crudup, and Kerwin Bell. As the pre-season practice came and went, so, too, went Sibbald, Crudup, Reynolds, and Whiting. With only days before the season opener against Miami, senior Dale Dorminey was announced as Florida's number-one quarterback. Dorminey was followed by Brewer, Bell, and Massingill on the depth chart. As fate would have it, Dorminey suffered a freak injury during practice, and the coaching staff moved Bell from number three to number one because he was more familiar with the offense as a red-shirt freshman. Thus began the career of "The Throwin' Mayoan" from Mayo, Florida – population 900. Bell went on to finish Florida's unprecedented SEC season being ranked the number-two quarterback in the nation and being named the Southeastern Conference's "Rookie of the Year." The Gators finished the 1984 season with a 9-1-1 record.

As 1985 rolled around, Coach Galen Hall was breaking in the previous year's prize recruit by inserting him in the lineup when Bell had built a comfortable lead. And so it was that during the second game of the season against Rutgers, Bell was pulled after building a 28-7 lead. Rodney Brewer will always be linked to this game by having a couple of interceptions and a fumble. Rutgers came back and tied the game 28-28. To this day Rodney is given the blame for this tie, although Rutgers had to sustain two drives of sixty-five and eighty-six yards for the tie. Even "The Animals of Section B" (FSU) wrote a song about Rodney. He was a good sport about it all when they serenaded him during football or baseball games.

It was not two or three hours after Rodney threw his first touchdown pass against Cincinnati in 1984 that he was talking about needing to find the time to get into the batting cage for some practice cuts. It was only a few weeks later when he joined Joe Arnold's Gator baseball team for 1985. Rod lettered for 1985-1987 with a batting average of .348. He still holds some pretty lofty records at the university. He is tied all-time for third place with David Eckstein with fifty-one doubles and is twelfth with a .568 slugging percentage.

Although there have been quite a few Gators who were two-sport athletes at the University of Florida in track and football, you can count on your fingers the number that played baseball and were quarterbacks on the football team. I can think of Herbert Perry, Doug Johnson, and Rodney Brewer. Then, of course, there was Haywood Sullivan back in 1951, fifteen years before Rodney was born. There may be more, but their names do not come to mind.

The St. Louis Cardinals drafted Rodney out of college in the 1987 draft (124th). He was sent to the St. Louis farm club in Johnson City, Tennessee, and batted .252 in his first season.

He spent time with the Springfield Cardinals and Arkansas Travelers and three years with the AAA Louisville Redbirds before being called up in the latter part of 1992 by the Cardinals. He finished that year with a .301 batting average. He had been called up two previous years in 1990-91, but did not see a lot of action. In 1993, he started out with St. Louis and had a .286 batting average for the year.

After his four-year stint with the Cardinals, Rodney spent time with the Buffalo Bisons, the Charlotte Knights, and the Phoenix Firebirds before retiring in 1997.

Northwest Orange County is proud of Rodney Brewer and all of the acclaim he has brought to himself and our end of the county. Whatever the situation, he always carried himself through his athletic career with honor and integrity. For this, we are proud.

Country Singer - John Anderson

A few years back, George "Jug" Anderson and I decided we were going to be good fathers and take our two sons, John and Robert, on a weekend fishing trip to Englewood. Jug swore the snook were biting and the ten-year-old boys would have the experience of their lives. Well, he was partially right; the boys had the time of their lives. From the time they hit the back seat, they were like two ornery bobcats. They fought all the way down and all the way back. To make matters worse, not only did we not catch any fish, but we did not even have a strike. Enough said about being a good fisherman.

One of the things that Jug could be proud of is the fact that his son John grew up loving to fish the lakes around Apopka and deer hunt with his friends. He probably remembers well his first deer and hunting with J.C. Hicks and his son Jim. Another thing he liked to do was play and sing with his favorite guitar that his dad bought for him at an early age. Generally speaking, John Anderson was the typical teenager growing up in Apopka.

When John graduated from Apopka High School, he moved to Nashville at the young age of seventeen. Being the son of a grounds supervisor at the University of Central Florida, he knew something about manual labor, and he hired on as a construction worker in Nashville. As ironic as it may be, one of his first jobs was putting the finishing touches on the new Grand Ole Opry House. He stayed busy during the day with his construction work and was singing in the honkytonks of Lower Broadway at night, hoping to be discovered.

His first step out of the honkytonks and lounges of Nashville was a record on the independent Ace of Hearts label. Then he got a songwriting contract with publisher Al Gallico.

Finally, in 1977, Warner Brothers signed him. He gained some recognition with his first album, but in 1981, he reached bona fide star status with his biggest hit up to that point, "I'm Just an old Chunk of Coal" By 1983, Anderson gave country music one of its biggest hits ever in "Swingin'," a masterfully delivered slice o' middle-class country life, for which he earned two Country Music Association awards. But you have to admit that Anderson's masterpiece was "Seminole Wind," a song about the Everglades in his native state of Florida.

John David Anderson has accumulated five number-one hits and twenty-three top-ten hits in his career. He also received the Academy of Country Music's Lifetime Achievement Award.

He and his wife, Jamie, and daughter, Brionna have settled down approximately fifty miles southeast of Nashville in the small community of Smithville. The house, which he designed with help from his wife, sits on 135 acres of beautiful Tennessee hill country.

In an interview with *Entertainer* magazine, John says when he is not making records in Nashville or playing concerts on the road, he is home, doing Smithville-type things. "I guess the most exciting thing that happens around here is when you go to the farmers' co-op, which is about twice a week," he says. "Of course Jamie goes to the grocery store every day, and sometimes I go along." He smiles. "That's pretty exciting, too."

He adds, "It just feels really great to be normal. You know, I enjoy going to the softball games with my kid, buying seeds at the co-op, and having people treat me just like everyone else. That kind of thing is a real treat for me."

The basically low-key Smithville is perhaps the perfect place for John to live his life. The hilly, partially wooded terrain around Smithville is thick with wildlife, including deer, as well as turkeys and other game birds. Prime wild-hog hunting territory can be found less than an hour from John's house. The fishing in the local lakes that dot the area is an angler's delight. "This place is like paradise for an outdoorsman," says John, with a big-as-all-outdoors smile.

It seems as though Jug's tow-headed son has found peace and contentment in the hills of Tennessee. His "flat-land" friends here in the Apopka area still wish him well and want him to remember that we still love him and are very proud that he is still considered one of us.

Glenn Hubbard

A small boy approached Mrs. Chambers, the Dream Lake Elementary School librarian, with the question, "Do you have any books on stocks and bonds?" Quite shocked with this type of question from a third-grader, she replied, "No, not really, but if you will give me some time, I will get you what you need." The small boy was quite exasperated when he said, "How do you expect me to learn about stocks and bonds when you have no books for me to read?" It did not take Mrs. Chambers long to come up with a couple of books on the subject.

This young man went on to join the faculty of Columbia University Graduate School of Business in New York City as a full professor at the age of twenty-eight. From 2001-2003, he was chairman of the U.S. Council of Economic Advisors under President George W. Bush. *Weekly Standard* executive editor, Fred Barnes, in *The International Economy*, called him, "the most influential chairman of the Council of Economic Advisers in two decades." By 2004, he was named the dean of the Columbia Graduate School of Business.

Glenn graduated from Apopka High School in 1976.

Glen graduated from Apopka High School in 1976. While he was there, he served as the state and chapter president of the National Honor Society and the National Beta Club, and was also the state president of the Teenage Republicans during his senior year.

This outstanding senior went on to attend the University of Central Florida, where he graduated number-one in the class of 1979 with a double major in business and economics and a 4.0 grade point average. In continuing his education, Glenn earned his master's degree and a Ph.D. in economics from Harvard University. Upon graduating, he accepted a position as a professor at Northwestern University in Evanston, Illinois. In 1988, after receiving a fellowship at the National Bureau of Economic Research, Dr. Hubbard joined the faculty of Columbia.

In addition to writing more than ninety scholarly articles on economics and finance, he is the author of a best-selling textbook on money and financial markets. He was deputy assistant secretary of the U.S. Treasury Department for Tax Policy from 1991-1993.

Dr. Hubbard was tapped by some media outlets to be a candidate for the position of chairman of the Federal Reserve when Alan Greenspan retired, although he was not nominated for the position. A supply-side economist, he was instrumental in the design of the 2003 Bush tax cuts.

In the spring of 2006, Columbia Business School students produced a parody video, "Every Breath Bernanke Takes," describing Hubbard's supposed disappointment at not receiving the nomination to be chairman of the Federal Reserve. The music is a mock music/video remix of The Police's song, "Every Breath You Take." The comedy troupe who produced the video also made one in 2005 about Hubbard, playing off the Vanilla Ice song, "Ice Ice Baby." These videos have been popularized by Internet sites and blogs. I would not assume the character used in the video was Dr. Hubbard, but if it was not, the Columbia Business School students should be commended.

In 2007, Dr. Hubbard signed on as co-chair of Governor Mitt Romney's Economic Advisory Committee in Romney's unsuccessful bid for the Republican Party's nomination to run for President of the United States. When asked why he supported Romney, he replied that he thought Romney was the smartest and understood the big economic problems we face. Dr. Hubbard does not shy away from expressing his opinion.

Dr. Hubbard is married to Constance Pond Hubbard, and they have two sons – Robert Andrew and William Charles. They reside in Manhattan.

Myrt and C.W. Hubbard must have had a busy time keeping their two boys supplied with reading material as they were growing up. The two boys were probably reading from two different books, as Glenn's brother Gregg, known as "Hobie," pursued a musical career in Nashville as part of the group Sawyer Brown.

As proud as "Ms. Myrt" must be of her boys, she can rest assured that this community is also very proud of them, and there will always be a place in our hearts for the boys who chose to do it their way.

Zack Greinke

Would you have believed in your wildest imagination that one of Apopka's own, Zack Greinke, is pitching his way toward a Cy Young Award for this 2009 season? Now, having him win that would really be something for our favorite hometown of Apopka. A couple of my dear ol' friends, Pellegrini, known as "Pal," and Tom Russell must be two happy campers. I do recall that every time Joan and I slipped out to see Zack play when he was in high school, there were Pal and Tom. Believe me, Apopka citizens are not the only ones sticking out their chests. Just listen to the management of the Kansas City Royals.

Royal's manager, Trey Hillman, recently stated that starting pitcher Zack Greinke is on track to join the game's elite pitchers. Greinke tossed his first major league shutout against the Texas Rangers recently and extended his shutout streak to thirty-four innings, dating back to last season. "He's on a roll," Hillman said. "That was about as good as it gets. I think Zack can be one of the premier pitchers in the major leagues."

After being named the Gatorade National Player of the Year in 2002, Zack was selected out of Apopka High School (he turned down a scholarship to Clemson) in the first round of the 2002 draft, and he spent the winter of 2002-03 in the Puerto Rican League. Afterwards, he played for the Wilmington Blue Rocks and Wichita Wranglers, where he was named the Royals Minor League Player of the Year, and *The Sporting News* Minor League Player of the Year, with a 15-4 record and 1.93 ERA. Greinke made his major league debut on May 22, 2004, against the Oakland Athletics.

He ended the 2004 season with a record of 8-11 (second-highest on the team, after Jimmy Gobble) and a 3.97 ERA. Greinke has been compared to Greg Maddux and Bret Saberhagen. He has sports endorsement deals with Adidas and Rawlings. However, Greinke's 2005 season was not as successful, as he went 5-17 with a 5.80 ERA.

In 2006, the talented Zack Greinke abruptly left the Royals spring training camp because he was bored and did not want to pitch anymore. He had made his debut at age twenty and was burned out by age twenty-two. Now, Greinke is twenty-five and has been diagnosed with depression and social anxiety disorder, and he wants to pitch and to excel. He is doing both.

As of the writing of this article, Zack will enter tonight's game against the Detroit Tigers a flawless pitcher. He is 3-0 with a 0.00 ERA, having not allowed a run in twenty innings. He has struck out twenty, walked five, and validated an organization that patiently waited for him to come to terms with his problems.

"I think there were a lot of expectations for Zack at a young age that were hard to live up to," said Bob McGuire, his pitching coach. "Zack is getting comfortable just being Zack."

These days, just being Zack means being one of the most dominant pitchers in baseball. Greinke has always had a superb array of pitches and has been diligent about peppering the strike zone. With an improved changeup and more tranquility, Greinke is becoming the ace he once tried to flee from being.

Jason Giambi, who has three homers in sixteen at-bats against Greinke, said he had wondered how daunting Greinke could be, "once he got it all together." Now Giambi, the first baseman for the Oakland Athletics, knows.

"There is something different about him," said Giambi, who hit against Greinke in the spring. "His location was better, and his pitches were sharper. He always had a phenomenal arm. He was really dialing it in." But just being Zack was not good enough for Greinke in February of 2006. He was a former first-rounder who was supposed to be a savior for the Royals. He had a ninety-five mph fastball, a vicious slider, a nifty curveball, and an impeccable delivery. With two major league seasons on his resume, the first one solid and the second suspect, Greinke needed time to blossom.

That blossoming had to wait. Greinke did not like dealing with people. He was restless and withdrawn. Baseball was something he did not want in his life any longer. The boy with the golden arm left the game and thought it was a divorce, not a trial separation. "When I left, I was leaving and never coming back," Greinke said.

Johnny Damon of the New York Yankees and a former Dr. Phillips standout, had worked out with Greinke in Orlando during the off-season. He theorized that Greinke probably missed being a kid. Damon said, "Once a player signs a professional contract, it can be jolting to go from hanging out with friends every day to rarely having a day off. When we were together, we talked about life more than we did about baseball. I think everything caught up with him. He wanted to surf more than play baseball at one time. That's why he needed that little break."

Well, that little break from baseball lasted only six weeks, although his separation from the majors lasted about seven months. The Royals brought him back slowly by sending him to Wichita in Class AA in 2006. Dayton Moore, the Royals' general manager, said Greinke told him he was having fun in the minor leagues and preferred to stay there. Greinke joined the Royals in late September of that year and pitched in three games.

As the Royals prepared for 2007, Moore said, "They did not consider Greinke as a definite member of their staff." But Greinke thrived and made the rotation. After Greinke labored, the Royals shifted him to the bullpen. Moore said Greinke benefited from being a reliever and, "learned that he had another gear." He went 7-7 with a 3.69 ERA. By 2008, Moore said Greinke, "had turned the pages on some things, and was a happier person and a happier pitcher."

Because of Greinke's solid season (13-19, 3.48) and the way that he interacted with teammates, Moore was confident enough to sign him to a four-year, $38 million extension in January.

Marion McDonald

Every town has a few "characters" that grew up and attended schools in the area, and Apopka had its share. In Apopka, we were fiercely proud of these guys because they were the ones that legends were made of. And so it was with Marion "Mad Man" McDonald. As he was growing up in the Plymouth area, his daredevil antics were legendary.

Marion McDonald was born in 1918 and was raised in a home built in 1887 in McDonald Station, Florida. "Mac" learned to drive in the family orange groves. "One day I hit the tracks, and my car jumped a gate on the other side, four feet off the ground. After that, I never opened that gate again," he said. By l936, Mac was racing in the hills of north Georgia.

Marion McDonald often took turns on two wheels.

In 1938, Mac went to work at Bill France's service station on Main Street in Daytona Beach, and that same year he entered the time trials for the Daytona Beach Road race. In a seventy-four mph dash, he posted a time two mph faster than France's time. At age twenty-one, he entered the Daytona Beach Race driving his personal car, a 1937 yellow Ford Phaeton (#14). Mac was tied into the car with a rope, and he had an open knife taped to the dash to free himself in case of an emergency. During the race, he pulled into the pits, shut off the engine for refueling, and noticed that one of his pit crew was eating a hamburger. As Mac pulled away, he grabbed the hamburger. The fans were surprised to see a driver racing into the north turn and down A1A while eating a hamburger. One fan said, "Look at the madman eating lunch while driving." The name stuck, and Mac became Madman Marion McDonald.

As he sped down the beach on a later lap, Mac suddenly drove up on Gus Sliger, who had stalled across the north turn. Gus was out of his car and running across the track toward safety, when he saw Mac speeding toward him. Gus froze -- he did not know whether to continue across the track or get back in his car. To avoid hitting Gus, Mac took the high side, climbed the dunes on two wheels, and drove on. Mac found that taking the turn on two wheels improved his speed, and thereafter, he entered the turns more often than not on two wheels. His daredevil style delighted the fans, but Mac described it as, "just Sunday afternoon driving."

Madman Marion McDonald raced the beach course in 1938 and 1939. In 1940, he got married, and at the request of his new bride, he tried to settle down. But the roar of the engines was too strong, and without his wife's knowledge, Mac raced on short tracks in Jacksonville, Casselberry, Orlando, and Deland in the White Ghost (a 1935 Ford). McDonald's last race was in Casselberry in 1946, and he still has vivid memories of the crash that ended his racing career. "A car in front of me hit a guardrail, and the rail came through my windshield and out the back window. It just kept coming and coming." Mac escaped without serious injuries, but even today, he flashes back to that guardrail. After the Casselberry race, Marion retired from racing and became a gentleman farmer in Plymouth, Florida.

The styles that Mac developed on the racetrack were unexpectedly revived in 1973. On February 27, he was driving on State Road 15 south of Okeechobee, Florida, when a station wagon with two women and two small boys left the road and overturned in the ditch. A three-year-old boy was thrown from the car and pinned under the center of the crankcase with approximately four inches of clearance from the car to the ground. Mac tried to dig under the boy, but failed. He then tried to flag down help, but again failed. He drove his truck, which was equipped with a power-lift tailgate, through the mud and up a steep canal bank. He lowered the tailgate, backed it under the car, raised the front, and pulled the child to safety. Mac received a commendation from the Florida Highway Patrol for his heroic action.

Ninety-year-old Marion McDonald is a member of the Living Legends of Auto Racing and presently resides in Port Orange, Florida. He was one of the honored guests at the Fireball Memorial Celebration held in Apopka in September of 2008.

Phil Orr

I think that most of us were of the opinion that Phil Orr was born and raised in Apopka, since we have always claimed him as "one of us." The truth is, however, he was born in Maitland, Florida, on September 30, 1926.

He attended Winter Park High School and played football under the legendary coach Jim Mobley. The team was known as "Mobley's gallant little band of Wildcats." That little band of Wildcats took on the Orlando Tigers in the game that dedicated Orlando's new $150,000 stadium, later to be known as the Tangerine Bowl. By the way, Orlando squeaked by that night, 31-0. Phil went to high school, and played football with teammates who went on to distinguish themselves in our local community. They included Bob Bishop, Larry Condict, and Allen Travillion.

Phil would later become one of the scat backs for Walter Hovater's Orlando All-Stars. This was a semi-pro team whose roster included a former All-Southern high school player from Orlando High School, Leroy Hoequist, as well as former Georgia All-American Ken McCall, "Kap" Winslow, and Aubine Batts.

Phil Orr served in the U.S. Navy from 1942 until 1945. While in the Navy, he began to box as a 136-pound lightweight. On returning home in 1945, he continued boxing at the old Orlando Legion Arena. His manager was Doug Barnes, who was Earl K. Wood's brother-in-law. I would not be too surprised if Earl K. was not the tax collector back in those days. It did not take Phil long to become a crowd favorite with his Rocky Marciano brawler style. Phil was known as the "Beak-Buster" from Winter Park for a reason. After a few years of fighting every lightweight available, Phil finally hung up his gloves in 1947, with a very respectable 25-2-3 record.

It seemed as though Phil had a passion for the rough-and-tumble sports, as he immediately turned his attention to auto racing. Although he raced on many tracks in the area, such as Volusia County Speedway, Barberville, Eau Galle, and the Orlando Speedway during the 1950s, he was also racing the old Beach Road Course in Daytona Beach. He was actually one of the founding fathers of Bill France's NASCAR. These "legends of racing" included Bill France, Marshall Teague, "Fireball" Roberts, Cale Yarborough, Ralph Earnhardt, Curtis Turner, and Marion McDonald. Phil raced the old beach course six times in the 1950s, including the Grand National.

One of the highlights of Phil's career was the 1958 Grand National Race on the 4.1 mile Beach

Road Course. This was to be the last stock car race on that historic course. Over 75,000 race fans broke all traffic-jam records that day. It took the fans longer to drive off the beach those days than it did for the legends to run the 160-mile Grand National over a very soupy course.

Phil was driving number 500 "Mayday Inc.," a 1958 Ford Fairlane sponsored by a group of Air Force officers from the Orlando Air Force base. He was bumped from behind on the first lap, which knocked his distributor out of time, and had to go to the pits on the third lap. He later went back on the track to finish a race he could not win.

In 1993, Phil attended the Living Legends of Beach Racing event in Daytona Beach. This event was to honor the drivers, owners, mechanics, and journalists who were involved in beach racing between 1936 through 1958. Some came in walkers and wheelchairs, but most looked fit enough to squeeze into the cars that were speeding around in 1993. Phil Orr was one of those.

Phil made this statement that day: "I think we had more fun racing on the beach. The turns from the sand into the highway, and then back again onto the sand were more dangerous. But they certainly weren't boring like some of today's tracks." That was our boy Phil.

After retiring from racing, Phil opened Florida Gator Motors and Phil Orr Reality in Plymouth, where he resided on the Mt. Plymouth Road with his lovely wife Annie. Although Phil has never been much of a spectator in sports, he has made an occasional exception by shouting, "Go Gators."

Phil Orr was one of our guests of honor at the Fireball Roberts Memorial Celebration event at the Northwest Recreational Park at Jason Dwelley Parkway in 2008.

Chapter XI – The Lazy 50's

Hickerson's Gorget

The Lake Apopka shoreline has a history of yielding artifacts from the Timucuan era. So it was when our good friend Norman Hickerson found a curious looking green stone (gorget) at his place of business on the east side of the Zellwood muck farms. Being the curious man that he is, Hickerson contacted Rollins College and the Central Florida Archeological Society in order to identify the gorget. It turned out to be a form of broach worn by the Timucuan Indians.

Rollins sent instructor Steve Hess, who also worked at Combank as a financial planning officer. Steve was so impressed with the site that he decided to explore it on his own. Norman allowed Hess and his group of thirty-five students to excavate the grounds on Saturdays.

"Through the first ten feet, we found one particular Indian's possessions, his tools and projectile points, for instance," Hess explained. "After four more feet of digging, we began to find some bone fragments." Hess said the primitive man was buried in a fetal position along with all his possessions. "The body is later covered with a mound of dirt as part of the religious burial ceremony," he said.

The mound, a few feet from what used to be the shores of Lake Apopka, has a large oak tree near its center. Hess believes the tree was purposely planted there by the Indians as a location marker for future tribes.

He believes there may be similar mounds in this same area.

Surprisingly enough, the early Paleo man was, on average, tall and stocky. "Food and water were abundant for the tribes," Hess explained. "All the hunter used, as proven by our findings, was a rough form of a spear."

A Hernando spearhead, invented in 3500 B.C., was exhumed from one of the holes. Hess said this particular find was important because it shows that some Indians occupied the Florida peninsular region far longer than originally believed.

After three to four years of excavating, Arthur Dreves, and his Central Florida Archeological Society members had to admit the "dig" had not produced any spectacular human bones, but they remained extremely proud of their findings. "This area we are now working was probably a campground for pre-Columbian civilizations," said Mr. Dreves, past president of the CFAS.

Almost 3,000 pieces of primitive pottery have been removed from the site. Much of the pottery, or potshards, contain intricate designs.

According to a report on the four years of excavations at the site, the area could be the oldest archaeological campsite yet found in the Central Florida coast area.

While a number of arrowheads have been recovered, the oldest is believed to have been used around 7500 B.C.

Crude stone knives have also been recovered.

"One of our members was digging and reached the white sand about four-feet below the surface. We believe it was the lake beach at one time," Dreves said. "And since we think it was once the beach, we usually stop digging at that point, but while he was smoothing the ground, he hit something and continued deeper."

That something was a group of twelve primitive knives, bunched together, "as if they had been left in some sort of carrying bag," Dreves said.

Dreves said one reason few human bones have been found is, "that would be like burying your relatives in your back yard. We are convinced these people lived here, at least seasonally."

Lake Apopka Fishing

Oh, how I seem to cycle back to that majestic body of water in our midst, Lake Apopka. I recall stating before, that when waterway transportation systems were overwhelmed by the railroads, it was not the end of the "queen." There were beautiful times yet to come. All through the 20th century, it became a world-renowned sport-fishing lake with twenty-one fishing camps operating by 1956.

Those of us who fished the ol' lake in those days will never forget Johnson's Fishing Camp, Fisherman's Paradise, Orange Fishing Lodge, Paradise Cove, and the many others. People came from near and far to enjoy the finest fishing anywhere. Lake Apopka was becoming the marvel of the nation's anglers.

Myers Boat Landing was sold in 1914 to Charles Wells of West Virginia, and he changed the name of the camp to Wells Gap. About the same time, Scott Searle of Indianapolis purchased the Stenstrom Boat Landing.

In the early 1920s, the city of Apopka built a dock, clubhouse, and picnic grounds at Lovell's Landing and urged E.T. Hawthorne, county road engineer, to build a road connecting it with the Ocoee-Apopka hardtop road. A committee composed of W.G. Talton, H.H. Witherington, and Leslie Waite finally secured the necessary right-of-way, and the community dock road was opened in 1922.

Fisherman's Paradise was somewhat affected by the 1920s prosperity. It was owned by a company of Apopka stockholders of which P.L. Starbird was president. Managed by G.M. Brown, the camp consisted of five cabins and twenty-five rental boats.

By 1923, Brown had arranged for daily bus trips between Orlando and the camp. In 1925, he sold out to G.A. Keene of Orlando who envisioned developing a, "playground for fishermen." Meanwhile, two large tracts were sold to out-of-state developers, and a California motion picture firm was negotiating for 1,000 acres on the lake.

While these activities were shortened by the end of the boom in late 1926, the Paradise Heights Project, which involved 126 acres adjacent to the fishing camp, was more substantial. A large auction was held in February 1926, with the usual entertainment supplemented with a fish fry by "Uncle Lee" Wells of Wells Gap. About 700 people attended the auction and festivities, and numerous lots were sold at, "good prices."

The lake was shallow, clear, and a pleasant ride from Johnson's Fish Camp to Hog Island. There, you would generally find Fred Odom and Rudy Kratzer quietly pulling in their big bass with their "jigger" poles. You might see Nell Jackson, Clem Womble or Lorena Smith with their string of specks. Most of Apopka took advantage of the bountiful waters between the 1920s and the 1960s.

The fishing sometimes turned social. After Uncle Lee opened Well's Gap in 1914, he started an annual picnic and fish fry that attracted several hundred people from Northwest Orange County for many years.

In the 1940s, Mayor C.H. Damsel and other Apopkans started an annual Lake Apopka Fish Rodeo to emphasize the lake as one of the community's most marketable attractions.

As I said at the beginning of this article, water transportation began losing its grip on Lake Apopka to the railroads. Do not shed any tears for Lake Apopka; there were beautiful times yet to come. Well, after those beautiful times came the nightmares and tragedies. The "queen" came very close to total death because she was too successful in what we asked her to do.

Martin Marietta

When people find out that you are a native Floridian, they generally say something to the effect that they would bet that you have seen a lot of changes in Orange County since the arrival of Walt Disney World. There is a lot of truth in that statement; however, I do not believe that Orange County was caught completely off guard with the arrival of Walt Disney World in 1965. You see, Disney was not the first large employer to end up in Orange County.

Nine years earlier, on September 14, 1956, the *Orlando Sentinel* had a blockbusting headline proclaiming, "Martin Aircraft Coming to Orlando." The banner headline was followed by, "Two million for land, but it's still a guess on how much for the plant." The story behind these headlines was that the Glen L. Martin Co. of Baltimore, Maryland, had selected a 7,300-acre site in Southwest Orange County for their proposed huge defense plant that would employ up to 10,000 people.

Reaction to this monumental announcement fell into one of two categories. The enthusiastic response of the promoter/speculator group translated roughly into, "What's in it for me?" Those expecting a profit from the many spin-offs of this industrial complex shared that attitude. The reaction of the other group was more cautious and translated into, "I wonder what all this activity will mean to my present and future way of life." These individuals wanted things to remain as they were and hoped that whatever took place would not affect them adversely.

By 1957, a full "military-industrial complex" was stimulating the Orange County economy, and when the Martin Company paid approximately $1,950,000 cash for some 7,000 acres of pasture, landowners realized that an era of speculation had dawned. When the unheard of price of $200 per acre was paid for 6,400 acres of pastureland and $750 an acre was paid for another 900 acres of pastureland just to "square off" the Martin tract, landowners, promoters, and speculators realized that the lid was off.

Following the announcement of the Martin Company project, Orange County commissioners and legislators enacted a series of courageous legislative acts to prevent the county from becoming engulfed in a haphazard building boom that would create a big urban slum as a result of the Martin Company building plans.

These public servants had the foresight and the intestinal fortitude to secure a countywide zoning act that prevented confusion. In 1955, the county passed a limited zoning act, but it controlled only land-use along major highways. Certain courageous community leaders tried to maintain the "City Beautiful" image, at least in a limited way, during the immediate post-war building boom. To do so required fortitude, because telling people what they could or could not do with their land was not at all popular.

However, with these modest land-use controls on the books, Mother Nature entered the scene and created a set of conditions that emphasized a new aspect for water control.

In 1959, the county recorded 63.77 inches of rainfall, roughly thirteen inches above the normal annual rainfall. This above-average rainfall spelled big trouble for several recent housing developments built in low areas. In 1960, the wettest year in more than thirty years dumped 17.37 inches of excess rainfall on the county. Hurricane Donna was responsible for part of this. At any rate, two back-to-back wet years caused flooding up to the eaves of houses in some urban developments in the county.

The public was outraged that the county commissioners had allowed building in these flood-prone areas. They realized that something had to be done. The County Water Control Act was pushed through the legislature, which gave the county the authority to control lake levels to prevent the urban encroachment in the flood-prone areas, and provided the means of building primary and secondary water control structures. To finance the construction of such structures, this bill authorized the county commissioners to levy a special ad valorem tax on all property in the county. The Water Control Act was passed in 1961.

From the time Orange County's boundaries were finally determined in 1913, no one told the landowner what he could or could not do with the land and water that he owned. Now, suddenly, when real estate prices for land were soaring, government officials had the audacity to try to play umpire in this new financial ball game. The critics reasoned that they owned the land, paid taxes on it, and it was their right to make as much money as they could from it for development purpose. So how did the county have the right to "nose" in on the deal?

This attitude may not have been the sole factor, but it certainly contributed to the defeat of every commissioner in office at the time these growth-control laws were enacted.

Progressive leadership invariably pays a heavy price for farsightedness, and these public servants deserve credit for their courageous actions. If some kind of planning and zoning had not been instituted during the "crash period" created by the Martin Company announcement, Orange County would certainly have not been in any shape to take on Walt Disney World in 1965.

The Ambs Family

The Ambs family traveled from Michigan to Apopka in this camper pulled by a tractor.

Some of you older citizens probably remember your family moving from your original home place to Florida. A lot of colorful stories generally emerged from these expeditions. These stories most often came from the 1800s or early 1900s, when most of your travel was by water or, maybe a little later, by train. Charles Stevenson left the Museum of the Apopkans the following recap of a diary kept by the Ambs family about their move from Leslie, Michigan, to Apopka in 1960 in a very unusual manner:

"Like so many other families in the 60s, the Ambs family decided to move to sunny Florida. So Mr. Ambs began by selling the family home on 2824 Olds Road in Leslie, Michigan. Finally he held a public auction on July 13, 1960, to give away to the local community all those things we can all use but hate to pay a decent price for. Included in these were several items of farm machinery, his boats, mowers and a garden tractor. Once the 1/2 ton pickup truck, refrigerator, freezer, washing machine, dryer and their best antique walnut furniture were gone, the Ambs family knew that there was no turning back. Mr. Ambs did hold out on two items during his selling spree. Most importantly were his beloved Oliver 550 Diesel Tractor and a 23 foot camper trailer of sorts. Mr. Ambs had modified the trailer to bring it up to what he considered to be the good living standards of the day. He had cut a large opening across the front into which he installed windows. A gas stove with 4 burners and an ice box-were installed. There was a sink, space heater, storage area for utensils, closets for clothing, and a sleeping area for the family. Over near the right front sat a table and sewing machine. Modern conveniences, power and air conditioning were not considered necessary in the '60s.

One begins to wonder why on earth the Ambs family would go to so much trouble and to such detail over a trailer that most families would not even want. Well, you see the Ambs family had a plan for traveling to sunny Florida in a most unusual way. They would not be traveling by car, by truck or by plane. They were planning to travel the entire 1300 miles from Leslie, Michigan to Apopka, Florida in this hopped up camper trailer. And by now you have figured out the other half of the story. Yes, Mr. Ambs was going to pull the trailer with his one remaining prized possession-the 550 Oliver Diesel, which by now had been fitted with a canopy to keep off the sun and rain. When questioned as to why they had chosen this manner of travel, Mr. Ambs stated, "I'm tired of the rush, rush, and it seems like a long distance but most farmers travel two or three times that distance just going around and around a field during the summer." Mr. Ambs had heard of another family who had traveled from the Atlantic to the Pacific and just thought that would be a more exciting way to travel.

The last ingredient to go into this 7 by 23 foot camper trailer would be the Ambs family consisting of Mr. Mark Ambs, Mrs. Anne Ambs and their five children-Lanette, Roger, Niela, Clark and Nancy. The children ranged in age from 1 1/2 to 12 years.

On August 5, 1960, the family left Leslie, Michigan heading for Apopka. It took them 21 days using back roads because they could only travel about 15-17 miles per hour and didn't want to have the stress of holding up traffic on major highways.

On August 25, the 21st and final day of the trip the skies were partly cloudy, but they didn't mind because everyone was very excited. Providing they don't have any breakdowns, they will reach their destination today. They were driving on route 19 through the Ocala National Forest. It is not very populated; however, the roads were very good.

As Anne continued in her diary; *Oh! Oh!* The road suddenly became very bumpy and it took a few seconds to realize that there was a flat tire on the trailer. Luckily, it wasn't the one Mark had been worried about. The first vehicle to pass was a Brink's truck, but naturally it didn't stop. The next car stopped and offered assistance, but there was really nothing they could do. We had to have something to block the trailer up but naturally there were no rocks, so Mark hunted back among the trees and found some old logs. Jacking the trailer up was no problem. Mark just used the hydraulic on the tractor. He dug a hole by the tire with the hub cap because the trailer couldn't be raised high enough to enable him to get the tire off. This done, he unhitched the tractor and took the tire and headed for a station. Mark was fortunate to pick up a used tire for $3.

Traveling a short distance we entered the citrus belt. The trees were laden with green fruit and we are looking forward to them ripening. At the Apopka City limits sign, we stopped to take a picture.

We have not minded doing without a Coleman lantern; in fact we rather enjoyed the early bed time hour. We managed very nicely with the flash light. I asked Mark how it felt at the end of the day and he replied, "A little tired, but I've enjoyed every minute of it." His answer to, "any calluses?" was,

"No, not one." The only time we had an anxious moment was on route 1 and 23 in southern Georgia when Mark observed a big truck approaching from the rear which was not slowing down or attempting to pass. So very quickly and skillfully, Mark pulled off the road. At that instant, the truck passed on the right side of the road.

Our fuel bill was $31.95. Our Tuesday evening overnight parking was $9.00. We have been swimming at Rock Springs and plan to go to the Atlantic Sunday with friends from Orlando. We were on Channel 6 on television in Orlando Saturday evening at 6:00 and 11:00. The *Orlando Evening Star* had pictures of our arrival.

We feel we have given a lot of people something to laugh at and a smile to a good many more, and if we accomplished no more than a lot of self pleasure and self satisfaction, we've given a lot of people something to talk about besides their neighbor's business. Our best regards to all. Anne, Mark Ambs and Family."

Gunnery Sergeant Carlos Hathcock

A few years ago, our friend and local Farm Bureau agent, Bill Morris, was browsing through a book entitled *Marine Snipers*. He was totally engrossed by an article on Carlos Hathcock. Carlos was, without a doubt, the greatest sniper our military has ever produced.

Bill began to wonder what it would take to get the Marine legend to come down and speak to a group of friends, so he called Quantico, Virginia, and they gave him Carlos' phone number in North Carolina. After he finally contacted Carlos, a trip down to Apopka was set up.

Old friends, Gy Sgt. Carlos Hathcock (seated) with GT Major Hank Hoffman.

Bill contacted ten of his friends who put up the funds necessary to cover the cost of bringing Carlos to Apopka. Some of those friends were Curt Haygood, Paul Faircloth, Sgt. Major Hank Hoffman, and Billy Long. A good ol' Fred Nix-style barbecue was set up at Paul Faircloth's boathouse on Lake Marshall.

The boys enjoyed themselves during the evening and were in hog-heaven conversing with Carlos about his exploits during the Vietnam War. Sometime during the evening, Carlos told Curt Haygood that his name was familiar to him. Curt replied that he too had done a little shooting when he was at Quantico. Carlos said he recalled seeing a plaque with Curt's name on it for his marksmanship. Curt replied that he was not aware of that.

Let's talk a little bit about their guest and some of the miraculous achievements that made him the legend that he is:

At only seventeen years of age, Carlos fulfilled his childhood dream by enlisting in the U.S. Marine Corps. It did not take long for the instructors on the rifle range at Camp Pendleton, California, to recognize Carlos' ability as a marksman. He was later transferred to Cherry Point, North Carolina, where he began shooting competitively. It was here that he set the Marine Corps record on the "A" course with a score of 248 out of a possible 250, a record that stands today.

This achievement led to his being sought after in 1966 to be part of a newly established sniper program in Vietnam. After his training was completed, Carlos began his new assignment. Operating from Hill 55, a position thirty-five miles southwest of Da Nang, Hathcock and his fellow Marine snipers renewed a Marine tactic which had been born on the islands of the Pacific in World War II. Within a short period of time, the effects of the Marine snipers could be felt around Hill 55. Carlos rapidly ran up a toll on the enemy that would eventually lead to a bounty being placed on his head by the Viet Cong.

As a result of his skill, Sergeant Hathcock was recruited three times for covert assignments. One of them was to kill a Frenchman who was working for the North Vietnamese as an interrogator. This individual was torturing American airmen who had been captured. It took only one round from Carlos' modified Winchester Model 70 to end the Frenchman's career.

On another occasion, Sergeant Hathcock accepted an assignment for which he was plainly told that his odds of survival were slim. He was dropped behind enemy lines by a helicopter and had to crawl on his belly for three days in order to put himself in position for a shot at a North Vietnamese general. He crawled through grass and only moved as the wind blew the grass. Ants were a constant problem, and on one occasion, he had to stare down a jade green Bamboo Viper coiled within six inches of his face. He knew this snake's venom was a neurotoxin like a cobra. Only by the grace of God, did the viper feel no threat, uncoil, and slither away into the tall grass. Night patrols came within touching distance on several occasions. Finally, on the third day, he came within 800 yards of his target. Early the next morning, the general came outside for his early morning stretch. It was the last stretch the general would ever take as Carlos hit him with one shot from the 800 yards. Luckily, he returned to Hill 55 unscratched.

It was at this point that the "game was on" as the Viet Cong put their ace sniper, "The Cobra," on a mission to exterminate Sgt. Hathcock. There was a $30,000 bounty put on the sergeant's head, and he was given the name Long Trang (White Feather) by the Viet Cong. This was because Carlos wore a white feather in his hat.

From Hill 55, Carlos, along with a spotter, took up a position from where they had many past kills. He had company awaiting him. They spotted a flash that they thought was the sunlight hitting a scope. Carlos did not wait long before he took a shot that passed directly through The Cobra's rifle scope, striking him in the eye at a range of 500 yards. They both had their scopes on each other, but Carlos pulled the trigger first.

Hathcock would eventually be credited with ninety-three confirmed enemy kills, including one Viet Cong shot dead by a round fired from a scope-mounted Browning M-2 .50 caliber machine gun at the unbelievable range of 2500 yards (1.42 miles).

In 1969, during his second tour of duty in Vietnam, Carlos was badly burned while rescuing fellow marines from a burning Amtrak. The other marines and Carlos had been riding in the vehicle when it ran over an anti-tank mine. Despite the severity of his wounds, it would ultimately be the ravages of multiple sclerosis that would bring Hathcock's extraordinary career to an end.

Carlos died on February 23, 1999. In the history of military and law enforcement snipers, Gunnery Sergeant Carlos Hathcock clearly rated as the greatest of them all.

Blackwelder's Department Store

Rexall Drug Store

Chapter XII - Seventies

Agriculture Lost Prominence In Apopka

It must be difficult for a lot of the newer residents in the area to realize how prominent agriculture was to this area's economy, even as recently as the '90s. There was fresh produce from the north shores of Lake Apopka, fabulous foliage plants scattered throughout Northwest Orange County, and the beautiful sight of rolling hills loaded with citrus trees. To drive through those citrus bearing areas and smell the orange blossoms was a delight beyond description.

All of these economically stimulated businesses had one adversary they shared in common. The businesses were out in the open and were particularly vulnerable to the weather. That may be in the form of hurricanes, droughts, freezes or excess rainfall. Also, insects, diseases, and pollution took their toll.

The citrus industry, which was probably the first to start losing ground in Northwest Orange County found itself "floating" into the end with rainfall showing 12.4 inches above normal. Then Hurricane Donna came with another 17.37 inches. In 1962, another one of those disastrous freezes with temperatures ranging around fifteen degrees came through. In 1964, Puerto Rico sent us a little gift in the sugarcane rootstalk borer weevil (Diaprepes Abbreviate) that devastated a portion of the citrus industry in Orange County.

All of this plus the Disney World land boom set the stage for the urbanization of much of the citrus land in the area. Businesses started moving to South Florida to escape the cold vise gripping Central Florida.

Plymouth Citrus Growers, Minute Maid Corporation, Zellwood Fruit Distributors, and Apopka Fruit Company were but a few of the companies that dissolved or moved to another location. Those jobs were gone forever.

Although the foliage plant industry shared the same demons with their sister agricultural commodities, it was more the Walt Disney effect and higher land prices that has moved the industry out of Northwest Orange County and more toward the northern counties with a lower tax base. This industry's efficiency improved so much over the years that they were actually selling product cheaper than in the 1950s. However, increased efficiency can only take you so far, and the land prices and taxes prevailed. Northwest Orange County is no longer the number one foliage producer in the state. At one time, Northwest Orange County had approximately 125 nurseries registered with the Florida Department of Agriculture. Today you would be lucky to find half that many. Those jobs are also gone forever.

By 1998, the State of Florida bought the muck farms on Lake Apopka due to the pollution of the lake. The St. Johns River Water Management maintained that the pollution was caused by agricultural discharges laden with phosphorus, treated wastewater from shoreline communities, and discharges from citrus processing plants prior to 1989. Approximately 2,500 employees lost their jobs.

The citrus workers may have moved to South Florida, and the foliage plant employees to another county, but a majority of the employees of the muck farms completely lost their jobs.

It seems strange, however, that the population of Apopka went up as manufacturing went out. According to the Census Bureau, Apopka had 26,960 residents in the year 2000, and by 2008 there were approximately 40,000. There is little doubt that a majority of this growth came from the "housing boom," but I suppose we are left to wonder just what affect did this agricultural move have on the economy of Apopka?

Ed "Possum Slim" Meyers

The information in this article came from articles written for the Sentinel Star back in 1975 by Chris Evans, Albion Land, and Ramsey Campbell.

Ed "Possum Slim" Myers was not a legend in his time because of his abilities at catching, skinning, and selling opossums as a young man in Virginia. He became a local legend in 1975, when he was banished from Lake County for killing a woman when he was 105.

The story goes that "Possum" was invited to the home of Mrs. Louise Stewart and Sammy Tolbert to celebrate Stewart's 51st birthday. Mrs. Stewart had asked Possum to bring a birthday present when he came. He showed up with $5, and a half-pint of gin. Then, Tolbert went to the store and returned with a six-pack of malt liquor.

According to Possum, they had a little more in mind than simply celebrating Mrs. Stewart's birthday. After he drank two cans of beer, he said Mrs. Stewart demanded more money, and she grabbed several bills from his hand. At that time, he said he went to his home to get a gun, and he returned to the Stewart home where he fatally wounded Mrs. Stewart and wounded her companion, Sammy Tolbert.

Myers was arrested by Lake County sheriff deputies that day in Sorrento.

Albion Land of the *Sentinel Star* interviewed Myers at the Lake County jail.

Possum's hands were shaking and his eyes stared straight ahead. 105-year-old Possum Slim Myers looked out of place clad in olive-drape prison garb.

With neither defiance nor remorse, the fifty-year resident of Sorrento poured out the frustration and 'righteous' anger he said led him to shoot Louise Stewart on the day of her birthday.

"They just take my money," he spat out in a raspy, barely audible voice. "I'd just done lost so much, I couldn't go no further."

But the last straw, he said, came Saturday.

He expresses no hatred for Mrs. Stewart. "Bein' a church member I couldn't have no hard heart for her. That wouldn't be livin' right'"

During the course of the last seven years, Myers said, he's been robbed eight times – as recently as last month. "They's just strong armin' me. A couple of 'em would hold me, and the other fella would take my money."

Expressing a strong faith in a righteous God, Myers said, "I believe I done right and still look up to him."

As for the future, he said emphatically, "I'm going to tell the truth. If they don't get me an attorney, I'll take Jesus and tell him to go into the hearts of the judge and the jury."

According to Albion Land, Possum Slim was found guilty of manslaughter -- a crime for which he could receive up to fifteen years in prison. He was released on bond. At this time, Myers moved to Apopka to stay with his long-time friend, fifty-eight- year-old Oscar Robinson. It was here that he would await his next court hearing for sentencing. His empty Sorrento home burned to the ground in March 1976, and he gave the bricks to a church in Mt. Dora. Although he had been a fruit picker and logger in his younger days, his health waned during the last five years.

His legend was chronicled on the front page of the *London Daily Telegraph*, and as he grew older, the stories about the frail, but irascible Possum Slim grew. His only medicines, he once said behind a toothless grin, were Geritol, aspirin, and whiskey mixed with strawberry soda.

"I don't eat meat. I like greens and beans," he said. "I like grits, but I don't like rice. It looks like little maggots in there."

Possum Slim also loves to talk about his way with women. Even at 107, he mused that, "I can still look."

At the sentencing, the judge placed Possum on a fifteen-year probation for the shooting death of Louise Stewart. Part of that probation was to ban the 105-year-old from Lake County and his beloved home of more than half-a-century for that same fifteen years. Of course, that meant the rest of his life.

A run-down shack in Zellwood, just across the Orange County line became home for Possum Slim during his exile, but there was never a time he did not long to return to Lake County.

"I don't care if I live another hour, I just want to go home," said Possum during the probation.

According to Jerry Jackson of the *Sentinel Star*, Possum returned home to Lake County in 1979. Death was the one thing that could nullify the 1975 court order.

Crippled with a bad leg and bowed by age, Possum Slim died alone and destitute at Florida Hospital in Orlando at the age of 110. He was buried at Edgewood Cemetery in Mt. Dora. The Lord granted his wish to return to his home in Lake County.

Corn On The Cob

*B*ack when Dick Burdette was writing for the Orlando Sentinel, he used to crank out some dandies. I think the following is one of them:

"There just isn't any delicate way to put this.

Another longtime, down-home slice of Americana is disappearing. Out along the back roads, out in the hinterlands, it's going the way of the kerosene lantern, the crank telephone, the dinner bell, the well dipper, the rumble seat, and the coal bucket. It's becoming little more than something you're surprised to remember you've forgotten, like washboards, slop jars, flypaper, pot-bellied stoves, straight razors, spittoons, porch swings and bath tub stoppers.

Any way you cut it, that good ol' standby, the handy-dandy corncob, is becoming a thing of the past.

You remember the corncob. Grandma's farmhouse? The out-house out back? Right next to the Sears and Roebuck catalog with a bunch of pages missing? Long before Mr. Whipple ever even thought of squeezing the Charmin, America counted on the corncob.

Oh, sure, some folks used those Sears catalog pages. Others in Sun Belt states preferred clumps of Spanish moss. But in those pre-bathroom stationery days, regardless of where they lived, Americans had two things in common: the outhouse and the corncob. Not that the corncob didn't have other uses, mind you.

Burke Leigh, a retired railroad man out of Coleman in Sumter County, remembers how folks used 'em for kindling or dipped them in oil to start the fire – or to fuel the fire, for that matter.

Down in Narcoossee in Osceola County, Pop Miles talks about how chunks of corncob were used as bottle corks. Pop's wife, Ethel, made candlewicks out of them.

Orlando fruit shipper, James Eaddy, who grew up in Linden in Hog County, he insists, will tell you when he was a young man, corncobs trimmed with brightly colored ribbons made dandy Christmas tree ornaments. They adorned scarecrows, too. And if the radiator in the old Model T sprang a leak, what better way to plug it than with a corncob? And if the rear end of your truck started growling, Eaddy said, the best way in the world to quiet it down was to insert some grease along with – you guessed it – ground up corncob.

If the corn crop was bad, Eaddy says, cobs were ground up to feed the cattle. Corncobs also made dandy homemade toys – wagons and dollhouses, Hunters used them to make turkey callers.

'I'll tell you what happened,' Eaddy said. 'People started having too many plastic toys. That and toilet paper came along and made the corncob obsolete.'

Of course, what's vanished is not the corncob, but its many uses. And, the kind of cob that was used came largely from shell corn, not the table corn variety produced here.

But for the record, courtesy of Bill Kelly, production manager of Zellwin Farms here, consider the following:

1. Last year, Zellwin produced 485,000 crates of table corn. At 52 ears per crate, that's 25 million ears shipped out of here for human consumption.

2. In the Zellwood, Leesburg, Sanford area alone, growers last year produced 11 million crates. That translates into 572 million cobs, uh, ears leaving the area.

3. "Seconds" – lower-grade table corn – amounted to an additional 25 percent in the Zellwood, Leesburg, and Sanford area – another 143 million ears. They're fed to cattle.

4. That means, all totaled, production last year in this area amounted to more than 700 million ears.

'I think you have to make the distinction that we're talking about table corn now and in the old days, people used the cobs from shell corn,' Kelly said.

OK, so what if all over the country, those 572 million cobs, representing only a tiny fraction of all the corncobs being produced throughout the state and across the nation, are being carted home in dozen and half-dozen packs and all those cobs thrown away?

Ask any old-timer. Somewhere, they'll tell you, amid all those millions of discarded cobs, *there's a right smart chance that there might some kind of moral to the story."*

Chapter XIII - From A Small Boy's Eyes: Memories Of Growing Up

Soap Box Derby

Since my mother worked full-time at the Plymouth Citrus Growers, we had what was called at the time, a "wash woman." Today, she would be known as a nanny.

Her name was Samantha, and she had two boys – Luther and Johnny. One was my brother's age, and the other was a little younger than I was. They lived across the Old Dixie Highway in the tenant's quarters of Standard Growers Groves. That location would be where the park is for Parkview Place in Errol Estates. Samantha did all our cleaning, washing, and ironing.

The thing that stands out so clear in my mind was "wash day." Samantha would build a fire under that big, black, iron pot full of water and let it boil the clothing for a while. She then took the clothes out with a long broom handle, and scrubbed each item with soap and water on the washboard. They were rinsed and then put on the clothesline to dry.

Sometimes a windstorm off the Zellwood muck would turn the sky black. I remember Samantha moving like Jesse Owens to take the clothes down from the line and get them inside. If she did not, all the day's work would have been in vain.

While Samantha was busy with her chores, the boys had no trouble keeping themselves busy. All kids dream about entering and winning the Soap Box Derby held in July of each year at the Derby Downs in Dayton, Ohio. My brother Gene, Luther, Johnny, and I were no exception.

In those days there was no way of going on the Internet and ordering a set of plans, so my chief engineer and I proceeded to raid the homestead junk pile for the proper material to build this supersonic jet we had in mind. Now, we figured that surely, these vehicles had to be built out of soapboxes, but regardless how hard we tried, we could not find one. I guess the people in our neck of the woods did not use much soap, so we moved on to the next best thing, and we raided our onsite junk pile.

My brother came up with some 2 x 4s for the frame; Luther found four tricycle wheels, and Johnny rustled up some plywood from Lord only knows where. I came up with enough rope for steering, and we were on our way.

In a few days, we were finished, and we selected Johnny as the driver because he was the lightest. Now came the big part, finding a hill steep enough for a trial run. The one we selected was known as "Babcock Hill." This eventually became the Blum house on the Old Dixie Highway. Today, this would be called a "dip," but to us it might as well have been the road to Pikes Peak.

We loaded Johnny up, gave him a good push, and away he went. The first thing that happened was one of the wheels came off causing the "missile" to start doing a figure eight. Johnny eventually ended up in the orange grove that ran parallel to the road.

When building started on "The Overview," they probably bulldozed that old contraption, because we left it in the orange grove and turned our racing careers over to Fireball Roberts.

Our Dog Jack

I have spoken in the past about those wonderful years growing up in Apopka with all the young lads in my neighborhood. I was thinking the other day that I have failed to mention the dearest and most loyal friend of all the gang. He was our dog Jack. Now to us, he was just a plain ol' dog. My Dad always said he had the looks of a German Shepherd but was just a cur, whatever that meant.

There was one thing you could be sure of, and that was that ol' Jack would always be with us boys wherever we went. He always seemed to be in the lead like a bird dog looking for a covey of quail. Sometimes, he might spot a black snake for us or some ol' gopher creeping along. When we went swimming at Dream Lake, he would sit along the bank like one of Queen Elizabeth's guards outside the palace. When we were ready to go, so was Jack.

I can recall one morning when My Dad and brother decided to go out to Hawthorne's Fernery to pull a few ferns to fill out an order they had. They decided that Jack and I could go along. In those days, if you needed some ferns from a certain nursery, you would go out, pull them yourself, and leave a note on how many you pulled. Later, they would bill you.

At any rate, my Dad and brother were busy pulling ferns, and I got a little venturesome. Just outside the fernery was a well. It was used for irrigation and had a three-inch intake pipe going out over the center that turned ninety-degrees down into the water.

I decided to walk that three-inch pipe. I did not do too well, as I slipped and went head first into the well. Ol' Jack started raising Cain and went down into the fernery barking, trying to raise as much attention as he could. It did not take my brother too long to realize what Jack was trying to tell him. He went up to the well but could not see too much because of the green algae on top of the water. But Jack would not let up. He kept barking into the well. Finally, my brother Jessie jumped into the well, found me on the bottom, and pulled me out. He stretched me over an old insecticide drum and pumped the water out of me.

From that day forward, Jack was number one from my point-of-view, and I think his rating went up a little with the entire family.

In addition to my neighborhood friends, I also spent a lot of time with the Cox boys down on west Fourth Street. James' and Bobby's dad was a butcher and ran a meat market on Park Avenue across from the crate mill. Every now and then, he would load up all us boys in his pickup truck and take us fishing for catfish down in St. Cloud.

On one of those trips, I decided to take Jack along. We were fishing in a canal, and Mr. Cox dropped me off in a pretty thick palmetto area. I was set up with my cane pole, can of worms, a peanut butter sandwich, and an RC Cola.

As time rolled on without a bite, I became a little mesmerized watching the cork. That did not last long because Jack jumped at something in the palmettos, and all hell broke loose. There was enough snorting and bellowing going on to wake the devil. I could see Mr. Cox and the boys coming down the bank, so I decided to go up and take a look. I really expected to see Jack battling a hog; however, I got the shock of my young life. Jack had a scrub cow by the nose and would not let loose. Believe me, that cow was not going anywhere.

The first thing Mr. Cox did was to check the cow for a brand. There wasn't one, so the cow was actually free game. Being a butcher by trade, I am sure Mr. Cox was drooling to take the cow home. The truth of the matter was that he had no way of loading that cow onto the truck with a bunch of little boys as his help. We had to hold Jack down as we released the cow.

That was when I realized that Jack was not really a cur, but a cow dog at heart.

Time moved on and Jack began to show his age. He no longer was the guard of the queen's palace or agile, and swift as he was in his younger days; instead, he sort of limped along. One morning, my mother sent me up the hill to pick something up at the Dixie Service Station, and Jack went along. An old model Ford came by, and Jack must have thought he had spotted another scrub cow, because he ran right under that car.

As he lay whining on the side of the road, I did the natural thing and lifted up his head to comfort him. He did the natural thing and bit me. I couldn't believe it. My best friend bit me. I forgave ol' Jack because he was crossing over the rainbow bridge into the good puppy land, and he was not aware he had bitten anyone.

The family and all the boys in the neighborhood missed him something terrible. Until this day, there is a place in my heart for ol' Jack.

Moss Yards

During World War II, when the Japanese cut off the American supply of rubber from the Far East, the United States had to come up with a substitute to make cushions for the automobile, especially military vehicles. One of the more prominent substitutes came from the Deep South, including the state of Florida. That little jewel was moss…yes, Spanish moss.

If my old memory is serving me right, Apopka had two of what were called moss yards. One was around Christiana Street, and the other was on the corner of Bradshaw Street and Johns Road. That was the one I was more familiar with.

A moss yard was laid out on the order of a grape vineyard. There were 4 x 4 posts with a 2 x 4 attached at the top, forming a T. There were about four wires strung the length of the field about two feet apart. Moss was hung on the wires until the sun dried it. Sometimes, the moss was laid on the ground; however, that was not a good idea in Florida because of the humidity. The finished product was used in cushions for military and civilian vehicles.

Keep in mind that this was during the tail end of the Depression, and any kind of work was a welcome event. A lot of locals had their trucks fixed with high sideboards in the back to increase the amount of Spanish moss they could carry per load. To gather the moss, they used bamboo-fishing poles with a hook on the tip. They simply hooked on to the moss, twisted the pole, gave a yank, and down came the moss. It did not take them long to fill their trucks, as the woods were full of large oaks loaded with Spanish moss. The moss pickers would deliver their cargo to the moss yard and receive much needed cash in return.

Since Apopka was known as the Fern City, there were a lot of Boston ferns grown in the area. In order to ship the ferns, they were wrapped in a moist sphagnum moss and wax paper. So naturally, there was a market for this moss as well, and generally, the same men harvested both.

My Dad had a small nursery growing ferns and used a fair amount of sphagnum moss. He purchased it from a gentleman named "Red" Russell, who also had a sawmill on the Piedmont/Wekiva Springs road. Now, Red was a congenial sort of guy, who always wore stripped overalls like a railroad engineer. He also wore an engineer's cap. One evening, I asked my Dad to ask Red if I could go with him some Saturday morning when he went to gather some Spanish moss. Of course, Red said he would enjoy the company.

Well, Saturday finally came around, and I ended up deep in some swampy area that was loaded with large oak trees, and a lot of Spanish moss. I did not get to operate the bamboo pole, but I would load the moss on the truck as Red pulled it down.

On one pull, a large clump of moss landed at our feet, and to our surprise, a large black snake hit the ground. Well, Red went one way, and I went the other. After the snake decided to go its own way, Red and I went back to work. Red was drinking something in a brown paper bag in order to settle his nerves. Since I was not old enough to be drinking anything out of a brown paper bag, my nerves remained unsettled for the rest of the day.

At any rate, we loaded the truck and headed back to town. On the trip back, I had the ride of my life. It was a blistering hot day. I was not wearing a shirt while I rode in the back of the truck on top of the moss. Man, was that the life, riding in a cool breeze and waving to anybody who might be looking our way.

I do not think that Red's nerves had quite settled down, because after he collected his money from the moss yard and dropped me off, he headed straight for the Mule Shoe Bar on Lake Marshall Road and Hwy. 441. That place had been known to settle the most shattered nerves in town.

Over dinner that night, I was ranting and raving about what a good time I had and how brave I was with that huge black snake. I don't think I impressed anyone, so I decided to go to bed. The heat continued into the night, and I slept with the windows open. During the night, I began to toss, turn, and scratch. Big red welts came up all over my body, so I ran into my mother's room begging for help. Sure enough, it was red bugs or "chiggers" picked up from rolling around in that Spanish moss. Back in those days, there was a home remedy for almost anything, and the remedy for red bugs was dipping a cloth into the kerosene from your lamp and dabbing it on the welts. The other remedy was to use finger nail polish to smother the red bugs, but I had no sisters living at home, and my mom doggone sure didn't use fingernail polish.

Yeah, the old moss yard and Red Russell would have to be in the classification of "the good ol' days;" however, those nights scratching the red bugs did not earn the same distinction.

Youthful Memories Of Growing Up

When I was but a wee lad growing up in the sandy scrub of my beloved Florida, I used to see, smell, taste, observe, and play with the things that only wee people can. Now that I have grown into a full-fledged adult, I often wonder what ever happened to those glorious events I used to observe and entertain myself with. Such as…

Doodlebugs

I remember so well crawling under the front porch to begin my search for the ever-elusive doodlebugs. I suppose this was a good spot because it was sandy and ultra dry. There you could find large numbers of little round holes dotting the ground. Supposedly, there was a doodlebug inhabiting each hole. Now, the name of the game was to get one of these rascals to come to the top.

You would have to find a broom straw or a stiff pine needle and insert it in the entrance of the hole. Patiently, you would stir and chant your lovely ballad, "Doodlebug, doodlebug wherever you are, please come to the top." There were many versions, and who knows the original? I don't know about the rest of the words, but we were quite often successful in bringing the little bugs up.

If I am wondering what ever happened to those good ol' days. I guess I have to ask myself how silly we would look at our age, under the back porch, leaning over a doodlebug hole like an Eskimo over a seal hole, trying to sing something that we could not even remember the words to.

Mulberry Trees

Oh, how I remember that ol' mulberry tree. But for the life of me, I just can't remember where it was. It seemed huge to us little guys, as we scaled to the top to get the very sweetest fruit we could find. I remember hanging upside down off some limb, stretching for that big, blackish-blue jewel just a little out of reach. We would eat until our little bellies would almost pop and then we would simmer down for some rest under the live oak next to the mulberry tree.

It was always a mystery to me how any tree that could produce the nectar of the gods, could be so messy and ugly. You had better watch where you walked underneath that mulberry tree because of fallen berries, and the fact that it was a favorite hangout for mockingbirds and blue jays.

I have read where Piedmont's Jackson and Larson Wineries bottled mulberry wine. I wonder how many trees they had to have in order to produce a large amount of this product. That would have been a rather messy orchard.

Fireflies

Once school was out, and the summer was upon us, we could hardly wait for the sun to go down and for the darkness to set in around the old oak trees in our back yard. It was time to break out the old peanut butter jars with the lids punched full of holes. The male firefly (actually beetles) would begin sending out patterns of lights to attract female fireflies, which meant it was time to fill our jars for the evening light show.

What a wonderful playmate we had there, as they did not bite, they had no pincers, they did not attack, they did not carry disease, they were not poisonous and best of all, they could not fly very fast and were easy to catch.

Every so often, we would squeeze the beetle a little too hard and get the luciferin (the chemical the firefly uses for its bioluminescence) all over our hands. We had hands that glowed in the dark.

You actually do not see many fireflies anymore, and I often wonder why. I suppose in today's world, filled with chemicals for treating lawns, etc., we have done away with a lot of God's little pleasures.

Foxfire

I could not have been any more than seven or eight years old when a mystery occurred in my young life, that stuck with me for many years to come. It was only after I took up golf and moved to Errol Estates did that mystery begin to unravel in my mind. Think back with me…

It was somewhere between 2:00-4:00 on a muggy summer morning when the Christmas household heard a loud banging on the screen door from our back porch. By the time I got awake, I heard my dad grumbling as he rambled down the hall on his way to the back door. I am sure he thought it was a motorist stranded on the highway; however, it could have been a member of our family in some sort of distress.

Upon opening the door, he found none of the above. There stood Elsie Kratzert with her small son. Both were completely consumed in fear and trembling.

After listening to Elsie's story, we had a household full of people all consumed with the same fear.

Elsie was the wife of Rudy Kratzert, who had a small son that I will call Billy because I have completely forgotten his name. Rudy was a popular local fisherman, who later had a bait and tackle shop on the corner of Central Avenue and Fifth Street. On this particular night, Rudy had gone to the coast fishing with some friends and left Elsie and Billy at home alone. Now, their home was maybe a mile from the Old Dixie Highway down Vick Road, heading north. It sat on a hill amongst some blackjack oak trees. There was a clay road leading down the hill to Vick Road.

On this particular evening, Elsie was awakened by a bright light shining into her bedroom window. Her first thought was that Rudy had returned from fishing trip early or maybe some foxhunters were looking for their dogs. On closer observation, she realized it was not headlights from a car but a ball of fire coming through the blackjacks. The ball of fire kept coming closer and closer to the house. Unable to stand it much longer, she grabbed Billy and ran for their car. As the crow flies, our house was probably the closest to hers, and she probably broke all records getting there.

For the rest of the morning there was a lot of jabber around the kitchen table about just what this ball of fire going through the woods was. Now, we speculated on everything from unidentified flying objects, ghosts, and goblins or just someone in the woods playing a hoax.

At any rate, it was agreed that when the sun came up, my oldest brother and my dad would go out and look for tell tale signs.

When the local investigators returned from their investigation on Vick Road, they reported there were no signs at all of a ball of fire being in the area. There was no scorching on the fallen blackjack leaves, no car tracks, no human tracks, and no nothing. You want to know something else?

From that day forward, when Rudy was out of town, the Kratzert home had no Elsie either. She was always a guest of the Christmas family.

****

As the years drifted by, "Sherlock" Christmas was never completely satisfied with the findings of the local investigators we sent out on the last investigation. My sidekick Watson (my brother Gene), brought to my attention that we never looked into the possibility of swamp gas, or shall we call it "foxfire," like they had in the Okefenokee Swamp in South Georgia. I asked, "How could we have swamp gas, since we don't have any swamps around here?"

"Not so," said Watson. "We have Banana Springs less than a mile north of the Kratzert homestead." Banana Springs lies just off the fourth green of the Grove Golf Course in Errol Estate. This spring was, and still is, a headwater to a creek running into the lakes of Errol.

Fox Fire, (a luminescent gaseous ball of fire) is formed from decaying organic matter that you would find around swampy areas such as Banana Springs. Swamp gas is comprised primarily of methane and carbon dioxide. The oxidation of hydrogen phosphate and methane gases produced by decaying matter could cause flowing lights to appear in the air. This could explain why our investigators never found any sign of a ball of fire, as the ball of fire was really luminescent. At any rate, my dear friends, this is Sherlock's "deductive reasoning."

Hobos

I am only guessing that the time frame was before World War II and at the tail end of The Great Depression. The time frame I speak of is the era of the hobos or, as we say today, the homeless.

I have said before that our home was adjacent to Hwy. 441 to the north, and the Seaboard Railroad to the south. I remember the hobos very distinctly traveling the highways and the rails. There was a steady flow of these "travelers" that would come to our door looking for a meal. I do not recall my mother ever refusing meals to anyone. My mother was very generous and always gave them a full plate. It seems like only yesterday, watching them sitting on the front steps scraping their plates.

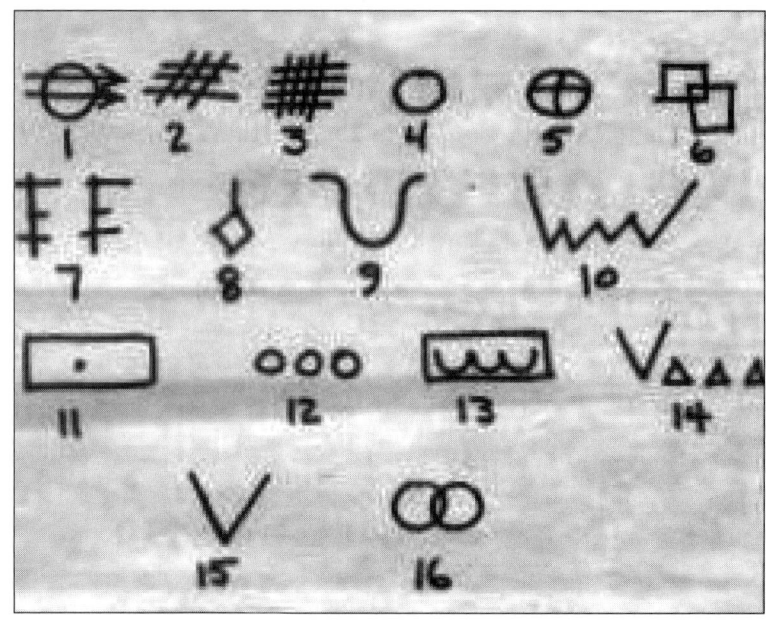

Symbols like these gave hobos valuable information.

Some were friendly and liked to talk, while others were quiet, and said nothing. They would say that the word on the street was that my mother was a good woman, and you could get a meal at her house. I never really understood what they meant at the time.

I now know that the hobos had left their own signs on the road as to what kind of a house ours was. You can see by the enclosed picture, one of the more basic charts used throughout the South. 1. Two hobos, traveling together, have gone the direction of the arrows. 2. Hobos not welcome. 3. This sign depicts the bars of a jail. 4. This means "GET OUT." 5. The town itself is no good. 6. This is a good place for hobos to meet other hobos. 7. All the ministers, mission heads, and Christian leaders are disposed to welcoming transients. 8. The pendulum indicates that the people here swing back and forth in their attitudes toward hobos. 9. This represents two rails and a cross ties which means "railway terminal" or "division point," a good place to board trains in different directions. 10. This sign represent teeth; it means the police and people are hostile toward tramps. 11. This means, "the jail is alive with cooties." 12. Keep on moving; the police, churches, and the people are no good. 13. This is a swell place to stop; these people are bighearted. 14. Food may be had for the asking. 15. This is the sign for "OK;" people are very good. 16. Best results are secured if two hobos travel together, not so good for a lone hobo.

I was not old enough to know what was going on, and I certainly knew nothing about the hobo "sign" language. If I had, and if I had looked out on Hwy. 441, I more than likely would have seen the sign #14, "Food may be had for the asking."

Three or four times a day, the old coal burning engines of the Seaboard Airline Railroad ran south of our home, chugging by to pick up oranges in Plymouth and plants from Apopka.

One very cold January evening, we were chopping wood to heat our fernery that went almost to the railroad in back of our house. As the train was slowing down for its Apopka stop, two young men jumped off. While we continued chopping wood, we saw them digging a hole in the side of the railroad bank for protection from the cold. Later they built a fire.

My ever-so-venturesome brother Gene just had to cross the tracks and find out who our new neighbors were. And that he did. They were two young boys about seventeen or eighteen years old from Detroit, looking for work. Their names were simply Kenny and Vernon. It did not take our family long to help those two boys. One of my sisters found a little apartment for the boys to stay in, and another sister rounded up clothing. My Dad found them a job in one of the nurseries, and slowly, they began to settle down to their new life.

They liked to hunt rabbits and would prepare a stew of macaroni, tomatoes, and rabbit. I would have to say, it tasted pretty good. I remember that they could not get over the fact that Florida rabbits were so small. Occasionally, they would catch the Florida tortoise and add that to their stew. They said it tasted like chicken. You could not prove that one by me.

Time moved on, and the boys worked hard and saved their money very diligently. It was not too long before they had saved enough to buy a Greyhound ticket back to Detroit. It was a sad day when they left, and actually, we never heard from them again. It was not long afterwards that Pearl Harbor was attacked, and they were probably drafted. To this day, I wonder what ever happened to Kenny and Vernon.

The "Hobos Chart" was reprinted with permission of Borderlands, a student writing of El Paso community College, El Paso, Texas. 79998, Ruth E. Vise, Faculty Editor, and David Uhl. All rights reserved.

Medicine Show

It was a lazy summer afternoon back around 1942, in the old school on Main St., as our sixth grade class was busy with a study period. This was Miss Kessler's class, and you dared not make a sound or look up from your books. All of a sudden, we began to hear what sounded like music coming from a little bit east on Hwy. 441. Soon, there they were – it was the medicine show making their yearly visit to Apopka. To those of us who had not strayed any farther from home than Zellwood, it seemed like the Rose Bowl parade.

There were three flatbed trucks. On the back of one truck were black-faced singers strumming their banjos, with a calliope blaring away on one of the other trucks. I think their main objective was to make a lot of noise and draw attention to their entrance into town. Miss Kessler was in one of her rare, sweet moods and allowed the class to open windows to watch the entertainment go by.

My guess is that the show manager made a point to go by the schools, so that the impressed young students would go home and beg their parents to attend the show that night. I fit right into their profile, and after school, I hit the home steps full blast, skidding down the hall on my knees, begging my mother to talk my dad into loading up the pickup truck and going to town for the show.

She was the only one who had any influence in such matters. It worked! That evening we loaded up.

The Medicine Show always set up on South Central Avenue across the railroad tracks, cattie-cornered from the icehouse. There was always an open field there, with plenty of parking for everyone. The show would set up a tent and use the back of one of the flatbeds as a stage for the performers. They always had a few sleight-of-hand tricks, a little comedy or some banjo solos between their pitches of whatever snake oil they might be selling. Their entertainers were not to be sneezed at, as a lot of vaudeville entertainers got their start in a medicine show. To mention a few, there were Buster Keaton, Red Skelton, Roy Acuff, George and Gracie Burns, Chico Marks, and Lester Flatt.

All this entertainment was to soften up the crowd so the pitchman could push his "cure all" medicines for whatever the market would stand. They claimed cures for nervousness, diabetes, cancer, gallstones, epilepsy, and weight-gain or there was just a plain old germ killer. The doctor (supposedly) would always tell a tear-jerking story about the fellow in the last town who did not buy his product and suffered the consequences.

The black-faced comic dominated most medicine show performances. They called him Jake or whatever name seemed appropriate.

You see, this character was borrowed straight from the minstrel show. Jake served as the chief comedian and master of ceremonies, acting in sketches, introducing specialty numbers, playing the banjo, and cracking jokes with the straight man. In most troupes, Jake also served as producer of the show.

All this commotion was well and good; however, my favorite time was when they started selling candy boxes, much like a Cracker Jack box. There was always one box containing a grand prize, maybe a watch. I always thought that redheaded boy who always won the prize was one of their own, because none of us had ever seen him before.

All of the great "cure alls" such as Kickapoo Indian Sagwa, Hamlin's Wizard Oil, and probably the last one to have a cure for everything, Hadacol, have pretty well faded away. Remember that old saying, they "hadda call" it something.

During its swan song, Hadacol was advertised on early television in order to reach its audience.

Due to medicine supply companies coming into their own, government regulations cracking down on outlandish claims made about the medicines, better forms of advertising, and drug stores coming into their own, the medicine show faded into the backdrop of progress and changing times. Even the old school house faded away and became Apopka City Hall.

City Gangs

You can't help but notice the outstanding campaign our Apopka City Councilman Kathy Till has going against street gangs in our community. Our town is definitely grateful for her efforts. This article certainly has no intention of making light of this subject, but only wishes to reminisce on how the gangs of my childhood and the gangs of today greatly differ.

My mind quite often drifts back to my pre-teenage days when our neighborhood had its own rendition of neighborhood gangs. We had the "B-B Kids," "The Booger Bottom Boys," and the "Jackie Bogar Gang."

I was fortunate enough to have been sworn into the B-B Kids (At least I thought so). Never get the idea that we were running around shooting up the neighborhood with B-B guns. Shoot, we didn't have the money to buy the B-B's much less a B-B gun. Our total mission was to find and destroy the other gangs "hideout." Now, that wasn't very difficult, as sometimes, the turbulence from a jaybird flying overhead would destroy their structures. We would leave a note saying, "The B-B Kids have struck again." Don't you suppose that left the fear of the Almighty in them? All of these meeting places were no more than a hole in the ground, with dried out dog fennel roofs. We were the envy of the local architects of the day.

The Booger Bottom Boys all came from around Main Street on the west side of town. I recall one evening; we were having a marble tournament in front of the Huggins' house. One on their gang got a little frustrated because he had lost his shooter and threw his marbles on Mr. Huggins' tin roof. Now that started a little commotion, and the last thing I saw was that chap running down the road screaming, "Daddy, Bodar did it."

The Jackie Bogar Gang was just that. It was a one-man gang consisting of the one and only, Jackie Bogar. He said he could not recruit anyone tough enough to meet his specifications. He had a good point there, as he was a ten-year-old boy in an eighteen-year-old body. We spent an awful lot of time avoiding him. We did not spend much time looking for his so-called hideout either. Even if we had, I guess we would have left a note saying, "Sorry to have missed you; have a nice day."

Actually, these gangs took the lighter side most of the time, by having their own football, baseball, marbles or any other kind of team that could compete against each other. Any vacant field was our football or baseball field for that moment, until the owner ran us off. I guess we were a little on the loud side. The Boy Scout Camp (Camp Wewa) in Plymouth let us use their softball field when they were not using it.

There was a boy that lived in Plymouth named Vance Williams, who was from Maine. Wow, could he hit a softball. The B-B kids tried to enlist him into our gang; however, he was not interested. He was probably the first holdout in our gangs' spring rush. We just drooled, as he continued to hit the softball into the woods (our rendition of over the fence). Being from Maine, Vance used to swim during the winter months in the lake behind his house. It's a good thing our gangs did not have a swim teams, as Vance would have won all the events during the winter months. Our gang members had a hard enough time taking a bath during those months.

I have written before about how Apopka has always loved baseball and has produced some pretty fair talent for the majors. Well, let me say now, none of that talent came from our side of town. Some of us did go as far as American Legion (managed by our Mayor John Land) and high school sports, but that was about the end of the line for us.

In the fall, football was king. Jackie Bogar created quite a problem. He was the Tim Tebow of our era. The big common denominator with Tebow was that Bogar was big and fast. The uncommon denominator was that he did not have much of a chance of getting a brain concussion.

We really tried to have our games on a field he could not find, but sometimes that was a little difficult. Jimmy Ustler was the little guy in our group, and he always had an open invitation. As his brother David grew up, we would have been smart to have avoided him, as he developed into one of the better linebackers to come out of Apopka.

The definition of gangs in our era was the development of a band of friends that lasted a lifetime. Many of our old friends are no longer with us, but those who are, still remember the days of the "B-B Kids" or "The Booger Bottom Boys." We all bonded together for a lifetime. I would suspect that most of you came from similar backgrounds in your childhood.

The activities of the gangs of today have changed dramatically. When you see the graffiti on the walls or read of drug related gangs, you can rest assured today's equivalent to "The Booger Bottom Boys" was not involved. Commissioner Till's campaign to bring community awareness of this problem should receive full support from everyone in this end of the county.

Dream Lake

How many of you remember the ol' swimming hole, where you probably learned to swim and spent a great deal of your summer breaks? Well, in my case, that ol' swimming hole is Dream Lake, and it's still here. That grand old lake was so prominent in our community that we named an elementary school in its honor.

When I first started swimming at Dream Lake there were no docks, and there were certainly no lifeguards. All we had was a magnificent old oak tree that spread its limbs out over the beautiful clear waters of the lake. The lake was so clear that you could see the fish swim by, and occasionally that majestic black bass would cruise by as if he owned that section of the lake. The depth of the water under the limbs was satisfactory for diving, and dive we did.

Now tagging along with your older brother isn't necessarily the smartest thing to do. Case in point was when I followed my brother out on that limb. I immediately got my first swimming lesson. He threw me out of the tree and told me I was on my own, in his nice way. Well, I made it to shore and never had a fear of the water again.

Then came the period of time when I met my first hero of the lake. We would all dive deep into the lake and see who could stay under the longest. I finally built my lungs up to the point that I could stay under for sixty-seconds, and I thought that might be a winner. We had a local lad named Earl Croom whom I am quite sure, had alligator lungs. I don't remember the exact time he spent under water; however, I think it was about three minutes. Now understand, he was the all-time Dream Lake champion. Bleed your heart out, Johnny Weissmuller.

If you wanted to hang around any lake here in Florida, you were going to pay the price. It was there that the ear fungi monster hung out. You might have a beautiful day swimming, but that night, the pain would strike. I do not know to this day what kind of warm oil my mother put in my ears, but it sure did the job. She warmed the oil, put it in with an eyedropper, and stuffed cotton in my ear to hold the oil in.

Our trips to the swimming hole were always a pretty eventful journey, as we would cut through the old Ustler Brothers Fernery and would stop at the other side for some berries from the blueberry patch. One day, we looked across the road and saw that Mr. Pittman's watermelons were about the right size for picking.

We reasoned amongst ourselves, that we would just "borrow" one of those melons and take it to the lake to chill it down a little. We went through the field thumping the melons, as if we knew what we were doing. Finally, we found one to our satisfaction, and about the time we were about to pick it, Mr. Pittman, who had been watching us all along, shot his shotgun straight up in the air. As the birdshot began to fall to the ground, we just knew we had been hit. We established a speed record back to the Ustler house. It did not take us long to find a new route to Dream Lake.

The trouble with this new route was that it was paved. No more dirt or clay streets to cool our bare feet. The asphalt was too hot to walk on, and when we moved to the side of the road, the sandspurs ate us alive. Even if it rained and the roads were cool, you had a tendency to stub your toe. If you used one of those wooden sidewalks, you would end up with splinters in your feet.

Something had to be done, and done fast. The only way out of this dilemma was, gulp, to start wearing shoes. The following weekend, I went down to George Kerr's shoe store to look around. Well, you might know I picked out the Converse Chuck Taylor All-Star Low-Tops. I had to learn how to walk in shoes, because in Florida, you had a tendency to get a lot of sand in your shoes. You had to stop, pour the sand out, and continue on your way. Shoot, when I played high school basketball, I still used the same low-top shoes.

Time moved on and Dream Lake finally got a dock. With the dock came the crowds, and soon there was a sign saying not to climb the old oak tree. Maybe now that I was a shoe wearer, it was time for me to look for another swimming hole. The gang in our neighborhood did not take long in deciding that we would start swimming at Sanlando Springs in Seminole County. They had the springs, a beach, slides, dressing rooms around a beautiful swimming pool, a dance patio at the top of the hill, and pretty girls. We did not have that at Dream Lake. The only problem was that we had no transportation to get there. We finally figured out that we could take a transit bus into Orlando and transfer to one going to Sanlando for only twenty-cents round trip. All this was so much better than the hot roads, sandspurs, splinters, and birdshot falling all around us.

History Of Apopka Foliage Industry

You quite often hear the question of how and why did the foliage industry end up in the Apopka area. To get to these answers, we would have to start our journey in a small town in Ohio somewhere around 1900-1910.

It was there at the Springfield Floral Company in Springfield, Ohio, that Harry Ustler worked as the company clerk. The company sales manager was a gentleman by the name of Mr. Powell. There was constant conversation between the two about the high cost of production on Boston ferns. It was Mr. Powell's belief that if they could lower the price, they would be able to sell twice as much product. Harry Ustler felt the only way to lower the cost of production would be grow the product in a place like Florida, where you would not have high heating or high labor costs. Since there was agreement of this, they decided to send Harry to Florida to see if he could find a location that would be suitable for the production of ferns.

Harry's objective was to find suitable land, plenty of lakes for a water supply, and weather conducive to growing Boston ferns. Central Florida met all the criteria, so Harry started his search by headquartering at the Altamonte Springs Hotel in Altamonte Springs, Florida.

While at the hotel, I am sure he met Charles D. Haines, a former congressman from New York State, who was also staying at the hotel at this time. Congressman Haines was the owner of The Royal Fernery in Altamonte Springs. He was in the process of building a lath shed for the production of Asparagus Plumosa ferns that would eventually total over sixty-five acres. I am sure Harry picked up a lot of useful information from Mr. Haines.

Also at that time, two of the nation's most eminent horticulturists were living in this area. They were Dr. Henry Nehrling of Gotha and Dr. Theodore Mead of Oviedo. Dr. Nehrling was best known for his work with caladiums, and Dr. Mead was an authority on orchids, gladiolus, and other tropical plants.

Transportation was a huge factor as to where Harry would want to locate. Central Florida had the Atlantic Coastline and Seaboard Railroads servicing the area at the time. Being perfectly satisfied that he had found the right location in Central Florida, Harry telexed his friend Mr. Powell to inform him of his findings. Much to Harry's dismay, Mr. Powell telexed back that he could not join him because of his lack of funds. This had to be a huge setback for Harry Ustler.

Being the stubborn German that he was, Harry had no intentions of abandoning his dream of growing Boston ferns in Florida. He applied for and got a job as a waiter at the Altamonte Hotel to bide his time. During his stay, he met a gentleman from New Hampshire by the name of W.P. Newell. Harry shared his passion about growing the Boston fern in Florida with Mr. Newell, and soon they agreed upon a partnership, with Mr. Newell providing the capital and Harry the expertise.

Immediately, they leased a Pinery (pineapples grown under lath), on Lake Eola in downtown Orlando. They had to start the production procedure from the very beginning. Learning how to handle the insects and diseases that were native to Florida, protecting these plants from the weather, as well as learning about packaging and shipping of the produce, were just a few of the kinks they had to work out.

But as time went by, they did very well. They were shipping a lot of produce back to Springfield Floral and other wholesalers in the Ohio area. As a matter of fact, they were doing so well, they needed to expand production, but they did not have any more land on Lake Eola. As fate would have it, Mr. Newell had purchased some land northwest of Orlando in Apopka, in the neighborhood of Park Avenue and Seventh Street.

About 1911, Newell and Ustler built the first lath shed for the exclusive purpose of growing Boston ferns in Apopka. From the very beginning, the venture proved to be very successful, with sales constantly outdistancing production. Newell and Ustler began to talk locals into growing ferns as satellite growers. W.T. Champneys came aboard in 1918, along with Bob Mitchell, Mallory Welch, Gillen McClure, and Harry Smith. Victor Pilat came from the Kings Ranch in Texas to grow ferns in Florida.

With all the rapid expansion in the growth of Boston ferns, in 1924, the City of Apopka adopted the slogan of The Fern City. From that day forward, all of the support companies, such as supply houses (boxes, pots, peat, etc.), fertilizer plants, and transportation began to locate near the production, making Apopka the hub of the Foliage plant industry for the State of Florida.

Slat Shed Heating

An interesting tidbit concerning the foliage industry is about the history of heating the nurseries and slat sheds, during the early days, from the cold weather to protect the ferns grown here in the "Fern City."

Keep in mind that the first Boston ferns were grown around the shores of Lake Eola in downtown Orlando somewhere around 1910. Harry Ustler and W.P. Newell leased a lath shed that had been used for growing pineapples for their first stab at growing the Boston fern in Florida.

I do not believe there are written records on how they protected their crops from the cold back when they grew ferns at Lake Eola; however; a good guess would be that they piled wood every so many feet apart and lit the piles when the temperature got close to thirty-two degrees. They soon used fifty-five gallon drums to contain the wood and fire. When I was a young boy in the 1940s, my brother and I would cut wood after school for my father to fire his heaters at night. All during the summer, we would cut and pile the wood outside the nursery. By the time cold weather rolled around, the wood had rotted a little and would be loaded with red ants and centipedes. It became a necessity to load the wood in a wheelbarrow and deliver it to the heaters.

Pushing a wheelbarrow in the dark, stepping on the plants beside the path you were going down, and burning the plants that were too close to the heat did not work out very well. The truth of the matter was that you actually damaged as many crops as you saved.

In about the late '40s or early '50s, the smudge pot came out. This was a small heater that was used in the citrus industry. This heater burned number two oil and created more black smoke than the community could stand. On a cold morning, you could hardly see your way through downtown Apopka because of the black smoke coming from the nurseries. Again, something better had to be found.

After that, there was the "jumbo" heater with a return stack that produced much less smoke, if any. It was taller and could be regulated to burn on low, medium or high. One of the problems was if you lit these heaters early in the evening, you had to refill it before the coldest period, which was about daylight. You had to put the cap of the heater about three quarters over the exhaust, open the bottom, and pour the cold oil directly in the burning oil, which was quite dangerous.

Not long after the jumbo heater, the nurserymen came up with the finest innovation yet. They started covering their sheds with 2-4 mil polyethylene. Holes were drilled in the polyethylene to let water through when it rained. The roof and walls were covered, and above all, it protected the crops from cold winds and low temperatures. You only had to light a few heaters on low, and they would last all night because most of the heat was retained by the plastic.

Things improved even more for the old slat sheds when growers started using a mist system inside the buildings, and the heat of the well water maintained adequate temperature controls. Also, it kept the plants cleaner due to a decrease of smoke and smut.

At one time, the old slat sheds were used for stock plants, and the greenhouses were used for the finished ones. Then a lot of the stock was moved inside the greenhouses in baskets, and some were imported from offshore.

Eventually, most of the smaller plants were grown inside greenhouses, heated from steam, hot water or unit heaters.

In the course of time, the slat (lath) sheds were replaced with saran cloth for shade, and larger plants were grown in the same manner as the large ones in south Florida.

I remember those old firing nights like it was yesterday. Norman Ustler, Mac Walters, Alvin Alcorn, and myself spent a lot of time putting out fires in nurseries where someone dozed off one time too many. Many nights were spent with Earl New, Lamont Marchman, Tom Mahaffey, Stewart Green, J.C. Hicks, and so many others. The big question at our early morning breakfast was, "How cold did it get at your place?" It was always the coldest at Lamont's Evergreen Gardens, because he always waited until last to announce his temperature.

Parris Island I

Sgt. Welcomes recruits at Yemassee

A couple of days after my graduation from high school, I dropped in on my favorite coffee table in Charlie's Restaurant on Main Street. Seated at the table was an old friend and local muck farmer, Mr. Bass. In conversation, Mr. Bass asked what I was going to do with myself now that I was out of high school. Very proudly, I said that I was going in the Marine Corps with my two best friends. None of the three of us had the funds to continue our education. The Marines had a program where you served one year on active duty and six years in the reserves. This entitled you to the G. I. Bill and its many benefits. I felt like this was a great deal.

There was a sparkling smile on Mr. Bass' face as he proceeded to tell me that he was in the Marine Corps in World War I, and he pretty much bet that it had not changed much. He continued on to tell me that he boarded a train in Jacksonville, and headed straight toward Yemassee, South Carolina. At that point, the train backed him into Port Royal. All the way, the porters kept saying they had better get their last poggie-bait (candy) and Cokes, because they would see no more of that for the next three months.

Mr. Bass said that when they arrived in Port Royal, they were met by a small corporal who said he did not want to see anything but a bunch of heels, or something like that. From there, buses took them to the barbershop on Parris Island, where their heads were completely shaved. He left his story telling at this point and said he did not want to spoil any of the fun we were in for over the next three months.

Well sure enough, Jack Gilliam, Jimmy Ustler, and I boarded the train in Jacksonville. Along the way, I related to them what Mr. Bass had said, and we all got quite a chuckle. After all, this was 1949, not World War I. The train finally arrived at Yemassee, and we switched over to another train bound for Port Royal.

It was on this leg of the trip that we began to hear things that made us a little nervous. Down the aisle came a porter shouting that we had better get our poggie-bait and Coca-Colas now, as we were not likely to have any more for the next three months. Well, as we were squirming, the train arrived in Port Royal, and sure enough, there stood a small corporal shouting at the top of his lungs for us to "fall in," and he did not want to see "anything but heels." We loaded the buses for Parris Island and the barbershop. This was the era of the Elvis Presley hairdos, and it was so sad to watch those beautiful locks of hair hit the floor.

They delivered us to our squad-bays, where all three of us stayed together. It took me a solid week to find Jack and Jimmy, even though Jack was only a few bunks down; recognizing him with no hair was not easy. It was here that we met our master for the next three months, our Drill Instructor. Sergeant Stevenson was not too bad, but Lord only knows where he got his assistants. They were the ones who taught us the difference between the left foot and the right foot, how to take a shower, how to address a superior, how to make a bed, and how to run the sand pits, even when the temperature got above 100 degrees.

The next morning we ran into one of those surprises that Mr. Bass failed to pass on. We were all lined up in front of the mess hall for breakfast. We were all at attention, and all the drill instructors were walking the aisles as if they were waiting on something to happen. About this time, our ranks were invaded by the infamous South Carolina sand fly. Now these little creatures were looking for a place to take a break, like in our ears, eyes, nose or wherever. We were at attention, with our thumbs neatly placed on the seam of our trousers, while three or four drill instructors watched our every move. Who would break first when the sand fly went up someone's nose? Sure enough, the confrontation came when a sand fly went up one of the Marine's nose. He tried to ease his hand up to swat the fly and was successful at that; however, the drill instructor caught him. The D.I. picked up the fly (or a piece of dirt) put it in a matchbox, and stuck it in his pocket. That seemed like the end of that little incident. However, we had another thought coming.

At 4:00 a.m., you would have thought a tornado hit our squad bay. The lights came on, and three drill instructors were shouting at the top of their lungs, "fall in, full combat gear, hit the streets, now, now, now!" I would say it took us about thirty-seconds to line-up in a perfect formation. Hut-two-three-four, down the street and out into the Geechie swamps we went. We finally arrived at a little clearing where the spoons were handed out to dig a little grave, six-by-three inches. One of the D.I.'s had a harmonica. The matchbox was taken out and wrapped in a little handkerchief, and with the harmonica playing its rendition of the taps, the little "coffin" was lowered into the grave.

The Marine who swatted this fly had to say a few words. A few words were the understatement of the year. I don't think he could utter a word. A cross was made of twigs. Our platoon marched quietly back to the base and took our position in the chow line. Thus, the saga of the South Carolina sand fly starts all over again, but to a much wiser platoon.

The one thing that has never changed about the Corps is their complete devotion to discipline. The sand fly episode is only one little incident of how the smallest possible detail cannot be overlooked.

Parris Island II

The Long Green Line

The last time I wrote about Parris Island, I promised you that I would write a few more lines on what my good friend Mr. Bass failed to tell me about the booby traps of the Island.

The Marines were probably the world's greatest propagandist. When we first arrived, I recall them telling us that no one had ever escaped the Island. Only two had tried, and they were both eaten by the sharks. It kind of sounded like Alcatraz to me; however, leave it to a bunch of eighteen-year-old kids to swallow it all, hook, line, and sinker.

We not only swallowed that, but I recall once during one of our open-air classes, that the Instructor started pounding on the table concerning the opening of the Panama Canal in 1914. The Navy claimed to have sent the first ship through the Canal; however, the Corps had pictures to prove two marines in a rowboat were just in front of the Navy ship.

You have heard it many times: never volunteer for anything in the military. Well, let's see just how dumb this same bunch of boys can be.

Once, a typist was needed for the Mess Hall, so they lined us all up in regular formation. They started at the left, which was me, and asked how many words I could type a minute. I answered the first thing that came to my mind, so I said forty. The next guy said forty-five, and so it went upward until it reached about 100. Finally, the drill instructor said, "the whole damn bunch of you are lying," so he gave it to the lowest one, which was me, only because I was first in line. Boy was that a good two weeks. All I did was answer the phone and type menus.

One day at the rifle range, a Sergeant pulled up in a pick-up truck and lined us up again. He wanted to know how many of us had a driver's license. Jack Gilliam beat me to it that day. He was chosen, and he disappeared behind the maintenance building. I can still see that sheepish grin on his face. It only took a few minutes, and he came back out with a wheelbarrow loaded with bricks. The grin had disappeared. I don't know why it was us Apopka boys that were so insistent on volunteering.

Jimmy Ustler had his bad days too. They marched us into the gas chamber, with our gas masks around our necks. When they threw the canister of gas into the chamber, we were simply supposed to put our gas masks on and continue to march around the room. You would be amazed how many of those boys could not slide the gas mask on. Now, Jimmy just got tired of fighting the mask, so he threw it on the floor and laid down in front of the exit door so he would be the first one out. Well, it did not work out exactly as he thought. When they opened the door, the rest of us also wanted to be the first out, and we nearly stomped Jimmy to death. Only an Apopka boy would think of lying down in front of the door.

On one hot day, we were strutting our stuff on the blistering asphalt, when it hit 100 degrees. Regulations state that all drills on asphalt must cease at 100 degrees. Well, those regulations did not bother the Corps at all, as they simply took us to the sand pits to finish the day. Our platoon held up pretty well for the day, so the Drill Instructor said he was going to let us go to the movies that night to see John Wayne in "The Shores of Iowa Jima."

All went well as we fell into formation with white towels around our necks. The white towels were so we could be easily seen, as it was in the evening and dark. Our field shoes were of a brogan style. When marching on a hard surface, we dug the heels in, making our platoon sound like the German Gestapo. With the Drill Instructor shouting, "heels, heels," the long green line finally arrived at our outdoor theatre.

After the D.I. gave us permission to be seated, someone lit a cigarette before the D.I. declared the, "smoking lamp is lit." He immediately marched us back to the barracks and put us on a work detail. We used old toothbrushes, soap, and water and scrubbed the cracks in the wooden floors. We did this until close to midnight. Finally, a Chaplin came in and gave the D.I. a real chewing-out for not having his troops in bed by that time.

There is only one Parris Island. With its funny, and yet tragic stories coming out of the island, it has become somewhat of a mystic legend. Regardless, there will always be a great deal of pride for those of us who embarked on our Marine Corps career on this little island somewhere south in the Carolina low country.

The Old First Baptist Church

I wonder how many of you remember the old Baptist Church that stood on the southwest corner of Main Street and Highlands. Yes…the one with the steeple and bell tower. I can still remember the rope at the entrance that would, you might say "Ring the Golden Bells" to remind the parishioners that it was time for Sunday school or church. I can still see the small choir all decked out in their blue gowns and ol' Charlie Bateman, Sr. taking his Sunday snooze in the back row of the choir. Lucy Goolsby directed that choir with all the pep and vigor of Arthur Fiedler of the Boston Pops, but in spite of her best efforts, she could not keep old E.J. Ryan from drowning out the rest of the choir with his deep base voice.

When I was growing up, my brother and I never had a vote as to whether we would attend Sunday school, BYPU, church or any other function that may have opened the doors to that old church. Our mother simply delivered us. Sunday school was just fine, mingling with other kids our age.

The old church stood on the corner of Main Street and Highland Avenue.

However, the good Lord knows, those Sunday mornings and evenings sitting on the back row with our parents was painful to the little guys. We were not the type that could sit on the edge of our seats listening to every word the pastor had to say. I know I was more apt to be listening to what my good friend Mark Junior Ryan was saying or doing on the other side of the church. During the evening services, I tried to sit where I could see who was coming or going across the street at the Midget Grill.

Deeply imbedded in my memory were the old-fashioned revivals, the ones where the visiting preacher delivered pure hellfire and brimstone. During one of those revivals, I was sitting on the third or fourth row with a playmate of mine. As the two of us were sitting there observing the excitement going on in the church, the preacher suddenly jumped down from his pulpit, marched straight to my friend and declared, "This young man is going to see the light and spread the gospel to the entire world." If a young kid could have had a heart attack, I probably did. Actually, my friend never had much of a chance to fulfill that prophecy, as he died a few years later in a car accident. I often wondered.

My family often talked about one of their favorite pastors by the name of Finley Edge. I do not think he served in Apopka very long, but during his short term, he certainly made an impression. I am sure the old church had a small congregation, because young Finley Edge seemed to make his home visits on a pretty regular basis. When my mother had her Sunday special fried chicken, the pastor was there. All of this was told to me, because I do not remember the pastor at all. Over the years, Finley Edge worked himself up as head of the Southern Baptist Convention. I suppose he ate a lot of chicken along the way.

Who could forget those wonderful Sundays when we had our dinner on the grounds under the beautiful oak trees? It was a time when every lady in the church brought her very best. They had the wooden tables laid out with a meal that would have fed the population of Apopka. On this table were black-eyed peas, turnip greens, green beans, deviled eggs, mashed potatoes, corn on the cob, fried chicken and dumplings, pecan pies, banana pudding, and a large keg of ice tea serving as a sentry at the end of the line. As a matter of fact, that meal would have fed the present population of Apopka. The ladies especially liked the dinner on the grounds because they did not have to prepare a full Sunday dinner for their family. My wife Joan always brought her family recipe of macaroni and cheese.

One of the last pastors of that old church was Miles Patterson. I suppose looking back, he and his wife were considered as pretty young by the congregation. Maybe he was, because he connected with the young people very well. He performed mine and Joan's wedding in 1953 in that old church, and we were always proud that we filled it for our wedding.

We probably neglected to say that it didn't take many to fill that old church on Main and Highland. Regardless of how small it may have been, it still holds a special place in our heart.

Gator Hunt

It was about 8:30 p.m. on a Friday night when we started our long trip down into Osceola County toward Lake Marion. It was a couple of nights before the full moon, and the sky was dark and cloudy. The rain was coming down pretty hard when we left Apopka; however, by the time we arrived at our destination, the clouds had moved on, and the sky was fairly clear.

Two very good friends of mine, Mark Hobson and Tim Landers, were very experienced alligator hunters who had just purchased their alligator hunting permits for the year. They paid $275 for permits that allowed them two gators for the year. They invited me to go along on their first hunt of the season that opened on August 24, 2007. To say the least, this was an honor and a thrill to be invited as an observer.

We arrived at the boat ramps about 10:00 p.m., and proceeded to launch for the hunt. Mark sat up front with a small light on his head, and Tim ran the big motors from the back. I sat in the seat next to Tim.

Jack and the Big Boy
August 24, 2007

When we arrived in the general area of the lake in which they wanted to hunt, Tim shut off the large motors, and Mark operated the trolling motor from the front. Mark was scanning the lake with his small light trying to pick up a large set of eyes. In the beginning, he said there were about thirteen gators to our left and maybe sixteen to our right. This meant there were about twenty-nine gators surrounding the boat. People ask me if I got sleepy on this trip. I would say definitely not. All of these eyes aimed at us were too small for the boys, so we moved out into deeper water (12-14 feet), where the big ones hung out.

I was warned that the blind mosquitoes might be bad when the heavy light came on. This was the understatement of the year, as they were so thick I had to put my windbreaker over my head to breath. The boys had grown used to all this and paid little attention to the mosquitoes.

It was about 12:30 a.m., when Mark told Tim to get ready to cast. Mark had spotted a good set of eyes. Tim had a salt-water rod with an 80-pound test line and a treble hook set in the casting position. Mark turned the big light on as Tim made the perfect cast, landing just behind the gator, and set the hook. Naturally, the gator took off like a scalded ape, but Mark moved the boat wherever the gator went. At last, the gator settled on the bottom, and we waited a while.

Finally, Tim started pulling the gator up. When it surfaced, Mark put a harpoon in the creature. The harpoon had a rope and Clorox jugs attached to it. It looked like "Jaws" when the gator took off dragging the Clorox bottles behind. The gator finally settled down. However, we knew where he was at all times because of the Clorox bottles. The boys said a gator usually stayed down about forty-five minutes before coming up for air. This one stayed down one-hour, and ten-minutes, telling us that he had a pretty big set of lungs, thus identifying him as a big gator.

When the gator came up for air, Mark hit him between the eyes with a .357 magnum bullet from a bang stick. Down it went again! After a few minutes, Tim started pulling him up. When his head came up, he still had life, so Mark hit him again with the bang stick. In a few minutes, they pulled the gator up and taped its mouth closed. At that time, Mark ceremoniously gave this big trophy a big smack on the snoot. This was fine because they were at the other end of the boat from me; however, about that time, the gator's tail hit my side of the boat to the left of my seat. That was the first time I realized how large this gator was. After taping the gator, they let him sink but left the rope and jugs so we could locate him when we were ready to return back to the landing. Then we went back to the mosquitoes and continued hunting for just one more big one.

We called it quits about 5:00 a.m., picked up the gator, and drug him on into shore. Mark backed his truck down the ramp, and they pulled as much of the gator as they could into the pickup. He then drove the truck down the ramp frontward and pushed the gator in the rest of the way.

We had seen several airboats cruising the shorelines, and they had been giving us a pain in the neck by cutting in front of us and scaring the gators away. Well, as we were loading the boat up to leave the lake, they came into the ramp next to us empty handed. I could not resist asking them how many they got. After they admitted to getting nothing, I invited them over to see what an alligator looked like. Tim and Mark got a kick out of that.

We left the lake and headed for the processing plant in Fort Christmas. The plant was actually an alligator farm where they raised gators and sold the meat and hides commercially. They were paying $30 a foot for gators over seven feet. The boys got over $300, which paid them more than the permit cost.

The following Sunday evening, Mark and Tim returned to Lake Marion and came out with a gator eleven-feet, eight-inches long. One foot larger than the one we caught. This one netted them approximately $330; however, it ended their season, as two was their limit.

I will say that night was one of the most memorable evenings I have ever spent. It was all new to me, and I will always be grateful to Tim and Mark for such a memorable night of adventure.

Stonebird

When we think of mountain men, we more than likely think of some romantic figure such as Robert Redford, who portrayed "Jeremiah Johnson" in the movie by the same name. Jeremiah Johnson was a take-off of one of the more famous mountain men of that era, John "Liver-Eating" Johnson.

After Lewis and Clark's expedition returned in 1806 with glowing reports of the abundance of fur bearing animals in the Northwest, the fur companies started sending brigades (a group of thirty to forty trappers) of men into the area until it reached a peak of about 2,500-3,000 men. These larger groups provided scouts, cooks, blacksmiths, and above all, safety in numbers. Mountain men like John Johnson operated as "free trappers," and were able to negotiate their own price for their trappings with the fur companies. These men helped open up the West to pioneer settlers. Their life was difficult, dangerous, and violent. One trapper in five died on the trails.

Curtis Stone took kids fishing and taught them about outdoors.

All of these traditions are carried on today by the American Mountain Men, an organization that covers all of the fifty states. They are committed to the preservation of the traditions and ways of our nation's greatest, most daring explorers and pioneers, the mountain men. They are dedicated to the conservation of our nation's remaining natural wilderness and wildlife, and to the ability of members to survive alone under any circumstances, using only what nature has to offer. It is very important that they pass their skills on to others, especially the younger generation.

Curtis Stone, Jr. of Clarcona is an American Mountain Man who has a cabin at Ft. Gates on the St. Johns River, a little north of Lake George. His neighbors at the river are Phil and Rebecca Coolidge of Atlanta who vacation at the river on occasion. They have three children – Luke, Ashley, and Joshua. Curtis quite often takes the kids fishing on the river and teaches them as much as he can about the wild outdoors of Florida.

Nearly every mountain man has a nickname, usually based on something dumb that he did. Fortunately, Curtis received the name of "Stonebird" because his last name was Stone, and everyone felt that when he played his guitar and whistled the songs, he sounded like a bird.

One week, young Joshua, who was twelve years old at the time, had to write an essay for his class. He chose to write "The Legend of Stonebird." He came in with a second place finish in a pretty large class in Atlanta. I thought he did an outstanding job of mixing the facts with fiction, if it was fiction. Here Is Joshua's essay:

The Legend Of Stonebird

"They say he sprung out of a croaker hole on the St. John's River somewhere between Lake George and Little Lake George. Homemade shoes out of tanned possum with deer sinew for laces, a gunnysack to carry his surprises, and his bedroll over his shoulder, he was a sight to behold moving out of the brush to the riverbank. As a boy he was called Curtis Stone, as a swamp man he was called Stonebird. He grew up on the shell banks of the St. Johns River in an area known as Ft. Gates. This is old Florida, when there were still plenty of gators lining the shoreline, and you would even hear the panther's scream through the night. If you were lucky you might even see one.

When he was only 7 years of age he wrestled the mightiest and biggest alligator you have ever seen. He was out one night frog gigging, wading through the lily pads and black muck of Lake Laura. His headlight reflected two yellow beads of light shining back at him across the water. Judging from the narrow space between the twin beads, young Curtis thought that this was just the right size gator for a pet to bring home and help clean off the table scraps from Aunt Gladys' cooking. So he silently moved through the black water like a fish, to a point where he could snatch by the neck what he thought would be a small one or two foot gator. To his surprise the water erupted in a froth of spray, scales, tail, and teeth of a 20-foot gator. Round and round, up and down they went with young Curtis hanging on for dear life trying to avoid the dagger like teeth and razor sharp claws. They wrestled for 3 days and nights until finally that big ol' malformed whump-eyed gator had had enough of Curtis and with a swat of his massive tail he sent Curtis flying through the air, whistling like a bird out of Lake Laura into a stand of palmetto fronds.

They say that Andrew Carnegie got the idea of carbonizing steel from a fishing trip with Curtis when he made his fishhooks. Curtis would wring the neck of a squirrel, twist paper clips into the shape of fish hooks, split open the squirrel and put the paperclip fishhooks inside and then stuff the squirrel, hooks and all inside an old soup can and throw it all into a fire. Once the squirrel cooked into nothing but ashes, he would remove the can and out came perfectly hardened fishhooks guaranteed to hold the angriest largemouth bass.

Curtis, or Stonebird as the swamp men called him would love to pass on his knowledge of the Florida wilds to young folks, teaching them how to fish and hunt and love nature. So if you are sitting around the fire in the woods of the Ocala forest or poling a johnboat up a creek off the St. Johns and hear the song of a mocking bird or a whippoorwill, look around for a kindly old swamp man with possum skin shoes, a gap between his front teeth, a scar below his left ear lobe, wearing a palmetto frond hat, it just might be old Stonebird himself whistling a tune while casting one of his paper clip hooks. Ask him how he got the scar. It was from a duel with a Spaniard, but that is a tale for another day, another fire lit night".

The Sycamore Tree

In the early years, Apopka should have been known as the city of beautiful trees, because that was the way it was. Entering Apopka on Hwy. 441 from the east, the street was lined with a beautiful canopy of oaks, as were Central Avenue, and most of the other side streets in the city.

When you emerged from under the canopy of oaks on Main Street, there on your left stood the most beautiful tree of them all, the majestic sycamore (Platanus Occidentailis). It stood in front of the old elementary school with its golden limbs outstretched as if standing guard over the many children who graced those halls.

You have heard it said, "A tree outlasts the man who planted it." Well, that certainly applies in this case, as this grand old tree was planted in 1902 by Parkinson Dodge Shepherd. There were actually two planted – one at the northwest corner of the Apopka Union School, and the other at the northeast corner. For the sake of this story, let's call the northeast tree, "the queen," and the northwest tree, "the king."

In the beginning, the trees stood on each side of the two-and-one-half story Apopka Union School, and for the first sixteen years, the school and the trees grew to handsome proportions.

However, on a chilly evening on January 11, 1918, as Apopka residents were finishing their evening meal, a light yellow cloud was forming over Lake Apopka. Observers said the cloud looked as though it had fire in it. Fire indeed, as a vicious tornado was coming off Lake Apopka and mowing down a half-mile path on its way to the center of Apopka. It hit Apopka about 9:00 p.m. and destroyed most of the city.

Many magnificent oaks were blown down or uprooted. W.G. Harris, a real estate man at the time, said Theodore Anderson used ropes and teams of mules to pull his trees back to an upright position. The school building was completely flattened, as was the king. Its mate was battered and torn but somehow withstood the mighty onslaught.

The queen was lonely for a while as her children were gone, and the king had moved on to tree heaven. However, in the early 1920s, the citizens of the County built a new elementary and high school. Once again, the queen had her children, and life moved on in its leisurely manner.

For all of us who attended the little green elementary school, each of us has memories of some description regarding the queen. I remember Jack Grossenbacher buzzing the school in his P-38 during World War II and clipping the top of the grand old sycamore. I know a little girl who received her first kiss under the tree, and the people whose initials still remain on the tree's trunk. The Mayor tells of a little girl who climbed too high up the tree and someone had to climb up and get her.

On October 22, 1982, the foliage industry added another member to the queen's court with a silver Boston fern monument honoring Harry Ustler and W.P. Newell as founders of the Apopka foliage industry.

Time rolled along, and around 1986, Father Time finally caught up with the little green schoolhouse. It was deemed unsafe for public use, and thus, the demolition crews were sent in. The high school was converted into the Apopka City Hall, and it still stands today.

On a lazy summer afternoon, not so many years ago, a windstorm came up with enough force to break off one of the queen's top limbs. Unfortunately, it landed directly in the middle of the Boston fern monument. It took a year or so before the repairs restored the monument; however, as you can see while riding by City Hall today, all is well with the queen and the Boston fern monument.

Keep in mind that a sycamore tree's life expectancy is roughly 100 years, and our beloved queen is 108. The City of Apopka has been the queen's caregiver over the years and must be congratulated for a job well done. The next time you are strolling past City Hall, don't forget to bow or curtsy to the queen for her many years of standing guard over the many children who attended the Apopka Union School and the little green elementary school.

Sycamore Bears Mayor's Name

This article was written by Diane Sears of the Orlando Sentinel on May 6, 1993, honoring John Land for his 40 years of service as Mayor of Apopka:

"One stands 97 feet tall; the other, about 5-foot-10. One is 186 inches around, while the other is, well, considerably slimmer.

But they have got something in common that's deep-rooted and promises to save them a spot in the history books. They're both Apopka champions, and now they both have the same name.

The 93-year-old sycamore that towers over City Hall was named the John Land Tree last week during a ceremony honoring Apopka's mayor of 40 years.

'This is the largest sycamore in the state of Florida...and the mayor is the longest serving in Florida,' parks Superintendent Mark Miller said as he unveiled a plaque at the foot of the tree.

Land, 73, also accepted a plaque from the state forester David Wentzel designating Apopka as a Tree City USA. The ceremony was on Friday, which is National Arbor Day.

The Sycamore is classified a state and national champion, which means it's among the oldest and largest trees in Florida and the United States.

'We know we've got two major champions within this city,' Miller told Land. 'This tree's been around a long time, and we know you have, too.'

The honor was a surprise for Land, who used to play under the tree when he was a boy and Apopka City Hall was a school.

He jokingly asked whether the sycamore's title was permanent.

'I thought you were going to say it had to run every three years like I did.'"

****

Petition For The Preservation Of Forest Integrity

For ninety-three years, this majestic symbol of quiet tranquility marched on its way to maturity providing shade and comfort to all who paused by the way.

It never made a political speech. It never asked anyone to vote for it. It never asked for a political contribution. It just went about doing its job growing to its own full potential.

Now along comes a young upstart twenty years after "Platanus Occidentalis" has been in business – crying and screaming for attention from everyone – even demanding that someone change his diapers daily. And yet some ninety-three years later, this well-intentioned, but grossly misled, cult group from the City of Apopka wants to name this towering giant after a mere upstart, John Land.

We concede that there are similarities between these two species, but that John Land learned from the tree--not vice versa.

Both stand tall.

Both have unquestionable integrity

Both have deep roots in the community

Both provide shade and comfort to their neighbors

Both are complimenters--not complainers.

Both are always cheerful.

But until John Land grows above ninety seven feet tall and over 186 inches in diameter, we cry out for--nay demand--that John Land's name be changed to John Sycamore Land, and this may it ever be.

Signed: SOCIETY FOR THE PRESERVATION OF FOREST INTEGRITY

Bill Morris, Benevolent Dictator

Earl Nelson, Armed Guard, and Charge D'affairs

May 6, 1993

References

Special thanks and appreciation to the following sources for information used in the writing of this book:

The Museum of the Apopkans

- Scrapbooks with articles by known and unknown authors.
- Pictures from their archives

Count Down for Agriculture in Orange County, Florida by Henry Swanson

The History of Apopka and N. W. Orange County by Jerrell H. Shofner

Story of Sneed from Dustballs by James Cox,

Crackers by Dana Ste. Claire

The Apopka Chief

The Orlando Sentinel

The Tampa Tribune

Thank You To Our Sponsors

Platinum Level Sponsorship
Family
Eric Hooper Family: Eric, Carolyn, David and Linda Hooper
Patrick and Sheila McGuffin: Reliance Media-Apopka Printing

Business and Civic
Apopka/Altamonte Springs Post #10147 V.F.W.
City of Apopka

Gold Level Sponsorship
Family
Bryan and Debbie Nelson

Business and Civic
The Apopka Chief and The Planter Newspapers
Rotary Club of Apopka - Bill Speigel/President

Silver Level Sponsorship
Family
Bill and Janine Arrowsmith
Arrowsmith Family
Cathi and Fred Brummer
Charles H. Damsel, Jr.
The Hobson Family - Mark, Sue, Ross, Laura, Ellen, Chad, Lily and Brent
John and Eileen Ricketson
Dr. Doyle Summerlin

Business and Civic
Apopka Citizens for Quality Law Enforcement, Inc.
Apopka Historical Society, Inc.
BankFIRST
Community Health Centers, Inc.
Foliage Sertoma Club of Apopka
GFWC Apopka Woman's Club, Inc.
McLeod Law Firm/Raymond A. McLeod and William J. McLeod
Rochelle Holdings
Walmart Apopka
World Class Installations, Inc.

Family Sponsors

ALLEGROE	Bob and Barbra Allegroe
ALLEN	Sarah, Graham and Brian Allen
ALSUP	Bill and Joan K. Alsup and Family

Family Sponsors *(Continued)*

ANDERSON	Karen and John Anderson
ANDERSON	Richard Anderson Family
ANDREWS	Hannah Dixon-Andrews and Herbert Andrews, Sr. Family
BAAB	Baab & Stout Family
BAILEY	Scott and Joan Christmas Bailey
BARNES	Family of Glenn and Deborah Barnes of Green Star Foliage, Inc.
BASS	Edward D. Bass II
BATEMAN	Charlie and Helen Bateman and Family
BECKERT	Howard M. Beckert Family
BENGIER	John and Pamela Bengier
BILETI	Joseph J. Bileti
BYRD	Beverly Gilliam Byrd
CHRISTMAS	Jack and Joanne Stone Christmas
CHRISTMAS	Cindy Christmas, Alex, Christian, Jack
CHRISTMAS	Robert and Patricia Christmas and Emilio
CHRISTMAS	Rick and Mark Christmas
COXWELL	Jim and Sandra Stone Coxwell
CROSTON	Croston Family
CUNNINGHAM	Tom and Carol Cunningham
DEWITT	Lorena Mahaffey Chambers DeWitt
DONNAN	Van and Sandy Donnan
DOUGLAS	Jack and Cherylyn Douglas
EDSTROM	Lennart and Britt Edstrom
GILLIAM	Belle Gilliam
GOFF	Michael and Kristen Goff Reilly
GOFF	Randy and Ginger Christmas Goff
GOFF	Ryan and Alison Goff and Carter
GOGGIN	Barbie and Jeff Goggin
HALL	Coaches Jack and Bob Hall/AHS Class of 46 & 43/ Sons of Dale and Gladys Hall
HAMRICK	Bo and Pat Hamrick
HICKERSON	Norman and Lillian Hickerson
HICKS	J.C. and Clemmie Hicks
HOOPER	Bob and Daphne Hooper
HUBBARD	Glenn and Constance Hubbard
HUNTSMAN	George W. and Betty Ann Huntsman
HUTH	Kay Huth
JANKUN	Bob and Betty Jankun
LAND	John Horting and Betty Hall, Suzanne, Betty Catherine and John H. Jr.
LAND	John H. Land Jr., Caroline and Samantha
LAND	Bennett, Jr. (b.1915 - d.1999) and Dorothy Haines (b.1914 - d.2000)
LAND	Josephine Horting Schneider (b.1890 – d.1980) and Bennett Sr. (b.1878 –d.1935)
LARKIN	Suzanne and Jon Larkin
LEUDENBURG	Larry and Hilda Leudenburg
LITTLE	Robert, Florence and Mary Catherine Little

Family Sponsors (Continued)

LOCKEBY	Ed and Mary Ann Lockeby
LOCKEBY	Lockeby Family
MacPHERSON	Don and Kathy MacPherson
McBRIDE	Family of Dr. Thomas E. McBride (Doc. Tommy)
McGUFFIN	Mac and Delores McGuffin Family
McLEOD	Raymond A McLeod and Sharon A. McLeod
MIXSON	Ann and Wayne Mixson
MORRIS	Mr. and Mrs. Bill Morris
MOORE	Christine E. Moore
NELSON	Bryan and Debbie Nelson and Family
NELSON	Earl and Flo Nelson
NELSON	Stephen Drew Nelson
	Brasher Parker (b.1924 - d.1998) and Catherine "Kit" Land (b.1923 – d.1996)
PALMER	Jim and Lisa Palmer
RANKIN	David and Gini Rankin
RICH	Dan and Sarah Rich
RICHARDSON	Elbert H. Richardson
RICHARDSON	Gerald and Amanda Richardson
ROBERSON	Sue and Robbie Roberson
RYAN	Patsy K. Ryan
SCHMIDT	Jack and Alice Schmidt
SHEPPARD	In memory of Leon and Florence Sheppard
SHEPPARD	Walter and Helen Sheppard
SIMPKINS	Don and Dorothy Simpkins
STALEY	Tom and Lou Staley
STARBIRD	Starbird Families
STARBUCK	Mrs. Jean Starbuck
STONE	Curtis and Betty Jean Stone, Jr.
SUMMERS	Jim Summers and Joy Summers
TALTON	John and Rudein Talton
TILL	Larry J. Till and Commissioner Kathy Till
USTLER	Jerry Ustler Family
WARD	Mary Moore, Judy M. Murdock and Peggy M. Ward
WATERS	Robert and Cathy Land Waters, Jordan Waters and India Waters
WEISS	Gerald and Trudy Weiss
WELCH	Jeff Welch
WILLIAMSON	Olie and Mary Williamson
YORK	Linda M. York

Business Sponsor

Beef O'Brady's Apopka

Need additional copies?

To order more copies of
Tales Of The Big Potato
contact NewBookPublishing.com

❐ Order online at NewBookPublishing.com

❐ Call 877-311-5100 or

❐ Email Info@NewBookPublishing.com

Call for multiple copy discounts!

Reliance Media